Justice Miscarried

Justice Miscarried

Inside Wrongful Convictions
in Canada

Hélèna Katz

DUNDURN
TORONTO

Project Editor: Michael Carroll
Editor: Nicole Chaplin
Design: Courtney Horner
Printer: Webcom

Library and Archives Canada Cataloguing in Publication

Katz, Hélèna, 1964-
    Justice miscarried : inside wrongful convictions in Canada / Hélèna Katz.

Includes bibliographical references and index.
Issued also in electronic formats.
ISBN 978-1-55488-874-0

    1. Judicial error--Canada. 2. False imprisonment--Canada. I. Title.

KE9440.K37 2011   347.71'012   C2011-901183-2
KF9756.K37 2011

1 2 3 4 5   15 14 13 12 11

Conseil des Arts du Canada   Canada Council for the Arts   Canadä   ONTARIO ARTS COUNCIL   CONSEIL DES ARTS DE L'ONTARIO

We acknowledge the support of the **Canada Council for the Arts** and the **Ontario Arts Council** for our publishing program. We also acknowledge the financial support of the **Government of Canada** through the **Canada Book Fund** and **Livres Canada Books**, and the **Government of Ontario** through the **Ontario Book Publishing Tax Credit** and the **Ontario Media Development Corporation**.

Care has been taken to trace the ownership of copyright material used in this book. The author and the publisher welcome any information enabling them to rectify any references or credits in subsequent editions.
                                                                J. Kirk Howard, President

Printed and bound in Canada.
www.dundurn.com

Front Cover Images: Top left: Guy Paul Morin (Rick Eglinton/*Toronto Star*/GetStock); top centre: David Milgaard, with his sister (left) and mother, Joyce (Ken Faught/*Toronto Star*/GetStock); top right: Donald Marshall (Rick Eglinton/*Toronto Star*/GetStock). Bottom: The Scales of Justice © Michael Park.

Dundurn	Gazelle Book Services Limited	Dundurn
3 Church Street, Suite 500	White Cross Mills	2250 Military Road
Toronto, Ontario, Canada	High Town, Lancaster, England	Tonawanda, NY
M5E 1M2	LA1 4XS	U.S.A. 14150

To the men and women whose lives have been stolen from them by wrongful convictions, and to the dedicated and passionate people who work tirelessly to free them.

Contents

Introduction

"You are asking the government for mercy, for something you have never done."
— David Milgaard, about his application to the federal justice minister to have his wrongful conviction for murder overturned.

A friend once confessed that it bothered her that people who have been convicted of a crime and imprisoned have the right to appeal their convictions and sentences.

"The appeals system wasn't made to protect the guilty," I said. "It was created to protect people who are wrongly convicted. Do you really want to have innocent people behind bars with no way to right the wrong when the justice system makes a mistake?" She nodded thoughtfully and agreed that the justice system needs checks and balances.

Behind the proud façade of Canada's criminal justice system lie the shattered lives of the people unjustly caught in its web. *Justice Miscarried* tells the heart-wrenching stories of twelve innocent Canadians who were wrongly convicted, and the errors in the justice system that changed their lives forever. The sad truth is that while laws may appear to be infallible, the people who apply them are not. No one is immune to error — not those who gather evidence over the course of a police investigation, nor those who conduct autopsies and forensic testing, prosecute and defend cases, and preside over trials. Wrongful convictions were once viewed as isolated occurrences, but that is no longer the case. More than a half-dozen inquiries, from Saskatchewan to Newfoundland, have highlighted systemic reasons why things can — and do — go horribly wrong. Unfortunately, the people in the justice system aren't necessarily good at admitting to mistakes and correcting them quickly. As lawyer James Lockyer told *The Globe and Mail*, "A wrongly convicted person becomes a victim on an express train without brakes."[1]

Canada doesn't have the death penalty, but the impact of wrongful convictions should never be underestimated. Life behind bars is dangerous, it's a world where being assaulted by other inmates isn't unusual. Ronald Dalton, who was wrongly convicted of murdering his wife, described prison life in an interview with *The Globe and Mail*:

> There was always a pervasive air of tension in prison. The first time you're in the gymnasium and a shotgun goes off from the gun tower, that gets to you. You develop a heightened sensitivity to what is going on around you. You learn to read the lay of the land, because you don't know who is having a bad day or carrying a shiv. You can't go around proclaiming your innocence in prison. Once you're there, nobody wants to hear your sad story, because they all have their own. But you never give up hope, because it's all you have to cling to. I've seen people go steadily downhill after they lost their last appeals, and had no more hope left.[2]

The prison system is not kind to people who have been wrongly convicted. Parole boards frequently perceive their continued statements of innocence as a lack of remorse, and evidence that they have yet to be rehabilitated. Consequently, they are frequently denied parole and end up spending many more years in prison than if they had admitted guilt for a crime they didn't commit. Meanwhile, the lost years away from their families can never be regained. Dalton spent more than eight years behind bars. He missed seeing his three children grow up. His daughter was in kindergarten when he went to prison; within days of his release, he watched her graduate from high school. As the cases profiled in this book clearly demonstrate, the assumption that every conviction is legitimate is incorrect.

The stigma of a criminal conviction follows its victims long after their incarceration. When Thomas Sophonow was acquitted in 1985 of murdering Winnipeg doughnut shop waitress Barbara Stoppel, he hoped that other people would give him a chance. But he knew what lay ahead. "The theory of the propagandist is that if you repeat something often enough, over and over again, people seem to accept it as being the truth."[3] A colleague at the manufacturing plant where he worked in 2002 hung a tag with the word "murderer" on his coveralls.

Wrongly convicted men and women aren't the only victims. What about their families and those of the injured or murdered victims? They, too, are often traumatized by wrongful convictions. The victims' families often feel some relief from knowing that the perpetrator is behind bars. But what happens when they learn that the real perpetrator continues to roam free? Do they relive the trauma of losing a loved one all over again along with not knowing what really happened? Nobody is held accountable if a murder remains unsolved. As time marches on and the trail gets colder, it can become more difficult to find the real killer. And what does it do for the confidence of the victims and their families in the criminal justice system? As Tim Orydzuk's mother Jane pointed out in a letter to the editor that appeared in the *Edmonton Journal*, "There have been compound losses for the two families. Not only did we lose our boys, but we lost our faith in the Canadian justice system…. In the eyes of the justice system, it's over. Nobody has been held accountable. There is still an empty chair around our table and a little girl who wonders why she has to grow up without her daddy."[4]

In some cases of wrongful conviction, such as the murders of Sandy Seale and Gail Miller, another person is eventually found guilty of the crime that was initially attributed to an innocent person, such as Donald Marshall Jr. and David Milgaard, respectively. Even in such cases, families have to relive the trauma of losing a loved one as another trial with yet another suspect takes place.

The book's first section profiles five cases where some of the most egregious errors were made during police investigations. Forensics experts are often called upon to testify, but as the four cases in the second part of *Justice Miscarried* demonstrate, experts sometimes misstate or overstate what they believe is evidence of a crime. From the Crown's failure to disclose evidence to the defence counsel to eyewitness misidentification and errors of law, errors can also occur in the hands of lawyers and judges. A variety of causes can lead to miscarriages of justice, but among the most evident are the use of jailhouse informants, bad science, the Crown's lack of disclosure, and eyewitness misidentification.

Advances in DNA technology have helped solve some murders and exonerate a number of wrongly convicted men and women. From gunshot residue tests to hair and fibre analysis and DNA testing, forensics are playing an increasingly important role in criminal investigations. Jurors place much weight on scientific evidence and expert testimony because of the air of infallibility and accuracy that science enjoys. This gives experts inordinate influence during criminal trials and makes the expert witness a powerful weapon in the Crown and defence's arsenal. However, it is critical that they remain objective in their analysis and avoid being influenced by the person who hired them. Remaining neutral and keeping an open mind is tricky business, particularly since medical examiners, pathologists, and other forensic experts work closely with police officers and Crown prosecutors. Experts could be influenced, however subtly, to find evidence that supports a conclusion the police have already reached.

Until 2003, forensic pathology was not a recognized medical subspecialty in Canada and there was no formal training or certification. Consequently, many forensic pathologists did not have training in their field of practice; they learned on the job. In addition to a lack of neutrality, lack of training, and lack of adherence to scientific conventions can lead forensic experts to peddle bad science as credible evidence, leading to wrongful convictions and lost years behind bars.

The flip side is that the advent of DNA evidence has opened prison doors, letting a number of wrongfully convicted people free. According to the Innocence Project in New York, the first person exonerated by DNA evidence was in 1989. Some 266 people have been exonerated in the United States thanks to post-conviction DNA. At least seventeen of them served time on death row.

While DNA evidence has been a boon for so many wrongly convicted people, it has also presented a challenge for individuals who don't have access to the evidence that could exonerate them. DNA evidence has become the gold standard for exonerations. Without it, it's harder to convince courts that a miscarriage of justice has occurred based on other evidence such as faulty eyewitness identification or bad science. This makes the fight for exoneration and compensation much more difficult.

Until a landmark Supreme Court of Canada ruling in 1991, the Crown prosecutors' failure to disclose evidence was an ongoing issue that could prevent an accused from getting a fair trial. Defence lawyers frequently felt ambushed during trials, as they were not given access to documents that could help them mount a full defence, or potentially exonerate their clients. With little duty to disclose, the Crown only had to provide defence counsel with the evidence that the prosecution considered relevant.

In 1991, the Supreme Court of Canada ruled that the Crown has a duty to fully disclose all evidence to the defence — not just the information it planned to present in court. In an adversarial justice system, securing convictions can take precedence over finding the truth. In a stinging comment, Justice Felix Cacchione told the Marshall inquiry that some prosecutors seemed to measure their success by the number of convictions they were able to secure: "Unfortunately, I found with certain persons it was a matter of how many notches did you have on your 'win' belt."[5] This raises the question: What is the role of the prosecutor in the criminal justice system? Is it to win convictions or to find the truth?

Judges bring their own level of knowledge and experience with criminal law to their positions. In Quebec, for example, lawyers need to have been in practice for ten years before they can apply to become a provincial court judge. However, the law doesn't require that they have courtroom or criminal law experience. That's why former Newfoundland Supreme Court of Appeal Justice William Marshall told a conference on wrongful convictions that trial judges can also make errors that lead to wrongful convictions. "It is difficult to perceive how any credible inquiry into a wrongful conviction could be commissioned without expectation that every stage of the judicial process leading to the miscarriage — including the judiciary's acquittal of its responsibilities — would be vetted," Justice Marshall told his audience.[6] Inquiries should also examine mistakes that judges may have made that could have contributed to a wrongful conviction. Respecting judicial independence shouldn't occur at the expense of examining their performances.

The road to exoneration is a long and costly one for victims of a miscarriage of justice. Once they have exhausted the appeals process, the final avenue is to appeal to the federal minister of justice to review their conviction under Section 696.1 (formerly Section 690) of the *Criminal Code*. The Criminal Conviction Review Group's lawyers review applications and make recommendations to the minister. If they find that a wrongful conviction is likely to have occurred, the minister can order a new trial, refer the case to a court of appeal, or refer specific questions to a court of appeal for an opinion. However, an applicant has to demonstrate they have new and significant information that was not available during the trial or appeals but which could have affected the outcome had it been available at the time. After determining that an application meets this criteria, a lawyer from the CCRG can conduct an investigation that includes interviewing witnesses to clarify or verify information, ordering scientific tests such as DNA testing, consulting police, prosecutors, and defence lawyers who were involved in the case's trial and appeals.

But much work happens before a file arrives in the hands of the CCRG. Canadian inmates rely heavily on the Association in Defence of the Wrongly Convicted in Toronto (AIDWYC). It includes a group of lawyers who volunteer their time to review cases on a pro bono basis and prepare Section 696.1 applications. The association was born from the Justice for Guy Paul Morin Committee, which was created in 1992 to support him after he was wrongly convicted of murdering the little girl who lived next door. Volunteers spend hundreds of hours sifting through files, re-interviewing witnesses, analyzing court transcripts, and searching for any information that may have been overlooked previously and could cast doubt on a conviction. AIDWYC has helped exonerate a number of people, including Nova Scotia's Clayton Johnson, Newfoundland's Greg Parsons and Randy Druken, Ontario's William Mullins-Johnson, Steven Truscott, and Gordon Folland, Manitoba's James Driskell, and Saskatchewan's David Milgaard. Prisoners also depend on the Innocence Project, a program run by the faculties of law at Toronto's York University and Montreal's McGill University. The Innocence Project at Osgoode Hall Law School in Toronto helped exonerate Gary Staples and Romeo Phillion.

Critics say the federal justice department's process for applying for possible cases of wrongful convictions is flawed because the people who review the cases answer directly to the Department of Justice — the same government department that is responsible for Canada's justice system. They claim that there is a real or perceived bias toward defending the justice system. The final decision on cases is left to a politician: the justice minister. In 1989, the royal commission into Donald Marshall's wrongful conviction recommended that Canada create an independent agency to examine cases of possible wrongful convictions. In the intervening twenty years, that recommendation has been made by other inquiries including, most recently, the 2008 Commission of Inquiry into the Wrongful Conviction of David Milgaard.

These recommendations call for an independent agency modelled after Britain's Criminal Cases Review Commission, which was created in 1997 to investigate suspected cases of wrongful convictions or unfair sentencing, sending those with merit to the courts. The staff of approximately 100 (compared to about six in Canada's CCRG) is accountable only to the commission's eleven commissioners. The organization receives about 1,000 applications to review each year and refers about 4 percent to appeal courts. About two thirds of those referred to the courts have led to quashed convictions. As of December 31, 2010, this process had resulted in 309 overturned convictions.

Once an exoneration has been won in Canada, compensation for a wrongful conviction doesn't always immediately follow. Marshall's case marked the first time that a Canadian was exonerated for a murder after serving a lengthy prison sentence. The idea that the justice system had made a mistake seemed inconceivable to lawmakers. Marshall fought for more than eleven years to clear his name — and another seven for compensation. When Marshall began fighting for compensation in the early 1980s, there was no precedent for awarding compensation in the case of wrongful convictions. A federal-provincial agreement was signed in 1988 that defined the circumstances under which someone can be compensated. Although the federal and provincial governments share the costs, it's left up to provincial governments to decide whether or not to award compensation and how much. A prerequisite for receiving compensation is known as "factual innocence": irrefutable proof that the person is innocent. An acquittal isn't enough, as was the case for Michel Dumont, who was acquitted of sexual assault when the victim recanted. He filed a civil suit, which entailed another lengthy battle. As Joyce Milgaard, David Milgaard's mother, said at a news conference in 2005, "After the first injustice for a crime he did not commit, Michel is now faced with the second injustice of having to face another trial to obtain compensation."[7] He was not the first to file a civil suit, and he likely won't be the last.

The indisputable truth is that people in the justice system will make mistakes. We need to accept that mistakes have been and will continue to be made. While a person who is accused of a crime is held accountable, the question remains: Who should be accountable when wrongful convictions occur? Is it enough to admonish police, prosecutors, pathologists, forensics experts, and judges who contribute to a wrongful conviction? Should prosecutors be disbarred for misconduct? Should pathologists lose their licenses or be suspended? Is there a better way to hold them accountable? It is difficult to win civil suits against those responsible for the wrongful conviction. Just how much protection should they have from decisions that lead to wrongful convictions?

Victims want someone to stand up and say they're sorry for what was done to them. All too often, the apologies are a long time in coming. If the justice system makes mistakes, we also need to spot them quickly, own up to and correct them. We owe it to the men and women who have been falsely convicted and languish for years behind bars waiting for justice. We also owe it to the victims of criminal acts and their families, who are re-victimized by knowing that the real perpetrator continues to go free.

PART I

Police Investigation: Making the Case

Chapter One

Unreliable Witnesses: The David Milgaard Case

In September 1968, twenty-year-old Gail Miller had just moved to Saskatoon, a city of 129,000 people, to take a job at City Hospital as a nursing assistant. On January 31, 1969 at 6:45 a.m., less than five months after she arrived, she left the boarding house where she was living in a working-class neighbourhood and headed to the bus stop. At about 8:30 a.m., Miller's body was found in an alley a block from her home. She was lying face down in the snow, the top of her nurse's uniform rolled down to her waist. She had been sexually assaulted and fatally stabbed more than a dozen times. Her bloodstained underwear, girdle, and stockings were near her left ankle. Her right boot and sweater were buried in the snow close by. The blade from a broken paring knife was found under her body, the maroon handle was discovered in a nearby yard. A few days later her purse was found in a nearby garbage can. Its contents had been scattered in backyards close to where her body was found.

Miller's murder came on the heels of three sexual assaults in the previous three months, all within ten blocks of where her body was found. On October 21 and November 13, 1968, a knife-wielding assailant grabbed the victims in early evening, took them to a nearby alley and ordered them to undress. The women weren't robbed or killed, but the circumstances surrounding the assaults were similar to Miller's rape and murder. The assailant in a November 28 attack was interrupted when a car came by. He fled before he could sexually assault his victim.

The Saskatoon Police arrived at the scene of Miller's murder after a schoolboy found her body. Murders were an unusual occurrence in the Prairie city. Police officers Lieutenant Joe Penkala and Thor Kliev of the Identification Division watched as Dr. Harry Emson, pathologist at St. Paul's Hospital, performed an autopsy on Miller's body. Dr. Emson noted that Miller had been slashed repeatedly in the throat and had stab wounds to her upper torso. She died from a stab wound to the lung. There was also semen in her vagina. He gave police samples of Miller's hair, pubic hair, blood, and clothing. The vaginal fluid that was removed was tested but not kept.

When Penkala returned to the scene of the crime on February 4, 1969, he found two frozen lumps in the snow. The Royal Canadian Mounted Police lab examined the lumps and other items the Saskatoon Police found near Gail Miller's body. In one of the frozen lumps, RCMP Staff Sgt. Bruce Paynter found pubic hair and semen containing A antigens. This suggested the donor had blood type A and secreted antigens into his bodily fluids. He also found human semen stains on Miller's underwear.

Police detective-sergeants Raymond Mackie and George Reid led the investigation into Gail Miller's murder, which involved more than 100 police officers. They concluded that the knife found underneath Miller's body was the murder weapon, but they couldn't find any useable fingerprints on it. Police canvassed the neighbourhood for about a six-block radius to find out if anyone had seen anything unusual the morning that Miller was killed. The police interviewed her roommates, family, friends, and co-workers in an effort to find possible suspects and a motive. The city's drycleaners were contacted to see if anyone had brought in bloodied clothes. They also investigated the many tips and leads they received, but none yielded any useful information.

The Saskatoon Police suspected that one man was responsible for all three sexual assaults and Miller's murder. They investigated known sex offenders as potential suspects. Police had investigated and eliminated more than 160 possible suspects by the time Albert Cadrain went to the Saskatoon Police on March 2, 1969. He told them he believed that his friend David Milgaard had murdered Miller. Sixteen-year-old Milgaard was a shaggy-haired hippie who had dropped out of school and was caught up in the free-spirited era of the sixties and experimenting with drugs. He had left Regina at midnight on Thursday January 30, 1969, with friends Ronald Wilson and Nichol John. They were driving Wilson's beat-up 1958 Pontiac to Saskatoon to pick up Cadrain before heading to Vancouver.

Milgaard, Wilson, and John arrived in Saskatoon at about 6:30 a.m. on January 31, 1969. Milgaard was the only one who had been to Cadrain's house, but he didn't have the address. All he could remember was that it was near St. Mary's Church, which, as it turned out, was halfway between Cadrain's and Miller's houses and half a block from where Miller's body was found two hours later. The trio stopped to ask a woman for directions, but she was unable to help. As they continued driving, the car got stuck in the snow. They couldn't dislodge it, so John stayed with the car while Wilson and Milgaard went in opposite directions looking for help. When they returned, two men in a cream-coloured car helped push them out. Sometime between 7:00 a.m. and 7:30 a.m. Wilson, Milgaard, and John drove to the Trav-A-Leer Motel and asked the front desk manager, Robert Rasmussen, for directions. On their way to Cadrain's, the Pontiac got stuck again, this time in an alley behind Sandra Danchuk's vehicle. They waited with the Danchuks in their house for a tow truck between 7:30 a.m. and 7:50 a.m. The Danchuks didn't see anything unusual about Milgaard or any blood on his clothes.

It was about 9:00 a.m. when the trio arrived at Cadrain's house. The crotch of Milgaard's pants had gotten ripped and they had holes from where battery acid had spilled. He and Wilson changed their clothes. Then Milgaard drove around the block by himself a couple of times. The car stalled again beside Cadrain's house. Milgaard, Wilson, John, and Cadrain left Saskatoon for Edmonton later that day, once the car was repaired. While they were driving along the highway, John pulled a woman's compact from the glove box of the car and asked to whom it belonged. Milgaard grabbed it and tossed it out the window. Milgaard later admitted that he had no idea where the bag came from or why he threw it out.

The group returned to Regina on February 6, 1969, when Wilson found out that his father was ill. The Regina Police picked up Cadrain the same day and charged him with vagrancy. When they learned that he lived in the same Saskatoon neighbourhood where Miller had been killed, and that he had left town that day, they asked him about the murder. He said he hadn't heard about it. Cadrain learned the details of Miller's death when he arrived home in Saskatoon on March 1, 1969, and his family told him about it. The police had no leads, but they were under pressure to solve the case and had posted a reward for information leading to the nursing assistant's killer.

Cadrain went to the Saskatoon Police the next day. That is when he first claimed that he saw blood on Milgaard's pants on January 31 and that his friend seemed to be in a hurry to leave town. Lieutenant Charles Short and Detective Eddie Karst questioned him and took his statement. During the two-hour interrogation, Cadrain told police that, on the day of the murder, Milgaard arrived unexpectedly at his house at about 9:05 a.m. and said they had to "leave town right away." Cadrain told them that he saw blood on Milgaard's shirt and pants before Milgaard changed his clothes and took Wilson's car for a drive by himself. He also claimed Milgaard talked a lot about cleaning the car and that others in the car seemed to be afraid of him.

On March 3, Karst questioned Milgaard. He told the teenager that he was a suspect in Miller's murder. Then he asked Milgaard to account for his whereabouts on January 31, 1969. Milgaard talked about stopping a woman in the street and going to a motel to get directions, getting stuck in an alley, and changing his clothes because of the battery acid on them. But he couldn't remember at what time various activities happened. He was cooperative but vague. He didn't know where his clothes were and they didn't turn up during a police search. There were no marks or scratches on his body consistent with what one might expect to find after a recent struggle.

Milgaard also told police that he drove Wilson's car around the block after reaching Cadrain's house. "I like to drive I guess," he replied when he was asked why he would do that after the car had just stalled. He explained that the reason he had been in a hurry to leave town was because he was excited about seeing his girlfriend in Edmonton. He admitted that he had taken drugs during the road trip, had received psychiatric treatment in Yorkton when he was thirteen years old, and that he tended to make impulsive decisions. He wasn't sure if he had been alone at any time the morning of Miller's murder. Karst asked Milgaard if he had a criminal record. He admitted that he had convictions for sexual immorality, trafficking, stolen cars, break and enter, escaping lawful custody, and that he had been deported from the United States.

Although Milgaard had not been convicted of a violent crime, Karst's interest in him as a suspect in Miller's murder grew. The teenager was in the vicinity at the time of the killing, he was driving in back alleys that morning, was at the Cadrain residence a block from where Miller's body was found, he and his companions were under the influence of drugs, he had a criminal record, and Milgaard tried to clean Wilson's car while it was being repaired. There also appeared to be gaps of time that were unaccounted for or that were vague. Milgaard denied there was blood on his clothing, but police couldn't find the clothes in question to either prove or disprove that statement.

While Milgaard was being interviewed by Karst, Wilson was being questioned by RCMP Inspector J.A.B. Riddell. Wilson said that he, Milgaard, and John arrived in Saskatoon between 5:00 a.m. and 6:00 a.m. They were driving around looking for Cadrain's house when their car stalled and became stuck in an alley. After getting a boost to restart their vehicle, they found their way to Cadrain's house. Wilson said that after they arrived, Milgaard changed his pants because of spilled battery acid and drove the car around the block. In his police statement, Wilson said that Milgaard was never out of his sight for more than a few minutes, except when he drove Wilson's car around the block. He wasn't aware of Milgaard owning a knife. Police searched Wilson's car but didn't find anything of interest nor did they see any bloodstains or find Milgaard's clothes.

Nichol John was questioned more than a week later, on March 11. She told police that she arrived in Saskatoon with Wilson and Milgaard between 6:30 a.m. and 7:30 a.m. They drove around looking for Cadrain's house, stopped at a motel for a map and directions, got stuck in an alley, and then reached Cadrain's home after daylight. Wilson changed his clothes because of spilled battery acid on them, while Milgaard put on a fresh pair of pants after the crotch of his other pants ripped. John didn't see any blood on their clothing. She said the car broke down after Milgaard drove it around the block, but he and Wilson were never out of her sight for more than a minute or two.

Wilson and John, who were travelling with Milgaard at the time of Gail Miller's murder, both told police their friend had no opportunity to commit the crime. Cadrain, whom they met up with later, was the only one to suggest that Milgaard was involved. Nonetheless, this didn't allay the Saskatoon Police's suspicions. A week later, on March 18, Karst and Short took Cadrain with them to Regina to conduct another interview with Wilson and John. They interviewed John and Cadrain together this time. John's story began to change. She told police that she was afraid of Milgaard and believed he was dangerous. She also said that he had forced her to have sex several times. Saskatoon Police also interviewed Milgaard's one-time girlfriend Sharon Williams in St. Albert. She had no information about the murder, but she provided an unflattering portrait of Milgaard. She talked of his criminal behaviour and his aggressive sexual behaviour toward her.

Then Gail Miller's wallet was found buried in the snow near Cadrain's house on April 4. Police speculated that Milgaard had tossed it there while he was driving around the neighbourhood. When John was interviewed a third time, on April 14, her story changed again. She insisted that Milgaard and Wilson hadn't been out of her sight the day of the murder for more than a moment or two and she didn't see any blood on Milgaard's clothes. She did think he was capable of sexual assault and murder.

When Saskatoon Police interviewed Milgaard on April 18, he was cooperative and gave them blood, saliva, and hair samples. He was eager to help them and clear himself. As he later said, "I was trying my best to help the police. This had to be resolved. It was a terrible crime." (He turned out to have blood type A, which was the same as the sperm found near Miller's body.)

Milgaard denied killing Miller or being involved in her death. Cadrain and Wilson were also tested. Cadrain was type O and Wilson was type B. This eliminated Milgaard's friends as potential suspects, but not Milgaard. Cadrain stuck to his story linking Milgaard to the murder despite the fact that he only became aware of the story of the murder after he returned to Saskatoon more than a month later. Police had no evidence linking Milgaard to the murder. There were two other problems: it appeared that he never had an opportunity to kill Gail Miller, since he wasn't away from his friends long enough, and police couldn't connect him to the three sexual assaults prior to Miller's murder, since he wasn't in Saskatoon at the time. The police needed to either find some evidence or eliminate Milgaard as their prime suspect.

In May 1969, under the strain of repeated questioning, Milgaard's companions began to change their stories. Wilson told the Saskatoon Police that Milgaard had left the car when they became stuck at about 6:45 that morning. When he returned, he seemed to be out of breath. Calgary Police Inspector Art Roberts, who was trained in interrogation and polygraph, spoke to John and Wilson before he administered a voluntary polygraph test. According to the inquiry report on the case, he showed the teenage girl some of Miller's bloodied clothing and appealed to her sympathy by asking her, "What if this had been your sister?" That's when John began to incriminate Milgaard. She suddenly claimed to remember seeing him stab the girl they had asked for directions moments before the murder happened. It was a claim that she never again repeated. Roberts didn't use a polygraph to test her statement. He turned her over to the Saskatoon police.

For his part, Wilson said the maroon paring knife found near Gail Miller's body was similar to one that Milgaard had with him on their road trip from Regina to Saskatoon. He said he'd seen blood on Milgaard's trousers when he was changing at Cadrain's house. He also recounted the incident when John found a woman's compact while she was looking in his car's glove compartment for a map, which Milgaard tossed out the window. Incidentally, Miller's compact was found with other items from her purse. Wilson also claimed that when they were in Calgary, Milgaard said he had tried to take a girl's purse in Saskatoon and that he'd jabbed her with a knife when she resisted. Roberts did not test the incriminating evidence by polygraph. It's not entirely clear why the teenagers suddenly changed their stories, but it proved to have devastating consequences for Milgaard. Now the police had the stories they needed to arrest him.

Milgaard was in Prince George, British Columbia, selling magazines when he found out the RCMP were looking for him. He went to the detachment. Police arrested him on May 30, 1969, after a four-month investigation. The pressure to find Miller's killer was finally over. Milgaard was brought to Saskatoon and committed to stand trial after a preliminary hearing on September 11.

The police did not disclose to the Crown that they had initially believed that the same person was responsible for both Miller's murder and the string of sexual assaults that preceded it. As was police practice at the time, they only sent the prosecutor the reports and witness statements that they felt were relevant to the case. In fact, neither the Crown nor Milgaard's lawyer, Calvin Tallis, were even aware of the sexual assaults.

The day before Milgaard's trial got underway, Wilson told police that Milgaard had re-enacted Miller's murder at a party in a Regina motel room in early May, shortly before he was arrested. Wilson had heard the story from Craig Melnyk and George Lapchuk. Detective Karst interviewed Melnyk and Lapchuk. They told him that they were at a party at the Park Lane Motel when a newscast about Miller's murder appeared on television. When Lapchuk suggested to Milgaard, who was under the influence of drugs, that he had killed Miller, Milgaard apparently grabbed a pillow and made stabbing motions. According to the two witnesses, he admitted that he killed the young nursing assistant. Milgaard told his lawyer that he had no memory of the incident. If he had done as his friends suggested, it was only intended as a joke. He had not killed Gail Miller.

Milgaard's trial by judge and jury began in Saskatoon Court of Queen's Bench on January 19, 1970, before Chief Justice Alfred Bence. Crown witness Sergeant Bruce Paynter testified that the frozen semen found at the crime scene was from someone who had type A blood and secreted antigens into bodily fluids such as semen and saliva. Milgaard had type A blood but no antigens were found in his saliva. This suggested he was not a secretor and the semen the police tested was not his. Tallis argued that Milgaard, therefore, could not be the person whose semen was found at the crime scene and this forensic evidence exonerated him.

However, testimony from Milgaard's friends suggested otherwise. Wilson, who initially told police that Milgaard was never away from the car for more than a minute or two, testified that he left the vehicle for fifteen minutes. The Crown's theory was that this was when Milgaard fatally stabbed Gail Miller. Although Wilson told police that he didn't see any blood on Milgaard's clothes, he testified during the trial that he saw blood on Milgaard's pants and shirt. Cadrain testified that he saw a bloodstain that was one or two inches in diameter and a few splatters on

Milgaard's pants and shirttail. Melnyk and Lapchuk recounted the story about the motel room re-enactment. Melnyk admitted that he didn't speak to the police until he was charged with armed robbery.

John testified that she couldn't remember saying that Milgaard had stabbed Gail Miller. This was inconsistent with the police statement she had given in May. Caldwell had the option of asking the judge for permission to cross-examine John on the previous inconsistent statement she had made in writing. This was a new provision in the *Canada Evidence Act*. Without the presence of the jury, Justice Bence received submissions from Tallis and Caldwell about the procedure to follow. Contrary to their submissions, the judge decided that evidence about the circumstances in which John made the out-of-court statement should be given in the jury's presence. Crown prosecutor T.D.R. Caldwell was granted permission to treat her as a hostile witness, before the defence had a chance to question her about the circumstances surrounding her police statement without the jury present. In the presence of the jury, Caldwell was allowed to read portions of John's police statement in which she claimed to have seen Milgaard stab a woman. When asked if her statement was true, John replied that she didn't know. Although the judge warned the jury to only use the parts of John's police statement that she had adopted on the stand, the damage was done. They had heard her police statement incriminating Milgaard. He didn't testify in his own defence after the Crown presented forty-four witnesses. His lawyer believed that Milgaard's drug use and previous brushes with the law would not make him a good witness.

Milgaard was convicted on January 31, 1970, and sentenced to life in prison with no chance of parole for ten years. He was seventeen years old. As his mother Joyce recounted in an excerpt from her book *A Mother's Story*,[1] David's conviction had an impact on the entire family. They lived in Langenburg, Saskatchewan, a tiny community of about 1,000 people, where Milgaard's father, Lorne, was a foreman at a potash mine. David's quiet fifteen-year-old brother came home showing signs of having been in fights, fourteen-year-old Susan suddenly no longer had friends, and children surrounded ten-year-old Maureen and taunted her with, "Your brother is a killer!" By May

1970, it became clear that the family would have to move. Lorne found a job running a quarry and the Milgaards headed to Winnipeg. The Saskatchewan Court of Appeal rejected Milgaard's appeal in January 1971, and the Supreme Court of Canada followed suit on November 15. He had reached a legal dead end.

But Larry Fisher's involvement with the criminal justice system had just begun. At the time of Gail Miller's murder, he lived in the basement apartment of the Cadrain house with his wife Linda and their infant daughter Tammy. Three weeks after Milgaard was convicted, a fourth victim was followed home and raped in Saskatoon on the evening of February 21, 1970. Another woman was assaulted in Fort Garry, Manitoba on August 2. Fisher was arrested in Fort Garry on September 19 while he was raping his sixth victim. He had no criminal record. The Saskatoon Police was alerted since Fisher had previously lived in that city. Perhaps they had unsolved rapes in that jurisdiction?

During an interview with Saskatoon Police Detective Eddie Karst in Winnipeg on October 22, 1970, Fisher confessed to two of the assaults in Saskatoon. Two months later, on December 30 (a month after Milgaard appealed his murder conviction to the Saskatchewan Court of Appeal), Fisher was charged with raping three victims in Saskatoon and one indecent assault. On May 28, 1971, he pleaded guilty to raping his final two victims in Manitoba, for which he was sentenced to thirteen years in prison. On December 21, he pleaded guilty to the four Saskatoon attacks and was ordered to serve his sentence concurrently with his thirteen-year sentence in the Manitoba attacks. In 1971, Crown prosecutor Serge Kujawa handled Milgaard's leave to appeal to the Supreme Court of Canada and Fisher's guilty plea in Saskatchewan Court of Queen's Bench. But neither the police nor the Crown made a connection between the series of rapes and Gail Miller's murder in the same neighbourhood around the same time period.

Fisher was released from prison on January 26, 1980, after serving ten years of his sentence. He was soon back behind bars after raping and slashing the throat of a woman in North Battleford, Saskatchewan, on March 31, 1980. He was sentenced in June 1981 to ten years in prison for rape and attempted murder. Fisher's first convictions ten years earlier had aroused the suspicions of his ex-wife Linda Fisher. In 1971, she confronted him while he was in the Prince Albert Penitentiary, but he denied that he had killed Miller. His denial, nor the fact that Milgaard had been convicted, didn't ease her suspicions. She even went to the public library to look for a picture of the murder weapon that was used in Miller's killing. She wanted to compare it with her missing paring knife.

On August 28, 1980, Linda Fisher went to the Saskatoon Police and told them she suspected that Larry Fisher was Gail Miller's killer. She thought David Milgaard was innocent. She gave her statement to Inspector Kenneth Wagner, the senior officer on duty. She told him that she was in the midst of an argument with Larry Fisher the day of Miller's murder when a news story about the killing came on the radio. She said he was shocked when she accused him of killing Miller. She also stated that she lost a paring knife around that time and believed Fisher might have used it in the killing. Larry Fisher had never been questioned about the murder. Her statement was sent to the police department's Investigation Division, but nobody followed up. It proved to be another missed opportunity to right a wrongful conviction. It would take another seventeen years for Larry Fisher to be linked to Gail Miller's murder.

While Milgaard waited for his appeals to run their course, he became depressed and attempted suicide. In March 1972, he was transferred to the notorious maximum-security Dorchester Penitentiary in New Brunswick, far from his family. He and two other prisoners escaped in 1973, but were caught as they fled through the woods when tracking dogs picked up their scent. He was sent to Stony Mountain Institution outside Winnipeg three years later, closer to his family. Prison officials felt that he needed to take responsibility for Gail Miller's murder in order to be considered rehabilitated. Since he continued to maintain his innocence, and refused to admit to a murder he didn't commit, he was repeatedly denied parole. As difficult as it was to be behind bars, Milgaard wasn't ready to trade his innocence for his freedom.

Milgaard went to visit his family on a temporary pass on August 22, 1980. Amid the excitement of a family barbecue to celebrate his brother's birthday, he escaped to Toronto. Under an assumed name, he found an apartment and a job. But his freedom was short-lived. His photo appeared in newspapers and he was described as a dangerous killer on the loose. Someone tipped off police. Milgaard was walking down the street in Toronto's Parkdale neighbourhood on November 8, 1980, when he spotted two burly men who looked like police officers. On his seventy-seventh day of freedom, the RCMP shot him in the back. As Joyce Milgaard sat with her son, handcuffed to his bed in St. Joseph's Hospital, she knew she needed to take action.

Joyce Milgaard issued a news release in December 1980 offering a $10,000 reward for information that would prove David's innocence. She bought court transcripts and, with her family, pored over them looking for holes in the Crown's case. Supporters began to rally around her. In 1986, Joyce Milgaard gave well-known criminal lawyer Hersh Wolch her last $2,000 to review the court transcripts to look for grounds to apply to the federal justice minister for "the mercy of the Crown" under what was then Section 617 (now Section 696.1) of the Criminal Code. This provision gave the minister the sole discretion to order a new trial or give Milgaard another chance to appeal his conviction to the Saskatchewan Court of Appeal. Finding enough compelling evidence to prove Milgaard's innocence and persuade the minister to overturn Milgaard's conviction proved to be an overwhelming task. No organization or agency existed to help the Milgaards gather the information they needed, and Legal Aid in Manitoba and Saskatchewan refused to fund lawyers and investigators. Wolch passed the file to David Asper, who had recently graduated from law school and was working at his firm.

Serendipitously, the Milgaards located Deborah Hall. She had attended the motel party at which David allegedly re-enacted Miller's murder. But police hadn't questioned her about the incident. She told them that she didn't remember Milgaard making a confession. If he had, "It would have freaked me right out," she said.[2] Hall said that any references he did make at the time about the murder were jokes. DNA testing and its application to criminal cases was just beginning to emerge. The Milgaards tracked down Vancouver forensic pathologist Dr. James Ferris. The field of DNA testing was not sufficiently advanced for him to help, but he did point out that the semen samples referred to during her son's trial were collected four days after the murder. This meant they were very likely contaminated after being trampled. He also concluded, as had argued Milgaard's trial lawyer, that serological evidence failed to link Milgaard to Miller's murder.

On December 28, 1988, nearly nineteen years after Milgaard was convicted, his lawyers applied to have the federal justice minister reopen his case. It was based on an affidavit from Hall and Ferris's report. While awaiting a response, Joyce Milgaard went to a Winnipeg hotel on May 14, 1990, and tried to hand federal Justice Minister Kim Campbell a copy of Ferris's report. As television cameras rolled, Campbell brushed past Joyce Milgaard. She said that seeing the report could jeopardize a review of the case. "I'm sorry, but if you want your son to have a fair hearing, don't approach me personally," Campbell said. The Milgaards were stunned. Joyce also enlisted the help of Paul Henderson, an investigator with Centurion Ministries. The American organization works to free people who have been wrongly convicted. Henderson tracked down Ron Wilson in British Columbia. Wilson recanted his testimony implicating Milgaard. He admitted that under repeated police questioning, he'd wanted out, so he had finally told the police what they wanted to hear.

On February 27, 1991, Campbell turned down Milgaard's request to reopen his case. The forensic report presented in the application was deemed to be similar to the argument that Milgaard's lawyer had made at trial. Wilson's recanted testimony was considered unreliable and Hall's story didn't alter what had occurred in the Regina motel room. Campbell felt there was no new evidence that would justify referring Milgaard's case back to the courts. His application for parole was refused yet again the following month. He had now spent nearly twenty-two years behind bars.

While the federal justice department was reviewing Milgaard's application, his lawyer, Hersh Wolch, received an anonymous phone call on February 26, 1990. The caller said that Larry Fisher was Miller's killer. The RCMP subsequently investigated Fisher but could find no physical evidence, confession, or witness that would give them reason to charge him with murder. The description of Linda Fisher's missing paring knife did not look like the one that had been used in Miller's killing. Nonetheless, this opened up a new avenue for Milgaard's lawyers to explore. They submitted a second application to the justice minister on August 16, 1991. It focused on Larry Fisher as the perpetrator of the string of sexual assaults in Gail Miller's neighbourhood prior to and immediately after her murder. It suggested that this information would have been admissible in David Milgaard's trial if the information had been known and available at that time. Miller's family joined Milgaard's in calling for a fresh look at the case.

Milgaard's supporters used a media campaign to gain public support for a review of his case. Since authorities didn't seem to be listening, they hoped that public support for his pleas of innocence would get attention for his case and influence the justice minister. On September 7, 1991, they held a candlelight vigil outside a Winnipeg hotel where Prime Minister Brian Mulroney was expected. The group lit one candle for each of the twenty-two years that Milgaard had spent behind bars. When Mulroney stepped out of his car, he greeted Joyce Milgaard and spoke with her briefly. She told him that her son's emotional state was deteriorating and asked if the prime minister might help get him transferred from Stony Mountain. She also asked if a speedy review of his case was possible. Mulroney told her she was courageous. A month later, David Milgaard was transferred to Rockwood Institution, a minimum-security prison beside Stony Mountain.

The justice minister referred Milgaard's case to the Supreme Court of Canada on November 28, 1991. This time, Milgaard testified during the hearings. Ron Wilson recanted part of his trial testimony and Milgaard's lawyers presented the pattern of assaults committed by Larry Fisher. On April 14, 1992, the Supreme Court of Canada, citing Wilson's partial recanting of his trial testimony and the string of sexual assaults committed by Larry Fisher, recommended that Milgaard's conviction be overturned and a new trial be ordered. The Supreme Court justices believed that the evidence could have affected the verdict at Milgaard's trial had it been available at the time. They also ordered that he be released. Two days later, the Saskatchewan government announced that it wouldn't retry Milgaard.

When Milgaard emerged from prison after twenty-three years behind bars, his lawyers were waiting for him in the parking lot. Wolch and Asper handed him a special birth certificate with his new birth date: April 16, 1992. Milgaard, who was just shy of his seventeenth birthday when he was arrested, was now thirty-nine years old. But he hadn't been acquitted nor exonerated for the murder. The Saskatchewan

David Milgaard on November 29, 1991, with his mother Joyce and his sister.
Photo: Ken Faught/Toronto Star/GetStock

government's attorney general said there would be no commission of inquiry nor would Milgaard receive compensation because his innocence had not been established by the Supreme Court of Canada. At the time, the guidelines for compensation for wrongful conviction required proof of innocence. On March 29, 1993, Milgaard filed a lawsuit against Saskatchewan justice officials and Saskatoon Police officers.

Fisher was released from prison on May 26, 1994. Three years later, DNA testing had advanced sufficiently to give the technology another try. A test was performed on semen found on Miller's clothes. On July 18, 1997, the results revealed that the semen on Miller's clothing didn't match Milgaard's — but it did match Fisher's. He was arrested on July 24 and charged with her murder, twenty-eight years after she was stabbed to death in a Saskatoon alley. Fisher was convicted on November 22, 1999, and sentenced to life in prison on January 4, 2000. The Saskatchewan Court of Appeal dismissed the appeal of his conviction and, on August 16, 2004, the Supreme Court of Canada dismissed his application for leave to appeal.

On August 19, 1997, a month after Milgaard was exonerated, the Saskatchewan government announced that he would be compensated for his wrongful conviction. They also made a commitment to hold a public inquiry into the circumstances that led to his wrongful conviction. Milgaard was awarded $10 million on May 17, 1999. The Commission of Inquiry into the Wrongful Conviction of David Milgaard got underway in Saskatoon before Justice Edward MacCallum of the Alberta Court of Queen's Bench on January 17, 2005. The inquiry examined the investigation into Gail Miller's murder and David Milgaard's trial, the information that emerged after Milgaard's conviction, how the case was reopened, and whether the investigation should have been reopened when police and justice officials received new information. It also examined systemic issues that led to Milgaard's wrongful conviction.

The inquiry wrapped up hearings on December 11, 2006. Saskatchewan Justice Minister Don Morgan released the commission's 815-page report on Sept. 26, 2008. Justice MacCallum believed the Saskatoon Police acted in good faith during its investigation of Miller's murder, but he raised questions about how Inspector Art Roberts questioned Ron Wilson and Nichol John. "But for the questioning of John and Wilson by polygrapher Roberts, David Milgaard would not have been charged and tried for the crime of murder," MacCallum said in his report. He didn't believe that Roberts induced John to lie about seeing Milgaard stab a woman. Rather, she may have been pressured to tell him what he wanted to hear. He was also critical of the trial judge, who incorrectly applied a rule of evidence, which led to the jury hearing information that prejudiced the case against Milgaard. The judge also intervened repeatedly when witnesses were testifying, which had a similar effect.

MacCallum noted that the Saskatoon Police should have investigated Linda Fisher's statement that she believed her ex-husband was responsible for Gail Miller's murder. He said that whether or not to follow up on these types of reports shouldn't be left to the discretion of the police. A policy should require these reports to be referred to the office of the Director of Public Prosecutions. Among his thirteen recommendations, he also called for the federal government to create an independent body to review allegations of wrongful convictions. "Had such an agency been in place in 1980, the investigation into the death of Gail Miller would probably have been reopened," MacCallum wrote in his report. His recommendation came more than eighteen years after Justice Alexander Hickman made the same one at an inquiry into the wrongful conviction of Donald Marshall Jr.

Chapter Two

Racism: The Donald Marshall Jr. Case

It was a Friday night on May 28, 1971, and seventeen-year-old Sandy Seale was playing pool with some friends in his family's basement in Sydney, Nova Scotia. At 8:30 p.m., the athletic teenager grabbed his jacket, said goodbye to his parents, and headed off to a dance at St. Joseph's Parish with a group of friends. But the dance was sold out by the time they arrived. After three unsuccessful attempts to sneak into the dance, Seale gave up. With his midnight curfew quickly approaching, he started walking toward Wentworth Park on his way to catch the bus home. When he reached the park, Seale ran into seventeen-year-old Donald Marshall Jr.

Junior, as family and friends called him, was from the Membertou Reserve. Following hearings in 1915, the Mi'kmaq band had been moved from highly-coveted land along the waterfront to a swampy site in a more isolated area. It took years for running water and electricity to be installed. A sewer system replaced outhouses only in the late 1950s.

The reserve of 125 band members was in the unusual position of being in an urban area, which made English the predominant language. But in the Marshall household, all the children spoke Mi'kmaq. Junior was the eldest of thirteen children. His father, Donald Sr., was the Grand Chief and spiritual leader of the 5,000 Mi'kmaqs who lived in the Maritimes. He also had his own plastering business. His mother, Caroline, worked as a cleaning lady at St. Rita Hospital in Sydney. The devoutly Catholic family was among the few on the reserve to have jobs; most people were unemployed and lived on welfare. Racism wasn't unusual. Police sometimes warned white parents when their daughters were seen in the company of Aboriginal youths.

Junior had enjoyed attending school on the reserve, but got into trouble in a white school. He was expelled when he was fifteen after a teacher grabbed him by the ear and he hit her. He barely had a grade six education. He joined a group of toughs and had minor brushes with the law, including a four-month stint in the county jail for giving liquor to minors. Seale and Junior had met when Donald Marshall Sr. did some drywalling for Seale's father. The two boys weren't friends, but they ran into each other from time to time. At about 11:00 p.m. that spring evening they stopped to chat on the edge of Wentworth Park.

Just before midnight, Junior and Seale were seen talking to two men. One was a small, older man with grey hair. The other, Jimmy MacNeil, was younger and taller. The two men were on their way to the older man's house after drinking seven beers each at the State Tavern, as well as some wine earlier in the evening. Roy Ebsary, the older man, was wearing a cloak and claimed that he was a priest from Manitoba. He asked if there were any women or bootleggers in the park. He invited the boys back to his house for a drink but they declined. They asked Ebsary for money. Seale was standing with his hands in his pockets. Suddenly, Ebsary pulled out a knife from beneath his cloak and plunged it into Seale's stomach. The youth crumpled to the ground. Then Ebsary turned to Marshall and slashed him in the arm. Fearing for his life, Marshall ran. Ebsary and MacNeil fled to Ebsary's house two blocks away.

Marshall ran into fifteen-year-old Maynard Chant, told him that a friend had been stabbed by one of two men, and showed him the cut on his arm. Chant, who had slipped out of a church service, was on probation for stealing milk money. He had been on his way home to Louisbourg when he bumped into Marshall. They flagged down a car and returned to the scene of the stabbing. Teenager Robert Scott MacKay, sixteen, and his date were walking to the bus stop when they found Seale on the ground. MacKay accompanied Marshall to a nearby house to call an ambulance. Chant took off his shirt and covered Seale's wound. Then he headed home to Louisbourg.

When the police arrived, Constable Richard Walsh was the first on the scene. He found Seale lying in the street, moaning in pain, his intestines bulging from his abdomen. He was bleeding profusely: the knife had penetrated so deeply that it had sliced through his torso, cut his bowel and severed the aorta. The dying Seale was rushed to Sydney City Hospital as two police officers followed the ambulance. Oddly enough, no officers accompanied him in the ambulance, in case he was able to make a statement about the incident.

Marshall gave Corporal Howard Dean a description of the two men who had attacked him and Seale, but Dean didn't write down the description in his notebook. Instead, the police officer placed Marshall in the back of the cruiser and brought him to the hospital to have his arm stitched up. Marshall also gave a description of the assailants to Sydney Police Sergeant-Detective Michael B. MacDonald. But he didn't make a note of it either because his notebook was at the office. None of the police officers stayed behind to cordon off the crime scene to preserve evidence, search for a weapon, gather names of those at the scene, interview possible witnesses, or conduct door-to-door checks of nearby homes for a possible suspect or eyewitnesses. In 1971, the force's officers didn't have specialized training in forensic investigation of crime scenes. Instead, all four officers went to the hospital.

Seale received twenty-two pints of blood throughout the night, but his kidneys failed and he was placed on life support. Doctors operated twice, but at about 8:00 p.m. on May 29, 1971, less than twenty-four hours after being stabbed, Seale died without regaining consciousness. Although it was the hospital's policy to notify the medical examiner when a patient died within twenty-four hours of surgery, surgeon Dr. Mahomad Naqvi, who operated on Seale, didn't remember having done so. No autopsy was performed on Seale's body to gather evidence for the police investigation.

It was Sydney's first murder in five years, and the force's police officers had little training in conducting investigations of this nature. Constable John Mullowney was dispatched to the park the morning after the stabbing to search for clues, but the crime scene hadn't been secured nor photographed, and Mullowney didn't have any training in handling evidence. He found a bloody Kleenex and turned it over to MacDonald without protecting it from contamination. Although the Sydney Police sometimes used the RCMP's expertise with investigations, this time they rejected the help. They didn't ask RCMP identification specialist John Ryan to photograph the park and the scene of the murder until more than two months later.

Sergeant of Detectives John MacIntyre took over the investigation the morning after the stabbing. Marshall spent much of that weekend at the police station in case officers had questions about the stabbing, but he wasn't asked to give a formal statement until Sunday May 30, 1971. At 4:50 p.m., Marshall spoke to MacIntyre for twenty-two minutes during which he recounted meeting Seale in the park, then standing and talking on a footbridge for a few minutes before two men called them over to Crescent Street asking for cigarettes. The men said they were priests from Manitoba. Marshall said the older man was short, stocky, grey-haired, wore glasses, was dressed in a long blue coat, and was about fifty years old. He said he didn't like "Indians" or "Negroes" when he stabbed Seale and slashed Marshall's left arm. The younger one was tall, had black hair, and wore a blue V-neck sweater. The only information police had was what Marshall himself had told them. Sergeant-Detective Michael MacDonald gave MacIntyre the description, but he didn't attempt to find the men.

MacIntyre had no evidence, hadn't searched Marshall's home for a murder weapon, nor had he taken any formal statements from witnesses. Yet he decided within hours of taking over the investigation on May 29, 1971, that Marshall had stabbed Seale during an argument. He discussed the case with the RCMP during a meeting at the Sydney Police station. He believed the cut on Marshall's arm was self-inflicted because it didn't line up with the tears in the yellow jacket he was wearing. Then he interviewed teenagers John Pratico, sixteen, Chant, fifteen, and Patricia Harriss, fourteen. The information they provided didn't support his theory. He interrogated them until they provided statements incriminating Marshall.

Pratico had consumed twelve to sixteen beers, and about one-and-three-quarter litres of wine before, during, and after the dance at the church hall the night of the stabbing. He first heard about the incident when it was mentioned on the radio the next morning. He learned more details when Marshall happened to walk by his house later that day. Another boy told police that Pratico had information about the stabbing. During questioning on Sunday, May 30, Pratico told MacIntyre that he knew nothing about the stabbing. But he sensed that the burly, intimidating, six-foot MacIntyre didn't believe him. It was standard police practice to have a parent present during questioning, but MacIntyre spoke to Pratico alone.

A week later, on June 4, feeling pressure from MacIntyre, the sixteen-year-old gave a different statement. MacIntyre told him he could go to jail if he didn't tell the truth. Pratico then told MacIntyre that he was sitting behind some bushes in Wentworth Park drinking more beer when he saw Marshall and Seale argue. Then Marshall took out "a shiny object" and stabbed Seale. Pratico, a jumpy, nervous teenager, had been under psychiatric care since August 1970. In 1982, Dr. M. A. Mian, medical director of the Cape Breton Hospital, would say in a sworn affidavit that Pratico suffered "from a schizophreniform illness manifested by a liability to fantasize and thereby distort reality" and a "rather childish desire to be in the limelight."[1]

On May 30, 1971, detectives MacIntyre and William Urquhart interviewed Chant. In his first statement to police, Chant said that he was walking through the park on his way home when he ran into Marshall. He said Junior told him there had been a stabbing and asked for help. The two detectives interviewed Chant again on June 4. As the interrogation progressed, police told his mother, Beudah Chant, that her son would talk more openly if she weren't present. She agreed to leave the room. The burly MacIntyre reminded Chant that he was on probation and that he could be sent to jail if he didn't tell the truth. The police were convinced that he had seen more than he was telling. As Chant sat alone, MacIntyre accused him of lying in his previous statement and said he could be jailed for up to five years for lying. He was told that another witness had placed him near the scene of the stabbing. That witness was John Pratico. As with Chant, he wasn't even in the park when Seale was stabbed. A frightened Chant just wanted to get out of the room. He decided to tell police what they wanted to hear so that he could get the interrogation over with. The fifteen-year-old signed a five-page statement in which he claimed to have witnessed Marshall stab Seale. The police brought him to Wentworth Park, where they helped him fill in the details of his testimony. "I didn't feel I was being told what to do, but suggestions were offered, such as 'Could you have been standing here, you could have seen it more clearly,'" he later said.[2]

Detective MacDonald had interviewed fourteen-year-old Patricia Harriss twice and her story was consistent. She corroborated Marshall's story again when she gave detective Urquhart a statement at 8:15 p.m. on June 17. She said that she and her boyfriend were on their way back from the dance at St. Joseph's when they saw Marshall talking to two men before the stabbing. Seale wasn't with them. She gave a description of Ebsary that matched the one Marshall had given police earlier. Harriss wasn't the only one to see Ebsary and his companion in the park the night Seale was stabbed. Teenagers George and Roderick McNeil went to the police station the next day. They said they were on their way back from the dance when they saw the two men ask a young couple for a cigarette. Sydney Police was given a detailed description.

Harriss didn't have a chance to sign her statement before MacIntyre entered the room and began interrogating her again. Her mother, Eunice, only spent about an hour of the interrogation with her daughter before MacIntyre asked to speak to her daughter alone because she might be more forthcoming. Police didn't believe Patricia had seen Marshall with the two men. Whenever she mentioned them, police crumpled up her statement and made her start over. She broke down and cried, but finally gave in. After five hours of questioning, she just wanted to leave. In her second statement, at 1:20 a.m. the next morning, she said she had seen Marshall and Seale together. But when she left the police station she was upset that police had told her what to say in her statement. As she later recalled in an affidavit to the RCMP in December 1982, "I found they (MacIntyre and Urquhart) were needlessly harping at me, going over and over telling me what they thought I should see ... They took statements and changed them ... My parents were not allowed in ..."[3]

Once the police had statements from Chant and Pratico, they moved in to arrest Marshall on June 4, 1971. The Marshalls had received threatening phone calls after the fatal stabbing, so they had packed up their family and gone to his maternal grandfather's home on the Whycocomagh reserve. The police drove to his grandparents' house that evening and picked him up. As they took him back to Sydney, they said they had two eyewitnesses who said they saw him kill Seale. Marshall couldn't believe his ears. He was placed in a cell at the Cape Breton County Jail.

MacIntyre believed that the gash on Marshall's wound was self-inflicted. Once Marshall was behind bars, he wanted to get a sample of Marshall's blood to strengthen his case. MacIntyre had the jackets Seale and Marshall had worn that fateful night, but there wasn't enough blood on Marshall's jacket to get a sample. MacIntyre asked a doctor at the Sydney hospital to take a sample while removing Marshall's stitches. But Marshall had removed the ten or twelve stitches himself using a pocketknife. MacIntyre had no murder weapon, but that didn't matter.

The case was handed to an experienced crown prosecutor, Donald C. MacNeil. He had been censured by the province's human rights commission the previous year for comments he made in court on the lawlessness of Aboriginals. To solidify Pratico's testimony, MacNeil and MacIntyre brought the teenager to Wentworth Park. They showed him where the mortally wounded Seale was found. They also said they had found a beer bottle with Pratico's fingerprints and offered details to help him remember his story. But the strain of carrying around a lie took its toll on Pratico. Following a preliminary hearing in July 1971, Marshall was committed to stand trial on non-capital murder. In late August, Pratico had an emotional breakdown and was driven to a psychiatric hospital 430 kilometres away in Dartmouth, Nova Scotia. He made the trip in a Sydney Police cruiser. A heavily-sedated Pratico was driven back to Sydney shortly before Marshall's trial got underway.

Marshall's family hired Sydney criminal lawyers Moe Rosenblum and Simon Khattar. Donald MacNeil didn't give them copies of the contradictory witness statements. The defence lawyers weren't aware that Chant, Pratico, and Harriss had given two different statements to police. For their part, Marshall's lawyers were dubious that their client was telling the truth about the events that led to Seale's fatal stabbing, including meeting two men who were dressed like priests. Although they were paid enough money to mount a proper defence, they didn't check out Marshall's story about being stabbed by an older man in a long coat, nor did they interview any of the Crown's witnesses before the trial or investigate their stories and backgrounds. Had they done so, they would've learned that Pratico was sent to a psychiatric hospital after the preliminary hearing and Chant was on probation when police interrogated him. Instead, they relied on an incarcerated Marshall to give them leads.

On November 2, 1971, Junior Marshall was brought, handcuffed, to the Cape Breton County Courthouse, just blocks from Wentworth Park where Seale was stabbed. People had lined up on the steps of the law courts hoping to snag one of the hundred seats in the second-floor courtroom where he would be tried. His trial for non-capital murder got underway in the Supreme Court of Nova Scotia before Mr. Justice J.L. Dubinsky.

Before Pratico, the Crown's star witness, was put on the stand in the Sydney courthouse, he made a last-ditch effort to tell the truth about what he really knew about the stabbing. During a recess, Pratico walked over to Marshall's father. Donald Sr. called over County Sheriff James MacKillop and the defence lawyer Simon Khattar to hear what Pratico had to say. They were soon joined by Detective MacIntyre and the prosecutor, Donald C. MacNeil. They all went into a small room to discuss the evidence. Pratico said that Marshall didn't stab Seale. But moments later a frightened Pratico went back into the courtroom and lied. He said that he was drinking beer behind a bush when he heard Marshall and Seale argue before Marshall pulled out a shiny object and plunged it into Seale's abdomen. Rosenblum tried to discredit Pratico's story by pointing out that he was drunk at the time of the murder and that he had said on other occasions that Marshall hadn't stabbed Seale. But when MacNeil and the defence tried to question Pratico about recanting his story in the courthouse hallway, Justice Louis Dubinsky told them to confine their questions to the night of the stabbing. Khattar wasn't able to find out why Pratico lied. That may have left the jury with the impression that Pratico had been intimidated by Marshall and his father into saying he hadn't seen the stabbing. Little did they know that Pratico hadn't been near the crime scene.

Harriss was having second thoughts, too, but police led her to believe that she would go to jail if she didn't stick to the second statement she gave police, which said that Marshall and Seale were the only ones she saw in the park before the stabbing. Chant, a fifteen-year-old grade seven student from nearby Louisbourg, who had repeated a couple of grades, said that was heading home when he saw Pratico behind a bush watching two people on Crescent Street and witnessed the stabbing. Under cross-examination he admitted that he couldn't positively identify Marshall as Seale's assailant. He was declared a hostile witness.

Marshall was the only defence witness that Rosenblum called to the stand. The judge had to repeatedly remind the soft-spoken Marshall to speak up and stop covering his mouth with his hand. He testified that he was talking to Seale in Wentworth Park at about 11:00 p.m. when two men in long coats or cloaks approached asking for a cigarette and a light. They said they were priests from Manitoba and asked if there were any women in the park. Then the older man said "we don't like Niggers or Indians," pulled out a knife and stabbed Seale in the abdomen. He then slashed Marshall's left arm with the knife. The trial was an ordeal for the young Marshall, who had just turned eighteen behind bars. He asked for and was given medication to help him through.

Jurors deliberated for four hours. Despite the absence of a murder weapon and the lack of motive, they ultimately chose to believe Pratico's testimony and the Crown's contention that Marshall's wound — next to a tattoo of the words "I hate cops" —was self-inflicted. On November 5, 1971, Marshall was found guilty of non-capital murder. He sobbed as he was convicted that afternoon and sentenced to life in prison.

Racial prejudice was an issue for at least one juror. In an interview with the *Toronto Star* more than a decade later, one juror said there was no racism at play during the trial, but he also told a reporter, "With one redskin and one Negro involved, it was like two dogs in a field — you knew one of them was going to kill the other. I would expect more from a white person," he said. "We are more civilized."[4] Marshall was taken to prison. Pratico returned to the Nova Scotia Hospital just before Christmas in 1971. He would continue to be in and out of psychiatric hospitals for the next decade.

Ten days after Marshall was convicted, a guilt-ridden Jimmy MacNeil went to the Sydney Police to tell them the wrong man was behind bars for Seale's murder. He never thought Marshall, an innocent man, would be convicted. On November 15, 1971, he told MacIntrye that he had witnessed the stabbing. Roy Ebsary was the real killer. Ebsary was a vegetable cutter who had served with the Royal Navy during the Second

World War. Under questioning, he admitted that he was in Wentworth Park that night but denied that he stabbed anyone. Police also interviewed Ebsary's common-law wife, Mary, and son, Greg. He told police that his father was fascinated with knives and often carried one with him. They didn't interview his sister, Donna, who had witnessed her father washing blood from a knife after Seale's murder.

On November 17, a criminal-records check revealed that MacNeil had no prior convictions. However, Ebsary had one breach of liquor laws and a conviction for possession of a concealed weapon — a knife. The file with MacNeil's statement was sent to assistant prosecutor Lewis Matheson. He informed Deputy Attorney-General Robert Anderson and handed the file to the RCMP. (At a public inquiry, Anderson admitted that during a private conversation with Marshall's lawyer Felix Cacchione in 1984 he may have said, "Felix, don't get your balls caught in a vise over an Indian." He claimed at the inquiry that his comment was based on Marshall's reputation rather than his race.)[5]

RCMP Inspector Ernest A. Marshall (no relation) and Constable Eugene Smith arrived in Sydney on November 16, 1971, and conducted a brief investigation. Inspector Marshall had been on the force for thirteen years and had developed a friendship with MacIntyre during the six years he worked in the Sydney area. He and Constable Smith spoke to MacIntyre, who was convinced that he had the right man. Constable Smith administered polygraph tests to Ebsary and MacNeil at a motel on November 23. Smith had been trained in polygraph science at New York's National Training Centre of Polygraphic Science but he wasn't yet certified as a technician. They concluded that Ebsary was being truthful but MacNeil's test was inconclusive. Constable Smith put an end to it because MacNeil was shaking badly from alcohol detoxification. However, he didn't resume the test when MacNeil's problems disappeared. The RCMP closed the case without further investigation. They never re-interviewed Donald Marshall Jr. or any of the witnesses who testified at Marshall's trial. As Constable Smith later admitted before an inquiry, they simply rubber-stamped the Sydney Police's investigation.

While the investigation cast doubt on Marshall's involvement in Seale's murder, his lawyers, who were appealing the teenager's conviction to the Nova Scotia Court of Appeal, were not informed about the new evidence. They also failed to raise a legal error that the trial judge had made when he stopped them from questioning Pratico about recanting his evidence. They lost the appeal in January 1972.

Marshall languished in county jail until June 20, 1972, when he was finally sent to maximum-security Dorchester Penitentiary in New Brunswick. He was transferred to the medium-security prison in Springhill in January 1975. While in prison, inmate 1997 went back to school and earned a certificate as a plumber. He passed the time playing hockey and baseball and running. Throughout his incarceration in Dorchester and Springhill penitentiaries, Marshall continued to maintain his innocence. A chain around his neck with an inscription from Isaiah, "No weapon formed against you shall prosper," helped give him hope that one day the truth would set him free.

An application for a three-day pass to spend Christmas 1977 with his family was turned down. Marshall believed it was because he refused to admit that he had killed Sandy Seale. They also refused to allow him to attend his grandmother's funeral. MacIntyre, who by then had become Sydney's police chief, was against allowing Marshall to receive unsupervised temporary absences. He said he was concerned that Marshall would seek revenge against witnesses.

For their part, prison staff continued trying to get Marshall to admit to the murder. Marshall refused. He wrote letters to politicians trying to get his case reopened, to no avail. In a 1972 report, while Marshall was incarcerated at Dorchester Penitentiary in New Brunswick, a staff member wrote, "Marshall is a typical, young Indian lad that seems to lose control of his senses while indulging in intoxicating liquor."[6]

In October 1979, he escaped while returning to Springhill Penitentiary from a wilderness camping trip for prisoners near New Glasgow, Nova Scotia. He made his way to his girlfriend's house in Pictou and was recaptured there several days later. He was charged with being unlawfully at large and sent to the maximum-security Dorchester Penitentiary in New Brunswick. While he was in prison, Marshall broke his wrist in a hockey game, but the prison doctor told him it was just a ganglion. Eight years later, an X-ray at a civilian hospital in Springhill revealed two broken bones in his wrist that had rotted away and died. He had surgery to repair the damage.

Marshall's incarceration also took an emotional and financial toll on his family. His parents were devastated and his father had nightmares. Marshall Sr. had to get an unlisted telephone number after his son was arrested because of threatening phone calls. His drywall and plastering business suffered. Each time he and his wife visited their son, they spent about $200 to travel more than 500 kilometres from the Membertou reserve to Dorchester, New Brunswick. At one time, the family had to rely on welfare to get by.

Meanwhile, the Sydney Police Department continued to receive information that they had the wrong man behind bars. In 1974, martial-arts instructor Dave Ratchford went to police a day after Ebsary's sixteen-year-old daughter Donna told him that her father was Seale's killer, not Marshall Jr. But Detective Urquhart said the case was closed.

While Marshall was imprisoned at Dorchester, a friend came for a visit and brought along a young man who had boarded with Ebsary. He said Ebsary admitted that he killed Seale. Marshall wrote Ebsary a letter. Ebsary replied that he knew Marshall wasn't Seale's killer and promised that he would get Marshall out of prison. Marshall sent copies of the letter to the parole board and the Sydney Police. He also contacted Halifax lawyer Stephen Aronson. On December 5, 1981, another stabbing occurred in Sydney. Ebsary was charged and convicted of the offence.

The RCMP began reinvestigating the case in February 1982 after Aronson wrote to the RCMP telling them that Mitchell Sarson of Pictou, Nova Scotia claimed Ebsary had committed the Seale murder. Staff Sergeant Harry Wheaton and Corporal James Carroll carried out the investigation under the supervision of Inspector Don Scott, commanding officer of the Sydney detachment. They were assigned to the case on February 3, 1982.

They met with MacIntyre, who produced two witness statements from Harriss and her boyfriend, Terry Gushue. A comment that MacIntyre allegedly made also raised eyebrows. MacIntyre said he wasn't able to get a blood sample from Marshall because Marshall removed his own stitches from the minor knife wound he sustained during Ebsary's attack. Wheaton asked why MacIntyre failed to ask Marshall's doctor, Dr. Mohan Virick of Sydney (who was East Indian), for the sample. MacIntyre replied, "Those brown-skinned fellows stick together." [7]

MacIntyre also claimed that Marshall had escaped prison in 1979 by paddling a canoe more than 250 kilometres to Pictou, Nova Scotia. In fact, Marshall walked and hitchhiked.

Wheaton and Carroll were stunned by what they uncovered. Pratico, Chant, and Harriss all recanted their testimony, saying that they had been pressured by the Sydney police to lie. Chant, a born-again Christian, had told his parents and his pastor that he lied during Marshall's murder trial. He was relieved to finally tell police the truth. Wheaton and Carroll interviewed Marshall at Dorchester Penitentiary on February 18, 1982, and March 3, 1982. The two concluded that Marshall was innocent.

When Wheaton and Corporal Herb Davies went to MacIntyre's office in April 17, 1982, to question him about his original 1971 investigation, the burly detective was less than forthcoming. When the two RCMP officers left MacIntyre's office, Davies told Wheaton that he had seen MacIntyre slip papers under his desk. Wheaton returned and confronted MacIntyre, who handed over the first statement that Patricia Harriss made to police in which she exonerated Marshall. But it wasn't the first time that MacIntyre had told the RCMP that he had handed over the entire contents of the file when in fact he hadn't.

Investigators finally found the murder weapon when Ebsary's estranged common-law wife allowed the police to search the basement of the home they once shared. Fibres from the clothing that Seale and Marshall were wearing the night of the fatal stabbing were found on the knife. The RCMP also interviewed Ebsary's daughter, Donna, who had seen her father wash the blood off his knife the night that Seale was stabbed. There was finally enough evidence to cast doubt on Marshall's conviction.

On March 26, 1982, the parole board informed lawyer Aronson that Marshall would be released. After spending nearly eleven years behind bars for a murder he didn't commit, Marshall walked out of Dorchester Penitentiary on March 29, 1982. He was twenty-eight years old. His parents were waiting to drive him from Moncton to Carleton House, a halfway house in Halifax. One of his first requests was to visit the fishing village of Peggy's Cove to see the ocean. The following day, on March 30, 1982, Ebsary, then aged sixty-nine, was sent to the Nova Scotia Hospital in Dartmouth to undergo a court-ordered psychiatric exam before being sentenced for the December 1981 stabbing.

Aronson appealed to federal Justice Minister Jean Chrétien to grant Marshall a full pardon, which would recognize that Marshall never committed the offence. Under what was then Section 617 of the Criminal Code, Chrétien could order a new trial, refer the matter to the appeals court, or ask the appeals court to rule on specific questions related to the case. Chrétien was apparently outraged about Marshall's wrongful conviction, but he was advised by his staff to refer the matter to the Nova Scotia Court of Appeal. In June 1982, Chrétien referred the case to the appeals court on the basis that new evidence uncovered by the RCMP had come to light. The court could order a new trial, declare Marshall not guilty or uphold his conviction. "All I want," Marshall told *The Globe and Mail* reporter Michael Harris, "is what belongs to me, my freedom."[8]

The Appeal Division of the Nova Scotia Supreme Court held a hearing on October 5, 1982, to consider the new evidence. Marshall sat quietly, dressed in a blue V-neck sweater, blue-gray slacks, a shirt, and tie. He had moved into an apartment and gotten a job as a Native education counselor with the federal Indian Affairs Department. The evidence was presented before Chief Justice Ian MacKeigan and Justices Gordon Hart, Malachi Jones, Angus L. Macdonald, and Leonard Pace, who was attorney general when Marshall was convicted in 1971. It included affidavits from John Pratico and Maynard Chant admitting they didn't witness the fatal stabbing and weren't even at the scene when it happened. Patricia Harriss recanted her testimony as well. She said her first statement to police about seeing Marshall with two men the night of the murder but not seeing Seale was the truth. The Sydney Police detectives filed affidavits saying the second statements from the witnesses were obtained because they believed Marshall had influenced the witnesses in their initial statements. The five justices heard applications from Crown Prosecutor Frank Edwards and defence lawyer Aronson. They decided to hear evidence from seven witnesses on December 1 and 2, 1982, including Marshall, Maynard Vincent Chant, and an RCMP fibre expert. James William MacNeil, the thirty-seven-year-old unemployed labourer who had been with Ebsary at the time of the murder, testified that Ebsary stabbed Seale during a scuffle when the teenagers tried to rob them. Then they went back to Ebsary's house and he watched him stand at the kitchen sink and wash blood off the knife. Ebsary's daughter, Donna, testified that she watched her father clean the knife and that he then took it upstairs to his room. She said he was fascinated with knives and had a grindstone in the basement. He was a violent man, she said, who had killed her cat and her budgie in a rage. Her brother, Greg Ebsary, identified the murder weapon as belonging to Roy Ebsary. Both Chant and Harriss recanted their 1971 testimony that helped convict Marshall and said they were pressured by police to change their statements. Marshall admitted that he wanted to get money when he was in the park, but he denied that he and Seale tried to rob Ebsary and MacNeil. RCMP forensics expert James Evers from the crime lab in Sackville, New Brunswick, said the knife had twelve fibres on the blade that were consistent with material from the coats that Seale and Marshall wore on May 28, 1971.

When the court hearing resumed on February 16, 1983, Crown prosecutor Frank Edwards and defence lawyer Aronson argued for just forty-five minutes that the five Supreme Court judges quash Marshall's conviction and acquit him of murdering Sandy Seale. Aronson argued that a miscarriage of justice had occurred. But Edwards argued that Marshall was "the author of his own misfortune to a very large degree."[9]

On May 10, 1983, more than a year after Marshall was released from prison, lawyer Stephen Aronson phoned the band office at the Membertou reserve to announce that the five judges of the Supreme Court of Nova Scotia unanimously acquitted Marshall of the murder of Sandy Seale. The band office emptied as people ran from one house to another to share the news that Junior was free. Marshall learned the news from his tearful mother when he went to Victoria General Hospital in Halifax to visit his father who was suffering from kidney failure. For Caroline Marshall, "It was the best Mother's Day present I've ever had, even if it was late."[10]

But in a portion of the sixty-six-page decision that would hinder Marshall's efforts to obtain compensation from the province, the judges picked up on the Crown's argument and blamed him for being the author of his own misfortune. They said that any miscarriage of justice in his case was more apparent than real. "In attempting to defend himself against the charge of murder Mr. Marshall admittedly committed perjury for which he could still be charged. By lying he helped secure his own conviction.... By planning a robbery with the aid of Mr. Seale he triggered a series of events which unfortunately ended in the death of Mr. Seale."[11] The judges made no reference to the perjury committed by three witnesses in Marshall's original trial. They also exonerated the police and the Crown while convicting Marshall for an offence for which he was never charged.

Aronson and Marshall were pleased with the decision but wanted a public inquiry to be called to determine how an innocent man came to be convicted of murder. Marshall had also amassed a legal bill of $79,000 for his acquittal, which he was unable to pay. Aronson said the Union of Nova Scotia Indians and the federal government both told him the bill would be paid. For its part, the provincial government refused to pay despite the fact that the administration of justice is under provincial jurisdiction. Having run out of money, Aronson left private practice and took a job with the federal government. But he didn't regret the work he did for Marshall's release. "I will always look forward to seeing this guy. What he's done in the last year, after spending 11 years behind bars is absolutely amazing. During the last year he's remained normal while I've grown less trusting and more cynical about the workings of the system."[12]

On May 12, 1983, two days after Marshall was acquitted, Roy Newman Ebsary was finally charged with second-degree murder in the death of Sandy Seale — twelve years after Seale was stabbed to death. The charge was reduced to manslaughter at his preliminary hearing in August 1983. Ebsary pleaded not guilty on the grounds of self-defence. On September 12, 1983, his lawyer, Luke Wintermans, tried to have the charges dropped on the grounds that too much time had elapsed between the offence and Ebsary's trial. Justice Lorne Clarke of the Nova Scotia Supreme Court dismissed the motion. Before a jury of eleven men and one woman, Wintermans claimed that Ebsary was defending himself when he stabbed the unarmed Seale. After a one-day trial and ten hours of deliberations, the jury couldn't come to a decision. Ebsary was released on his own recognizance pending a new trial. This was in contrast to twelve years earlier, when Marshall was taken from the courtroom in handcuffs and shackles. Noel Doucette, then president of the Council of Nova Scotia Indians, and a fourteen-year member of the provincial Human Rights Commission, was upset. "It's a sad irony. Twelve years ago Donald Marshall (a Micmac) came into this same courtroom in shackles.

It took a white jury only 45 minutes to convict him. Then you see Ebsary, a white man just walk in and out of here as if he had done nothing at all. It's justice for the white man and for the Indian; it's the law."[13]

Ebsary's second trial began two months later, on November 4, 1983, before Mr. Justice R. McLeod Rogers of the Nova Scotia Supreme Court. This time, prosecutor Edwards played a tape recording of a twenty-minute conversation between Ebsary, seventy-one, and Corporal James Carroll, a twenty-three-year veteran of the RCMP. In it, Ebsary described the sequence of events that occurred in Wentworth Park on May 28, 1971, and how he stabbed Seale and slashed Marshall's arm, then went home, fired up a barbecue, and cooked up some steaks. Ebsary claimed Marshall had fatally stabbed Seale to "finish him off." He was found guilty of manslaughter. Donald Marshall Sr. raised a clenched fist in victory. After years of public shame about his son's conviction, the right man was finally convicted. On November 24, 1983, Ebsary was sentenced to five years in prison in the same courtroom where Marshall was sentenced to life behind bars twelve years earlier.

But it was not over. Ebsary was released on bail pending an appeal of his conviction. The Nova Scotia Supreme Court Appeals Division ordered a new trial on September 11, 1984. Chief Justice Ian MacKeigan ruled that the trial judge in November 1983 gave the jury incorrect instructions on whether Ebsary acted in self-defence when Seale and Marshall confronted him. Ebsary's third trial got underway in January 1985 before Justice Merlin Nunn. As Ebsary was found guilty on January 17, 1985, Marshall sat in the back of the courtroom and wept quietly. On January 30, 1985, Ebsary was sentenced to three years in prison but his lawyer appealed. On May 12, 1986, the Nova Scotia Supreme Court upheld Ebsary's manslaughter conviction but reduced his sentence from three years in prison to one year in county jail. The Supreme Court said it reduced the sentence because of Ebsary's advanced age and failing health and because there was an element of self-defence. On October 9, 1986, the Supreme Court of Canada refused Ebsary leave to appeal the conviction. He served his one-year sentence at the Cape Breton County Correctional Centre near Sydney. The tiny, frail eccentric lived the final years of his life in Sydney rooming houses, estranged from his longtime common-law wife and their two children.

Compensation for Marshall's eleven years behind bars and a public inquiry into his wrongful conviction proved to be another battle he would have to fight. The federal government argued that it was up to the Nova Scotia government to compensate him since the administration of justice is under provincial jurisdiction. Nova Scotia's attorney-general initially said that Marshall's Aboriginal status made him a federal responsibility. Marshall wanted $1 million in compensation, taking into account his loss of freedom and pain and suffering during his incarceration. During negotiations with the provincial government, which began in June 1984, Marshall's lawyer, Felix Cacchione, also cited a New Zealand case in which a wrongly convicted person received $1.3 million in government compensation and an American case in which $1 million in compensation was paid. But the provincial government's position was to pay Marshall as little as possible. The final settlement wouldn't take into account the botched police investigation. They didn't believe that a miscarriage of justice had occurred.

Cacchione was denied access to the provincial government's files on Marshall's case, giving the government an advantage during compensation negotiations. As Reinhold Endres, the government's chief negotiator, later testified at a royal commission into Marshall's wrongful conviction, the province wanted a settlement that was as low as possible. "My concern was not that justice be done for Mr. Marshall," he said. "The way I approached it was how far down we could come from that figure."[14] In the appeal that acquitted Marshall, the Nova Scotia Supreme Court justices said that a miscarriage of justice in the case was more apparent than real because the murder occurred when he was involved in an alleged mugging. (The word "alleged" is used by the author because Marshall was never tried for the offence and there were questions as to whether a robbery even occurred.)

In September 1984, tired of fighting what seemed like yet another uphill battle, Marshall settled for $270,000 in compensation from the province of Nova Scotia. He agreed, in return, not to take any legal action against the Crown for his wrongful imprisonment. Compensation included $97,000 in legal costs he incurred to prove his innocence and get compensation. Cacchione and Aronson reduced their legal bills. Aronson received $70,000 and Cacchione got $27,000, but this still left Marshall with only $173,000 for nearly eleven years behind bars. That amounted to $43.79 a day for nearly 4,000 days in prison. The federal government agreed to cover half of the compensation. A fund that Montreal United Church minister Robert Hussey set up collected another $45,000 for Marshall. As Cacchione told *The Globe and Mail* in an interview, "This is not a happy ending. This is partial repayment of an unpayable debt."[15]

Fifteen years after Marshall was wrongly convicted, the Nova Scotia government appointed a royal commission, in October 1986, to examine the circumstances that led to Marshall's wrongful conviction, as well as the administration of criminal justice in the province. Alexander Hickman, chief justice of the Newfoundland Supreme Court's trial division, headed the commission. The other members were Associate Chief Justice Lawrence Poitras of the Quebec Superior Court and Chief Justice Gregory Evans of the Ontario Supreme Court.

About eighty people packed the basement hall of St. Andrews United Church, just blocks from where Seale was murdered, when the inquiry got underway in Sydney on September 9, 1987. During the inquiry, the three commissioners learned that the police investigation was shoddy: the crime scene wasn't sealed off and searched for clues, bystanders weren't questioned, no autopsy was performed, a description that Marshall gave police wasn't circulated to officers on patrol, and police didn't search files looking for someone fitting Ebsary's description. The Crown also failed to give the defence copies of witnesses' contradictory police statements, and defence lawyers failed to request them. Witnesses agreed that full disclosure did not exist in Nova Scotia. The trial judge didn't allow the defence to question a witness about his admission in the hallway outside the court that his testimony about witnessing Marshall stab Seale was a lie. Marshall's lawyers failed to raise this legally incorrect ruling during their 1972 appeal. A 1971 RCMP re-investigation of the case simply rubber-stamped the original Sydney Police investigation. Frank Edwards, the prosecutor in Marshall's 1983 appeal hearing, wanted to argue for an acquittal on the grounds that there was a miscarriage of justice. But he was directed by deputy minister Gordon Coles to argue that Marshall was partly to blame for his wrongful conviction. The five appeal justices who blamed Marshall for his wrongful conviction reached their conclusion in 1983 based on statements and affidavits that were

Justice Alexander Hickman headed the Commission of Inquiry into Donald Marshall's wrongful conviction. Courtesy of Justice Alexander Hickman

filed but weren't formally introduced before the court. This meant that the Crown and defence counsel couldn't make submissions about them or cross-examine people who made the statements to which the judges referred in their ruling.

The inquiry also heard about allegations of racism and a two-tiered justice system. Lewis Matheson, who was by then a Provincial Court judge in Nova Scotia, was still a Cape Breton County prosecutor when he said that a fence should be built around the nearby Eskasoni reserve to prevent the Natives from going to Sydney to cause problems. Bernie Francis, who was a court worker from 1970 to 1974, told the inquiry that Mi'kmaqs often pleaded guilty to charges they didn't understand, because judges often denied the use of Mi'kmaq-English interpreters and some lawyers were more attentive to white clients than Native ones. Meanwhile, senior officials in the attorney general's department intervened to nix charges in the case of provincial cabinet minister Roland Thornhill, who was believed to have received personal benefits from four banks that did business with the government. They also initially said no to charges against cabinet minister William Joseph (Billy Joe) MacLean after allegations of misusing his expense account surfaced. He was charged four years later, in 1986, and pleaded guilty.

The inquiry wrapped up in October 1988 after fourteen months of hearings from 112 witnesses. The seven-volume report was released on January 26, 1990. The commission's three judges criticized the Sydney Police for a botched investigation and coercing witnesses to fabricate evidence against Marshall, the Crown for failing to disclose key evidence, Marshall's original defence lawyers for failing to do basic legal work to challenge the prosecutor's case and not raising an incorrect trial judge ruling on appeal, the trial judge for incorrect rulings that denied Marshall a fair trial, the 1983 Court of Appeal for blaming Marshall for his wrongful conviction without evidence to substantiate it, and the attorney general's department for treating Marshall unfairly during his fight for an appeal, compensation and an inquiry. It also found that racism played a role in Marshall's conviction and that two provincial cabinet ministers received special treatment during police investigations into possible criminal activity.

On February 7, 1990, nearly nineteen years after Marshall was wrongly convicted, Attorney General Tom McInnis apologized to Marshall and his family on behalf of the Nova Scotia government. Within a month of the report criticizing Gordon Coles for abusing his power as deputy attorney general, Coles resigned his $94,000-a-year job as special

*Donald Marshall Jr. with David and Joyce Milgaard. Photo: Rick Eglinton/
Toronto Star/GetStock*

adviser to cabinet on constitutional affairs. He was given a settlement of $145,000. The RCMP re-opened a criminal investigation into cabinet minister Roland Thornhill's 1980 deals with four banks that led them to write off about $100,000 in personal debts.

Within days of the report's release, Nova Scotia Premier John Buchanan asked retired Supreme Court of Ontario judge Greg Evans to head an inquiry into compensation for Marshall. Unlike its previous compensation inquiry, the premier said the government would accept the new inquiry's recommendation. In July 1990, Justice Evans recommended that Marshall receive more than $1 million in additional compensation for his wrongful conviction. It included an annuity of $292,000 that will pay him $22,000 a year for life, rising by 3 percent a year to $53,000 per year for a total of just over $1-million if he lived to age sixty-five. Evans also recommended that Marshall receive an additional $199,872 for pain and suffering, plus $50,000 to cover rehabilitation expenses if Marshall chose to seek help for alcohol abuse. Marshall's parents, Donald Sr. and Caroline, were to be given a lump sum payment of $94,242.09, and an annuity worth $80,000 to give them payments of about $7,200 a year, increasing 3 percent a year.

As part of a formal agreement that the federal government signed with the provinces in 1988 to share costs for compensating people who suffer a miscarriage of justice, the federal government paid half of the cost of compensating Marshall and his parents. The agreement between the federal government and the provinces had been prompted by Marshall's case.

In 1996, Marshall was convicted for catching and selling eels out of season and without a licence near Antigonish. Three years later, the Supreme Court of Canada upheld a centuries-old treaty signed in 1760 between the Mi'kmaq and the British Crown allowing the Mi'kmaq and Maliseet in New Brunswick and Nova Scotia to earn a modest living from hunting and fishing. He suffered from chronic obstructive pulmonary disease and received a double-lung transplant in 2003, but suffered from kidney failure linked to the anti-rejection drugs. He was surrounded by family as he was taken off life support in a Sydney hospital at 1:30 a.m. and slipped away on August 6, 2009, at the age of fifty-five. About 200 visitors had come to see him that final evening. Hundreds of people packed Saint Anthony Daniel Church in Sydney and 100 more stood outside to pay their final respects at his funeral. John MacIntyre died two months later at the age of ninety. His funeral was held in the same church.

Chapter Three

Cooking up Evidence: The Jason Dix Case

Jason Dix's two-and-a-half-year marriage wasn't going well. Seven months after he started working at Pacific Industrial Scale Co. Ltd. in Edmonton in May 1993, he started an affair with his attractive and gregarious co-worker, Lucienne Payette. His wife, Lori, suspected he was having an affair and confronted him. In August 1994, Dix promised that he would break it off with Payette. But he didn't. That fall, Payette began pressuring Dix to leave his wife. She was not interested in being the other woman. She gave Dix an ultimatum and, in late September, ended their relationship.

On September 30, 1994, Dix returned from a business trip to High Level and called Payette to invite her out for drinks. But she had already accepted an invitation from James Deiter, who worked at the Crown Packaging Paperboard Limited recycling plant, where he was an equipment operator and did maintenance. Payette had recently sold an industrial weigh scale to that company. Deiter, twenty-four and a married father of two, was also Dix's friend. He had arrived at Payette's office to pick her up when Dix called. Payette didn't want Dix to join them, but Deiter grabbed the phone and invited him along.

The trio went out drinking and dancing. As they chatted throughout the evening, Deiter mentioned that he was going into work the next morning to fix the plant's paper baler. Just before the three of them went their separate ways at about 11:00 p.m., either Deiter or Payette suggested they get together again. Payette handed him her business card and home telephone number. Then Dix drove her home and arranged to pick her up the next day.

On Saturday October 1, Deiter and Tim Orydzuk, thirty-three, arrived at the plant sometime after 7:00 a.m. and began fixing a huge piece of machinery that packs recycled paper into bales. Orydzuk, the plant manager, was married and the father of two children. He had returned home the night before after spending much of the previous two weeks in Vancouver taking a course. Sidney Ferguson saw them when he was working across the street from Crown Packaging in the Strathcona County industrial park. He came over at about 9:20 a.m. to help them fix the paper-baler. When he returned to the plant later, it appeared the men hadn't made much progress with the repairs after he last saw them.

Meanwhile, Dix left his house at 10:30 a.m., picked Payette up at her house, and drove her to work, where she had left her car. He told Lori that he had to drop off a manual for the new scale with Deiter at the Crown Packaging plant later that day. He dropped Payette off at Pacific Scales at 11:40 a.m. Lori met him there at about 1:00 p.m. as planned. He was wearing the same clothes as earlier in the day. Lori dropped him off at G. B. Diesel to pick up his truck, which had been brought in for repairs.

Deiter's wife, Pam, had told her husband to be home by 1:00 p.m., in time for a party for their son Dylan's first birthday. "Jamie was kind of famous for being a bit late," she later told Crown prosecutor Arnold Piragoff. Pam and her mother, Gladys Good, didn't begin to worry until about 4:00 p.m. Pam started calling the plant, but there was no answer.[1] By then, Stephanie Orydzuk was also worried. She had phoned the Crown Packaging plant at about 10:00 a.m. to confirm that her husband Tim would pick up their daughter Colm at their home at noon. Deiter answered. When she asked what the two men were doing, he joked "I'm just trying to kill your husband." She replied, "Well, remember, he's worth more to me dead than alive."[2] Tim had a life insurance policy and benefits worth nearly $700,000.

When Orydzuk didn't show up as planned, Stephanie left several angry voice mail messages on his cellphone. "You better be either dead or have something broken or have stitches," she said in one message.[3]

Just before 6:00 p.m. Pam Deiter sent her brother-in-law, Bernard Deiter, to Crown Packaging. Bernard spotted his brother's truck and

Orydzuk's Jeep parked in the yard. He tried the shop door, but it was locked. A phone was ringing inside, but no one answered. He left. Stephanie Orydzuk took her daughter and drove to the plant between 6:30 p.m. and 7:00 p.m. Her husband's Jeep and James Deiter's truck were parked outside. The door was locked but, much to her surprise, the office door was open. While her daughter played in the office, Stephanie walked around the plant searching for her husband. There was nothing amiss, but when she still hadn't found him after about forty-five minutes, she got her daughter and left.

Stephanie returned to the plant at about 9:00 p.m. with neighbours Dave and Ted Adams. They searched the plant. Stephanie found the bodies of her husband and Deiter beside a large paper baler. Tim still had a screwdriver in his hands. Dave Adams was right behind her. They raced back into the office. As Stephanie wailed in the background, Dave phoned 911. "We have two fatalities," he told the operator. "There's been two men electrocuted."[4]

Royal Canadian Mounted Police Constable Kim Ross, who was a new Mountie still undergoing field training, was one of the first officers on the scene. She arrived with auxiliary Constable Greg Preston. She had no experience investigating violent deaths. RCMP Constable Donald Drissell, who had fourteen years of experience, arrived at 9:41 p.m. He had been told the two men had been electrocuted. He saw no signs of foul play. Within two minutes, he agreed with the assessment of the 911 caller that this was an industrial accident. He didn't question the blood where the men lay, nor blood on one man's face. Preston didn't mention blood spatters that went about 60 centimetres up a plywood wall near Deiter's body because it didn't seem important. He believed that it was part of the electrocution theory.

Drissell and Ross phoned RCMP watch commander Corporal Randall Marchand to tell him that paramedics believed the men had been electrocuted. They couldn't find the power source. Drissell didn't mention the blood spatters because he didn't think it had any bearing on the investigation of an industrial accident. He believed that blood on Deiter's head might have occurred from hitting a beam. Ross, however, did mention that there was blood at the scene. But Marchand agreed that they call in Occupational Health and Safety inspectors.

Not everyone at the scene was convinced. Michael Nicholson, a Strathcona County paramedic, later testified that a wound on Orydzuk's forehead could have been the electricity's point of entry or exit, but there were no other obvious signs of electrocution. "I said at the scene, 'If this is an electrocution, we should call in the *X-Files*,'" he recalled.

The men had no flash burns on their bodies or burn marks from rings or watches, and their shoes hadn't been blown off from the force of an electrocution. There was also blood everywhere, but electrocutions produce little blood. According to Preston, none of the three electricians at the scene could find a source of live power in the huge paper baler the two victims had been trying to repair. Nicholson said he told the police of his concerns with their assessment. Occupational Health and Safety Officer Arnold Lorentz wasn't convinced that the electrocution theory was accurate either, but treated it as such to be on the safe side. Later, Drissell said in court that he couldn't remember if Nicholson and Lorentz had shared their concerns with them and discussed the need for an autopsy. Marchand violated policy when he failed to go to the scene to provide advice and support.

Since there were no signs of a struggle, the police and occupational safety officers weren't concerned about preserving any evidence at the scene. They were more worried about turning off the power to ensure it was safe to move the bodies. Drissell gave permission for the bodies to be moved. Then he turned the investigation over to Alberta Occupational Health and Safety.

The following morning, Stephanie Orydzuk phoned the plant and asked company officials if Ted and Dave Adams could return to the plant for another look. Although the officials thought the request was strange, they agreed. The two men arrived that Sunday afternoon. Ted walked up to the baling machine near where the bodies had been found less than twenty-four hours earlier. He peered inside the machine and touched the screwdriver that Orydzuk was holding when he died. He told other people that an electrical current had discoloured the tool.

Assistant Chief Medical Examiner Dr. Bernard Bannach began examining the bodies on Monday morning, October 3, 1994. He wondered why one of the men had dried blood on his face. He quickly discovered that each man had been shot three times, execution style,

Sherwood Park RCMP investigated the double murders. Photo: Michael Di Massa,
Sherwood Park-Strathcona County News

on the right side of the head. All but one bullet was fired at close range. Hair covered the wounds, making them harder to see. Bannach's autopsy didn't find any signs of electrocution burns. He alerted the RCMP that they had a double-murder on their hands. What appeared to be an industrial accident quickly turned into a homicide investigation. Edmonton Police Constable Michael Sweet, a blood-spatter analyst, was called in.

But by then the crime scene had been contaminated; it had been left without police presence for more than twenty-four hours. Any potential forensic evidence, such as hair and fibre samples, had either been destroyed or was so tainted that it was useless. This proved to be a huge embarrassment to the Sherwood Park RCMP. "We really screwed up," the new Mountie, Ross, told Corporal Gerard Mallett that day.[5]

Dix was stunned and upset when he read about Deiter's death in the newspaper. He had planned to visit Deiter at work the morning of the murders but slept in and then had to pick up his truck. He and Payette decided to attend the funeral to pay their respects to the man with whom they had gone out drinking the night before his death.

Based on information from Sidney Ferguson, the last person known to have seen the men alive, the police concluded that the men had been killed between 10:00 a.m. and 11:00 a.m. The RCMP turned their attention toward Ted Adams, the Orydzuks' neighbour who had been at the plant when the bodies were found. Police found his behaviour bizarre and Stephanie told them she believed that he had a romantic interest in her. The RCMP questioned Adams and also administered two polygraph tests. The first test results were inconclusive, but he failed the second test. The polygraph examiner then interviewed Adams, who apparently got up and left the room without responding when he was accused of killing the two men.

Adams had moved from Shaunavon, Saskatchewan. Lead investigator Sergeant Ed Comaniuk sent two officers to the community to interview people who knew Adams. When they got there, a message was waiting for them at the local detachment to return to Edmonton: investigators no longer believed that Adams was a suspect. He had been looking after his five-year-old nephew the day of the double murder. Police didn't believe he would leave his nephew alone in his vehicle while he went inside the recycling plant and shot the two men. They didn't think he had the mental capacity, or the time to plan and carry out the crime since he only found out that morning that Tim Orydzuk had gone to work. Besides, they had a new suspect in mind — Jason Dix.

Before leaving Shaunavon, the two officers nonetheless conducted interviews with people who had known Adams. They found out that he was familiar with firearms and owned several weapons. People described Adams as being aloof and a loner. The police interest in Adams was briefly rekindled in January 1996 after Pam Deiter phoned Corporal Robinson. She had learned during a lunch with Stephanie Orydzuk that she was buying silk sheets for Adams and that he had just moved into an apartment building beside hers. But Stephanie insisted to police that the two weren't romantically involved.

Dix and Payette attended Deiter's funeral, but police were suspicious because Dix wasn't a close friend. They took the pair in for questioning on October 13, 1994, after they learned that Dix and Payette had spent the evening before the murder with Deiter. Dix had a solid alibi for the period during which the murders were initially estimated to have taken place.

The time that he left home and that it took to reach the Crown Packaging Plant made it impossible for Dix to have committed the double murders. But the police, led by Mallett, weren't convinced he wasn't the culprit.

Police believed the gun enthusiast and former army reservist had killed Deiter because he was either perceived as a rival, or Dix was worried that Deiter would tell his wife that the affair with Payette wasn't over. Orydzuk was killed to cover up Deiter's murder. Police believed that Dix had an opportunity to commit the murders between the time he dropped off Payette at 11:40 a.m. and when he met his wife at Pacific Scales at 1:00 p.m. Police needed evidence or, even better, a confession.

About six weeks after the murders, the RCMP launched a sting operation called Operation Kabaya. It would last thirteen months, involve fifty-two police officers from Alberta, British Columbia, and Ontario and cost taxpayers about $1.5 million. They placed Dix under surveillance; they followed and photographed him, bugged his house, and tapped his phone for six months. Undercover officer Corporal Harvey Jones, using the name Brian Anderson, went to Pacific Scales in November 1994 posing as a contractor and pretending to be a potential customer. Jones had long hair, wore flannel shirts and dirty jeans, but Dix and Payette were suspicious. When Dix accused Jones of being a police officer, Jones got angry and pulled out parole papers. Jones consulted Dix about buying scales and later gave him lumber for a new deck for his house.

The scenario for Operation Kabaya involved introducing Dix to an undercover agent who claimed that he was part of a gang, led by "Mr. Big," that was involved in drugs, money laundering, and other illegal activities. The agent would buy a scale from Pacific Scales claiming that it was going to be used in their legitimate business that was actually a cover for illegal activities. Then the agent would recruit Dix into the alleged criminal organization, gain his trust, and try to get him to confess to the double murders in an effort to impress the phony crime bosses. It took a lot of convincing before Dix would take the bait and join the alleged organized crime network.

The RCMP sometimes uses Mr. Big sting operations to try to nab killers. They build the suspect's trust by making them believe that a powerful criminal gang is trying to recruit them. They start off by delivering what they believe are illegal goods. Various scenarios make them believe they just have to come clean to an alleged crime boss in order to access money and power. The characters are all undercover police officers waiting to arrest the suspect as soon as they confess. Although these types of sting operations are used in Canada by the RCMP, they are not permitted in the United States or Britain because they are considered entrapment. It's believed that these operations also have the potential for false confessions by suspects who want to impress their new friends with how tough they are.

Based on Dix's taped phone conversations in April 1995, it became apparent that he believed Jones's story about being an ex-con who was part of a gang involved in a money-laundering operation. Dix needed money, so he agreed to help Jones. "If my finances had been past what they were and I didn't need money, I wouldn't have got involved with these guys," he later said. "I knew what I was involved with wasn't legal and I shouldn't have been involved with it, but the money was a bigger draw."[6] Jones paid Dix $200 to $500 to be a lookout while he picked up mysterious envelopes. As Dix became more involved in the fake criminal activities, Jones pressured him to prove his commitment to the organization.

In May 1995, the two men flew to Toronto. Dix was put up in an expensive hotel and driven to a warehouse where he was introduced to an undercover officer masquerading as the mob boss. Amid the gangsters with slick suits and fat cigars stood a man holding a rifle over a table covered in stacks of money in a smoky back room. Dix watched as $1 million from a fake payoff was counted in front of him to demonstrate just how important and big the criminal operation was. Although Jones and Dix talked the following month about a contract killing in which a man in Revelstoke would be run over with a bulldozer and made to look like an accident, nothing came of it. Police staged fake car and motorcycle thefts, but it wasn't until December 1995 that Operation Kabaya's most elaborate ruse occurred.

Jones and Dix drove to Yahk, a small town 60 kilometres from Cranbrook in southeast British Columbia for a drug deal that was to involve 10 kilograms of cocaine. When they arrived, Jones went inside the trailer. A shotgun blast broke the silence moments later. Jones ran back to the car. The alleged drug deal had gone bad; Jones and Dix fled. Within days, Dix met with two gang bosses in a hotel room on Vancouver

Island to tell them why a gang member had shot someone at Yahk. They pressured Dix to confess to the double murder at the Sherwood Park plant because they were worried that he would tell police about the fake murder at the trailer if police picked him up in connection with the double murder at the recycling plant. "I knew James and he was a good guy. He was a really nice guy," he told the two gang bosses. "I wouldn't kill him. I have never done that in my life. If you want a killer, I'm not." Dix made $4,500 during the sting operation and got a new deck, but Operation Kabaya didn't lead to a confession.[7]

In March 1996, Corporal Rick Pasker and his partner, Corporal Doug Workman, took over the investigation. They reviewed the evidence that the investigation had gathered and then decided how to move forward. While the previous investigators believed that Dix had committed the murders before he picked up Payette and dropped her off at Pacific Scales at 11:40 a.m., the new investigative team decided the murders had been committed afterward, even though there was no evidence the men were alive after 10:00 a.m.

Workman and Pasker re-interviewed Payette on May 21, 1996. Although Dix had told police that he couldn't remember what he and Payette had talked about the morning of the murder, they told Payette during the interview that Dix had said an important conversation had occurred. But Payette couldn't remember her conversation with Dix. The officers also tried to tell her they were building a team and that she was a part of their team. "You're very important to the equation," Workman told her. "We have to work on this together as a team ... We can't get this guy without you."[8]

On May 30, 1996, several RCMP investigators went to Baptiste Lake to look for the murder weapon. Dix and Payette had stayed at a cabin there twelve days after the murder. It wasn't the first time they searched the area and they didn't have a search warrant, but this time they struck what they thought was pay dirt. A metal detector indicated that there was metal buried near the base of a tree close to the cabin. Police began digging and found a toolbox buried six inches underground. Inside were four revolvers smeared in grease and wrapped in a plastic bag. One was a .22 calibre, the same type of weapon that was used in the double murder. The weapons were brought to the Edmonton RCMP crime lab.

Civilian employee Scott Kashuba examined the .22-calibre revolver. He compared the bullets from that gun with the slugs removed from the murder victims. He couldn't conclude that they matched. He went to Oregon, where more sophisticated equipment was available. While he told Workman that they had the murder weapon, the written report he sent the RCMP told a different story. It said that it probably was the murder weapon, but he couldn't be definite and he couldn't offer any scientific degree of probability to what extent it was likely to be the murder weapon. But the police were more interested in Kashuba's verbal conclusions than his written report. It was the only piece of physical evidence they had linking Dix to the murders. It appears that Workman may not have read the written report.

The police believed that Dix had buried the .22-calibre Taurus revolver at the lakefront property when he went to the cabin for a weekend with Payette, her friend Sadie Stevenson Trebell, and Sadie's two-year-old daughter. They headed out to the cabin 150 kilometres north after work on October 14, 1994. Payette later testified that she had a hard time carrying his bag into the cabin because it was so heavy. Sometime that weekend, the two women and Sadie's daughter went for a walk. Dix said he would catch up. Trebell said he joined them five or ten minutes later, but Payette testified that he joined them half an hour later as they walked back toward the cabin. When Payette asked where he had been, he told her that he had gone to look at the well. On the Sunday afternoon, Payette's friend and the owner of the property, Doug Wilson, arrived with his brother Larry Gale to store Gale's belongings after he'd been forced to move out of his Edmonton apartment. Gale went to the shed and left behind mostly tools, tackle boxes, and toolboxes. He initially told the RCMP that he didn't recognize the toolbox they had dug up. After going back to check the shed, he changed his mind. He told them it looked like one that had been a gift from a friend and that had gone missing along with a stereo. But in court the friend didn't recognize the toolbox.

The four guns were among forty-four weapons that were stolen from Arnold's Gunshop in Vancouver in September 1989. Two Vancouver men were arrested four months later in connection with the holdup of a Brinks armoured car. The two men, Eugene Fengstad and Wayne Stewart, had seven of the stolen guns with them. Police found a buried cache of guns from the gun shop robbery — and several had the two men's prints on them. The question was how the four weapons found at the Baptiste Lake property got there. Wayne Blackley sold the cabin to Wilson in September 1994. Blackley's brother, Rodney "Rusty" John Blackley, was a friend of Fengstad's. The RCMP interviewed Rodney Blackley at least twice, and he denied knowing anything about the guns. He pointed out that if he had buried any weapons, he would have done it in the bush — not on his brother's property. In early July 1996, the Sherwood Park RCMP told the media they had found what they believed was the murder weapon. They informed Wilson that they planned to set up surveillance at the cabin to see if anyone turned up following the media reports.

In July 1996, the RCMP told Crown prosecutor Arnold Piragoff that an expert believed the Taurus was the murder weapon. The grey-haired Piragoff had been a prosecutor for about twenty-five years and was known as the Silver Fox. He gave them the green light to arrest Dix. It was the final piece of circumstantial evidence that Piragoff believed would help him convict Dix on charges of first-degree murder.

Dix had been laid off from the Crown recycling plant in August 1995. By July 1996, he had found a new job at an oil-well drilling site near Bonnyville, 200 kilometres northeast of Edmonton. Lori, an intensive-care nurse at the University Hospital for twelve years, was planning to accept a nursing position in Galveston, Texas. The RCMP arrested Dix on July 10, 1996, and charged him with two counts of first-degree murder in the deaths of Deiter and Orydzuk. During a ninety-minute interrogation, a RCMP sergeant claimed that the police had planted "misinformation" about mistakes the RCMP had made at the scene of the double murder in Sherwood Park. Sergeant Don Szymiec told Dix he would be portrayed as another Paul Bernardo if he didn't confess to the double murder.

Corporal Gary Steinke told Dix during the same interview "I don't want you to get the impression that we screwed up and we're trying to make amends for it now." The two Mounties told Dix they believed he had killed Deiter in a fit of jealousy over Payette and that Orydzuk was shot to cover up the killing. "You have screwed up, you have really screwed up, and right now your life is hell," Steinke told Dix. "Your life from that day forward has been a living nightmare." But Dix told officers a half-dozen times "on the advice of my lawyer I have nothing to say."[9]

As they drove back to the Sherwood Park detachment, the officers stopped to help with the "arrest" of two prostitutes and their pimp. All three were, in fact, undercover police officers. A sergeant, who played the role of the pimp, was placed in the same cell as Dix for the next six days. They hoped Dix would confess to the double murder, but he didn't. On July 16, 1996, six days after his arrest, Dix agreed to be interviewed without the presence of a lawyer.

Over the next eleven hours, six police officers subjected him to an intense and gruelling interrogation. They fed him false information, including telling him that they had a witness who could place Dix and his car outside the Crown Packaging plant the morning of the shootings. They also falsely claimed that he was seen burying the murder weapon at Baptiste Lake. Corporal Doug Workman interrogated Dix for five hours, but Dix repeatedly denied he was involved with the murders. "Whoever did it is walking around laughing at you guys," he told Workman on July 16, 1996. "I did not commit these murders, these godawful murders. I would never do that to anybody. I wouldn't do that to my cat." He said that his biggest mistake was to have an extramarital affair. "I'm sorry for me because my family life has been destroyed. I did most of it with the affair and the hookers," Dix said. "That's my fault, my stupidity, but I'm not a murderer, not for drugs, not for money, not for women, not for gold, not for a Mercedes-Benz, nothing."[10]

Corporal Gary Steinke was the third officer to interview Dix that day. He brought what was believed to be the murder weapon into the room and offered to let Dix hold the .22-calibre handgun. "Jason, it's yours," he said. "It's OK. You can hold it. It's got no bullets. I feel fairly safe." Dix sat with his arms folded across his chest. He refused to touch the gun. He suspected the officer was trying to get his fingerprints on the weapon. "On the advice of my lawyer, I have nothing further to say," he repeated yet again.[11]

In the middle of the interrogation, Dix decided to stop answering questions. "On the advice of my lawyer, I decline to answer that question," he told officers about a hundred times over the next six hours. But the interrogation continued. Corporal Bruce Jackson sat down across from Dix, their knees facing each other. He was the fourth RCMP officer to take a crack at Dix. He began to insist that Dix believed Deiter was involved with his girlfriend, Lu Payette. In a fit of jealousy, he continued, Dix had gone to the recycling plant to kill Deiter. Orydzuk was killed because Dix hadn't anticipated him being at the plant that day and he witnessed the shooting. Jackson repeatedly called Dix a liar. He claimed that Dix's previous statements were filled with discrepancies. "You're not going to paint a very good picture of yourself [in court]. The picture that will be painted is a liar ... and a person with a motive to kill."[12] Dix's only response was to invoke his right to silence.

Corporal Mike Ritchie, the last officer to interrogate Dix became frustrated with Dix's silence. He jumped up, grabbed the arms of Dix's chair, and shoved his face within inches of Dix's. "Are you a ... parrot? I asked you a ... question ... answer me, you fucking parrot!" he yelled.[13] Dix, who was leaning back in his chair with his arms crossed over his chest and his feet stretched out in front of him, remained silent. "You would lie to your mother, your father, your minister," Ritchie said to him. Workman ended the interview.

Police brought Dix back to his cell at the Sherwood Park detachment, but there was more in store for him. Soon after, at midnight, police removed him from his cell and handcuffed him. They marched him into the back of a cruiser and told him he was "going for a ride." Dix had no idea where they were going and what was about to happen to him. He said that he didn't want to go with six armed police officers.[14] They drove Dix to the Crown Packaging plant and the paper-baler machine hoping to get a confession. They fed him false information that they had physical evidence linking him to the murders, but Dix did not confess.

Unbeknownst to Dix, RCMP Corporal Craig Smith had already interviewed Dix's four-and-a-half-year-old son in an attempt gather evidence against Dix. Less than a week after his father was arrested, James Dix sat alone holding a stuffed donkey as he talked to Smith for about thirty minutes. James said that police "took my dad to a safety place" because they thought he killed someone. Smith asked if it was true that Dix had killed someone. James replied "I never knew that ... he was out of town."[15]

Dix was sent to the Edmonton Remand Centre on July 21, 1996, to await his preliminary hearing. The remand centre, for inmates awaiting trial, was designed to hold 300 inmates in single cells but severe overcrowding meant prisoners were doubled up in cells measuring 3.8 by 2.2 metres. They shared an open toilet, had no privacy, and were confined to their cells for as many as twenty hours a day. They were fed small portions of poor-quality food.

Having been unable to pry a confession from Dix, the police decided to try their luck with three jailhouse informants who had criminal records. Mark Robert Simpson was a drug addict and small-time thief with a penchant for selling information to the police. He netted more than $1,100 from city police over two years for information that led to more than a dozen arrests. Most were for petty crimes. The Crown also stayed a sexual assault and a drug charge he faced in two separate cases. Simpson was arrested on July 8, 1996, in connection with a drive-by shooting. Within hours, he offered to act as an informant while he was being held in the remand centre. The police agreed.

Within days of Dix's arrival at the remand centre, Simpson contacted police with information. He claimed to police that Dix had confessed to the double murders and wanted to find someone to "babysit" (slang for murder) Payette. Police consulted Piragoff, who gave them approval to write Dix a two-page letter from "Mark Smith" offering the services of an experienced "babysitter" who's "real good with problem kids." The letter puzzled Dix when he received it in jail on August 21. He gave it to his lawyer, Peter Royal.[16] Meanwhile, the RCMP paid $500 to bail Simpson out of jail.

Jeffrey Allan Harris contacted police on August 27. He had fifty-eight convictions for armed robbery, drug trafficking, assault, obstruction, and a five-year sentence for sexually assaulting a twelve-year-old girl. Harris was initially told he wouldn't receive any benefits for information he passed on to police. That changed within three days, when Sergeant Joe Mamela hinted that Harris could testify under a new name or anonymously. Dix's bail hearing was held on January 28, 1997. During the proceedings, Crown prosecutor Piragoff presented the letter from "Mark Smith" as evidence that Dix was a threat to potential witnesses and shouldn't be released on bail. He wanted to keep Dix behind bars. He failed to mention that police were the ones who wrote the letter, Simpson's only role was to sign it. Court of Queen's Bench Justice Joanne Veit denied Dix's bid for bail.

Less than three months later, on April 13, 1997, Dix sat in jail at the remand centre reading a transcript of the interview that police had conducted with his young son the previous summer. He was angry and sad that police had involved his preschooler. Dix crushed 150 Tylenol pills that he had bought at the remand centre's canteen over a number of weeks and hidden in a can of foot powder. He sat down and wrote a one-page farewell note to his family. "I just can't continue," he wrote. "I feel like I am going insane. One minute I feel OK, the next I just want to curl up and die." He apologized to Lori, saying: "I guess you were right, I am a crumbler, a non-survivor." Then he ended with a message for the RCMP. He said that he didn't murder the two men. "But you can now close the file, eh?" he said. "I hope whoever did this doesn't get one of your family members!" Dix didn't want anyone to think that he had killed himself out of guilt for the killings. That night in his cell, Dix swallowed the pills he had crushed in an unsuccessful suicide attempt.[17]

Then another jailhouse informant stepped forward on May 13, 1997. Blaine Paul Jerabek had a long record of robberies, thefts, and escapes. When Constable Steve Marissink found out that Jerabek might have gleaned information from Dix, his former cellmate, the police officer told him that it could be "financially beneficial" to share it with police. He believed Jerabek could offer useful information in the case if he stayed sober. Jerabek discredited the other two informants. He said Simpson only had a brief conversation with Dix, while Harris was "too bombed up on medication" to be aware of what was happening. Jerabek said he could help the Crown with their case. "I'm not saying the Crown is grasping at straws or anything," he told police. "But from what I know, it's mostly circumstantial evidence. I could give the Crown probably a pretty strong foothold in convicting him."[18]

Both Harris and Jerabek claimed that Dix confessed to the murders and told them he wanted to get rid of Payette to prevent her from testifying against him. Yet, Dix needed her to testify since she gave part of his alibi for the morning of the murders. They said Dix killed Deiter to prevent him from telling Lori Dix about her husband's affair with Payette. However, Dix's wife knew about the affair before the shootings and there was no evidence that Deiter knew about the affair. Harris claimed that Dix told him he had hidden the murder weapon at his house before burying it inside a toolbox at Baptiste Lake while he was visiting with Payette. However, Jerabek said Dix told him that none of the guns police found at Baptiste Lake were the murder weapon and police would never find it.

Both men claimed that they were passing along information about Dix because they wanted to clear their conscience, were trying to turn their lives around, and, Jerabek claimed, wanted to ease the pain of the families of the two victims. Corporal Gary Steinke, who interviewed him, was convinced of Jerabek's story. "If you're lying you're doing an excellent job," Steinke said in a transcript of an interview with Jerabek. "I think you're a credible individual and that's going to be my story … Because, you know, I look for certain signs of deception when I talk to people, especially in this place … You've got to have that sixth sense and be able to judge people or else you get screwed." Although other potential witnesses had to take a polygraph test, the jailhouse informants didn't.[19]

Jerabek was entered into the witness protection program and Simpson was also set to enter the program. Simpson received bail money, cash, food vouchers, and $500 toward paying a $2,500 fine for driving without insurance. Harris was transferred from jail to the RCMP detachment in Sherwood Park when he said he was worried about his safety. The Mounties placed him in a private cell with a television, VCR, books, magazines, cigarettes, and snacks. They also bought him clothes, and took him out a number of times to restaurants and a video store. Six weeks later, Harris was transferred to a jail outside Alberta; the RCMP covered his long-distance calls. He signed a witness-protection agreement the day he was released. He received a new identity including a birth certificate, social insurance card, medical coverage, and $5,000 over the next four months. Harris had threatened to recant his statement if the prosecutor didn't get him bailed out of jail. "I've been straight with you guys and you're [messing] me around," Harris told Mamela. "I'm calling it quits. I'm going to call Dix's lawyer and let him know."[20]

The claims of the three prison informants were at odds with Dix's repeated denials to his wife, girlfriend, parents, boss, and the police that he was involved in the double murders. Neither wiretaps on his conversations at home and work, nor Project Kabaya, led to a confession. He also voluntarily took two polygraph tests and provided fingerprint and hair samples. As Dix later said, "From a year of undercover operations, all they got was lots of, 'I didn't do its.' And all of a sudden, I'm thrown in jail and I'm singing like a canary? That's just incredible."[21] A twenty-month investigation yielded no direct evidence against Dix. Piragoff thought the jailhouse informants strengthened his entirely circumstantial case against Dix.

Dix's preliminary hearing began in August 1997 before provincial court Judge John Maher. The prosecution and defence presented evidence for six weeks. Mark Simpson was the only informant to take the stand. This professional informant maintained that he wasn't looking for favourable treatment in exchange for his statement. "I'm doing this so I can sleep good at night," he testified. "This is one of those things that I'm doing to straighten out my life."[22] Dix's lawyer questioned why Simpson had asked about a $10,000 reward the victims' employer had offered for information about the double murder. Simpson said that he wanted to keep $2,000 of the money and donate $8,000 of the money to the families of the victims.

Justice Maher didn't consider the jailhouse snitch to be a credible witness; he didn't believe that Dix would confide in him. Simpson was an "agent of the state" rather than a true police informant. The courts define an agent as an inmate that police have directed to collect evidence against a particular accused. The Supreme Court of Canada has ruled that this type of evidence is inadmissible in court. In November 1997, the judge committed Dix to stand trial even though he thought it was unlikely there was enough evidence to convict. Besides the informants, the evidence against Dix was all very circumstantial.

Dix made another attempt to get bail. During the hearing on November 21, 1997, before Justice Joanne Veit, defence lawyer Peter Royal accused prosecutor Piragoff of misrepresenting the source of the Mark Smith letter. A week later, the judge denied Dix bail to protect the public, she said, but she was "very troubled by the prosecution's lack of candour." The Crown then tried, in March 1998, to have Peter Royal dismissed from the case because he once represented one of the jailhouse informants. Their request was denied.

Jailhouse informant Blaine Jerabek would be the Crown's star witness. There was just one problem: he planned to sabotage their case by testifying that he lied about Dix's confession to the murders. That's what he told Dix in a letter on February 26, 1998. "When I'm done, no judge will believe any jailhouse rat," he wrote. "It's the only way for me to get my stupid … ass out of this mess, help you, and save face by sticking it to the Crown and RCMP by exposing their corrupt tactics in convicting people."[23] Dix was stunned. He and Jerabek had shared a cell. "My heart went up into my throat and I just about died," Dix later told reporters.[24]

Harris blew his chance for a fresh start in life mere weeks after entering the witness-protection program. In a police statement, Harris's girlfriend said that he stole a new truck just a few days before he was supposed to receive the final payment of $1,000 from the witness-protection program. He said he planned to flee to the United States just before Dix's trial. His girlfriend said he beat, choked, and threatened her with a knife before he disappeared four days before Dix's trial got underway.

The jury trial opened before Court of Queen's Bench Justice Peter Costigan on April 27, 1998. It was expected to last seven weeks. People walked through a metal detector as they entered the courtroom. Dix sat in the prisoner's dock near his lawyer, Peter Royal, dressed in a dark suit and white shirt. Prosecutor Arnold Piragoff admitted that his case was largely circumstantial, but he cited evidence from three informants. Jealousy was the motive for the killing: Deiter was shot to death the day after Dix saw his mistress Payette hand Deiter her home telephone number. The Crown believed Dix drove to the plant and shot the two victims after he had dropped Payette off at Pacific Scales at 11:40 a.m. Then Dix drove back to work to meet his wife an hour later. None of the evidence gathered from Operation Kabaya would be admitted at trial.

On May 5, 1998, the trial moved from the courtroom to a basement conference room at the Telus tower to hear from witness Kimberly Mackay in New York who testified via live videoconference. The former escort worked for Edmonton Entertainment Group when Dix phoned the escort service from his workplace just before midnight the night before the double murders. He said his name was Don Bourk. The place was dark when the blond Mackay arrived. At her request, Dix turned on the lights and invited her into the back office. She described him as being fidgety, defensive, or frustrated. They discussed the services she would provide and the cost, but Mackay left before things went any further because she felt uncomfortable with Dix. She gave her testimony as part

Crown prosecutor Arnold Piragoff. Photo: Edmonton Journal — Larry Wong/
The Canadian Press

of a *voir dire* — a hearing within a trial that allows a judge to listen to testimony and then decide if it is admissible and the amount of weight it should be given in the case.

Payette, Dix's former mistress, testified that police suggested Dix had killed Deiter either because he thought Deiter was interested in Payette, or he was worried that Deiter would tell Dix's wife about the affair. Neither motive made sense to her. Dix liked Deiter and he was not a jealous man. There was no animosity between the two. Besides, there was no indication that Deiter wanted to be anything more than friends — and he knew nothing of her affair with Dix. "I think James went to his grave not knowing about my affair with Jason Dix."[25] The affair had ended a month after Deiter and Orydzuk were killed.

The case against Dix continued to fall apart. On May 15, 1998, defence attorney Royal said that the prosecutor, Arnold Piragoff, had failed to disclose that the letter he presented in the January 1997 bail hearing as being from a jailhouse informant was a fake. During a break in the bail hearing, Corporal Workman had reminded Piragoff of the letter's true origins — that it had, in fact, been written by police — but Piragoff failed to inform the court when proceedings resumed and Dix was subsequently denied bail. Piragoff denied that he had misled the court, but Court of Queen's Bench Justice Peter Costigan said the evidence raised "serious issues" about "the conduct of the Crown." He indicated that Piragoff had a right to respond to the allegations. However, Piragoff couldn't respond to the allegations against him without becoming a witness in the very case he was prosecuting. He withdrew from the case on May 21. Costigan had heard evidence from fifty-one witnesses during the three-week trial, but the three jailhouse informants were not among them.

Veteran prosecutor Bill Pinckney replaced Piragoff. The judge agreed to postpone the trial until September 8, 1998, to give the new prosecutor a chance to review the case and prepare for the trial. It was of little solace to the families of the victims. "The delay is disheartening," Orydzuk's mother Jane told reporters. "We were just looking for closure."[26] Citing both a weakened prosecution case and prosecutorial misconduct, Justice Joanne Veit granted Dix $10,000 bail on June 1. She also noted that Lori and his former mistress had completed their testimony in the case. Conditions included that he live with his mother Jane Robertson, report to a probation officer twice a week, and not leave the province without permission. After spending twenty-two months in jail, Dix left the Remand Centre and climbed into a blue pickup truck beside his father.

Over the summer, Pinckney spent six weeks reviewing the evidence against Dix. It was thin. Just before returning to court on September 3, 1998, he and RCMP investigator Corporal Rick Pasker met with the families of the two victims to break the news. There wasn't enough evidence to get a conviction against Dix. Deiter and Orydzuk's relatives were stunned. Police had told them the prosecution had a great case and that "Arnie Piragoff doesn't back a loser." Pasker hesitated when the family asked if he thought police had the right man. He finally answered that he did, but it wasn't his job or his position to decide.[27]

Several hours later, Pinckney returned to court and requested that the charges against Dix be dismissed due to lack of evidence. He could find no evidence that the two victims were alive after 10:15 a.m. on October 1, 1994; Lori Dix told police that he didn't leave home until 10:30 a.m. that day. Pinckney didn't believe the three jailhouse informants would provide any useful testimony against Dix. Four other experienced prosecutors and the assistant deputy justice minister agreed with his assessment. So did Court of Queen's Bench Justice Costigan. The charges against Dix were dropped. He was a free man, but his life had changed significantly since he was first arrested. He'd lost his job, nearly two years of freedom, 60 pounds during his incarceration, and his wife had divorced him and moved to Texas with their two children, James and Elizabeth, whom he hadn't seen since his arrest on July 10, 1996.

In February 1999, Dix filed a $14.2-million lawsuit against the RCMP and provincial Crown prosecutors. The suit included $10 million in punitive damages for malicious prosecution, false imprisonment, conspiracy, abuse of process, and negligence. His lawyers said that Dix spent $93,000 in legal fees to defend himself and he also believed he was owed $122,000 in lost income and interest for the twenty-two months he was in jail. Dix gave his first lawyer, Mike Clancy, his 1977 Chevy Malibu worth $5,000–$6,000 as payment.

The defendants contended they did nothing wrong. The twenty-one-page statement of claim was filed in Alberta Court of Queen's Bench. It named fifty-five defendants including twenty-two RCMP officers, four Crown prosecutors, the RCMP commissioner and assistant commissioner, the provincial and federal governments, and several of their cabinet ministers. Dix alleged that police defendants "conspired" and "intentionally abused their powers" in the investigation and prosecution for the purpose of, "covering up the incompetent investigation and satisfying the public that a person had been charged and convicted for the two murders in question, without regard for the actual guilt or innocence of the plaintiff."[28] He also alleged the RCMP recruited jailhouse informants to give false evidence against Dix; they lied to, cajoled, and intimidated witnesses into changing their statements to implicate Dix. Crown prosecutors suppressed evidence of Dix's innocence and failed to disclose evidence to the defence; and the lead prosecutor withdrew from the case because of "prosecutorial misconduct" during a bail hearing.

The trial in the civil lawsuit that Dix launched opened on October 1, 2001, seven years to the day since Orydzuk and Deiter were murdered. Lawyers presented 437 pages of written arguments before Court of Queen's Bench Justice Keith Ritter. It included a three-page memo dated August 27, 1998, from former Crown prosecutor Arnold Piragoff urging senior prosecutor Pinckney to make it clear that Piragoff wasn't to blame for the case's collapse. "Remember, Bill, it is my reputation on the line, not yours!" he wrote. "It cannot be left to suggestions that: a) the case collapsed because of an allegation of misconduct on my part, and/or b) the Crown was proceeding blindly with this case in the face of its case falling apart: it is not a question of proceeding in such a fashion, rather I had no opportunity to reassess the case after the 'disappearance' of a witness."[29]

The civil trial ended on February 14, 2002. Justice Ritter handed down his 144-page judgment on June 17, 2002. He found seven Mounties, as well as Crown prosecutor Arnold Piragoff, and the provincial and federal governments liable for malicious prosecution. Dix was awarded $765,000. Ritter criticized the RCMP's tactics. "The police dealt with the plaintiff in an aggressive, offensive and high-handed manner, which not only offended the sensibilities of a court …. but which would offend and often shock the sensibilities of most Albertans," Judge Ritter said. "This is certainly not the way we expect the Royal Canadian Mounted Police to conduct themselves." He concluded that the investigating officers were desperate to cover up for their initial mistake that the two men had died of electrocution. "The file itself is permeated with an overriding concern about the image of the RCMP resulting from this initial error," his wrote in his judgment.[30]

The judge also criticized the misconduct of Crown prosecutor Arnold Piragoff. "To knowingly mislead a court is grave misconduct, to do so as a Crown prosecutor is particularly grave, and for a Crown prosecutor to mislead a court on a liberty issue is egregious."[31] He said there was lack of probable cause to charge Dix, and his right to counsel and to remain silent were violated repeatedly during his long police interrogation. In a scathing decision, Ritter wrote that "The defendants are, quite simply, legally cloaked in malice." Ritter held Piragoff personally liable for $200,000 in punitive damages.[32] The award called for $200,000 in general damages, $93,000 to cover Dix's fees for his criminal lawyer, Peter Royal, plus interest, $121,000 for pre-trial and future loss of income, $100,000 in punitive damages against the federal government, $200,000 in punitive damages against the provincial government, and $50,000 for false imprisonment.

The justice minister rejected calls for an inquiry into the case, citing the fact that the Crown halted the prosecution when it realized it had insufficient evidence to proceed. One issue was clear: the Dix prosecution had relied heavily on the evidence of jailhouse informants. The three men had lengthy criminal records, including one man who had received money in the past for being an informant.

In July 1999, Alberta Justice unveiled guidelines to limit the use of evidence from jailhouse informants in criminal trials in an effort to prevent wrongful convictions. They limited use of the evidence to "instances where there is compelling public interest." However, it did not define what constituted compelling public interest. The guidelines listed eight principles that judges, prosecutors, and police should use to determine public interest, such as the seriousness of the crime. The guidelines included rules to assess the reliability of informants, required that a senior department official outside of the Crown's office evaluate and approve informant evidence before it was presented in court, and full disclosure of an informant's background to the defence. However, the guidelines didn't do away with deals for jailhouse informants in exchange for providing information.

Piragoff left the Edmonton prosecutor's office in 2001 after a thirty-five-year career during which he handled more than 150 murder trials. He became a defence lawyer. Following a hearing in 2005, the Law Society of Alberta decided that he had acted recklessly, but did not knowingly mislead the court. Piragoff was reprimanded and ordered to pay a fine of $15,000 within a year. The RCMP conducted an internal review of the investigation into the double murder and why it targeted Dix. It concluded that none of the police officers breached the RCMP's code of conduct. The only officer to be sanctioned was Corporal Randall Marchand, for not going to the scene of the double murder and for releasing the cause of death to the media before it was confirmed.

For the families of the two murdered men, there would be no closure. "We are still wondering why he is gone," Jane Orydzuk said. "We are still wondering who killed him. If Jason Dix didn't, then there's somebody else out there who did."[33]

Chapter Four

False Confession: The Simon Marshall Case

For the Sainte-Foy Police, Simon Marshall was the dream suspect. It was the winter of 1997, and a man had been terrorizing the Quebec City suburb for nearly two years with a string of more than thirty sexual assaults. Dubbed the Sainte-Foy attacker by the media, most of his victims were young women between the ages of seventeen and twenty-five. The attacker would grab them from behind, pull their blouse or sweater over their head, and force them to perform oral sex and other lewd acts. One woman was assaulted by a man who broke into her home at night. Despite the number of assaults, police didn't even have enough information to create a composite sketch of the man who had stalked and attacked so many women.

In the wee hours of January 3, 1997, patrons at a Subway restaurant hurled insults and roughed up Marshall after they caught him peeping under stalls in the women's washroom. His hat was torn in the scuffle, but he continued to hang around. The Sainte-Foy Police were called. Constables Nathalie Blais and Roger Ferland arrested Marshall, twenty-three, for voyeurism and read him his rights. He said he didn't need a lawyer. He wasn't a pedophile, he told the two officers, referring to one of the insults that patrons had yelled at him. He said that women had consented to whatever acts he had committed with them.

Constable Ferland found the comment intriguing. He started asking Marshall for details. The intellectually disabled man was sitting in the police car when they drove past a wooded area on their way to the police station. It was the site of one of the sexual assaults. Ferland asked Marshall about the location of the assaults. Marshall pointed at the wooded area, but he claimed that the woman had consented. Constable Blais was puzzled about his willingness to confess. She couldn't figure out if he was making it up, enjoying bragging, or whether he really had committed the assaults.

Once the trio reached the police station, Ferland and Detective-Sergeant Raymond Matte interrogated Marshall. They concluded that he was the real deal. He had given them some details of the attacks that — they believed — hadn't been released to the public. These included that one victim had her period, another one was wearing a Walkman, and a third woman's flat was broken into by a man claiming he had entered the wrong house by accident.

Police also prompted Marshall. Detective-Sergeant Matte asked Marshall what was unusual about a particular incident. Marshall couldn't remember. It was only when Matte gave him a hint, the word "bra," that Marshall said the man had tried to unhook the bra in the front, but the clasps were in the back. It was only when the local newspaper Le Soleil reviewed the case seven years later, in 2004, that it demonstrated that the media had reported the details, along with dates and locations of assaults, before Marshall was picked up by police and confessed.

The police were pleased to finally catch a suspect — and get a confession — in this high profile case. "Female citizens will finally be able to sleep in peace," an investigator told a news conference that was called to announce the arrest.[1] Police had a DNA sample from sperm in one of the assaults, on a seven-year-old girl. But those charges were withdrawn when Marshall's information didn't match that given by the victim. The DNA sample wasn't tested to see if it matched Marshall's. Since they had a confession, there seemed no need to use forensics to confirm that the police had the right man. Crown attorney Jean-Pierre Dumais authorized the charges. Marshall was placed in remand at the Orsainville detention centre.

Marshall had trouble learning. He finally completed grade nine when he was twenty years old. He was taking anti-psychotic drugs, and had received psychiatric care for his behavioural problems as early as 1992. He'd been diagnosed as being schizophrenic. Psychiatrist

Dr. Richard Laliberté examined Marshall on January 13, 1997, and concluded within ten minutes that he was fit to stand trial and that he was a danger to society.

Defence lawyer Jorge Armijo felt there was little he could do to keep Marshall out of jail. In June 1997, he said his client insisted on pleading guilty to thirteen counts of sexual assault, assault, breaking and entering, and uttering threats for attacks on nine women. But none of the victims were able to identify Marshall as their attacker. One of them didn't believe he was her attacker. Psychiatrist Dr. Sylvain Faucher, from Hôpital Robert-Gifford, testified that Marshall had a melodramatic ("histrionic") personality. It manifested as a craving for attention and a desire to impress people. Armijo didn't present any expert witnesses to support Marshall's intellectual handicap, nor did he invoke a defence of mental defect.

During his sentencing hearing, probation officer Suzanne Lamy testified that Marshall tended to make up stories in a bid for attention and an eagerness to please people. He would tell people what he thought they wanted to hear. He even denied that he was responsible for the crimes for which he was charged, then changed his mind. "Even in the same conversation he could say two contradictory things within 15 minutes ... you could almost make him say things," she said.[2] But that apparently didn't set off any alarm bells for Quebec Court Judge Pierre Rousseau and the two lawyers.

On the morning of November 28, 1997, Marshall was sentenced to five years behind bars in addition to the eleven months he had already served in detention on remand. Judge Rousseau recommended that he be sent to the Philippe-Pinel Institute or the La Macaza detention centre for treatment. Instead, he was sent to the Sainte-Anne-des-Plaines federal penitentiary in Laval to serve his sentence. The National Parole Board rejected his three applications for parole. In an unusual move, Marshall was forced to serve his entire sentence behind bars. Assaults similar to those for which Marshall was convicted occurred during his incarceration but they received scant publicity.

In an interview, a former inmate told Quebec television network TVA that Marshall was beaten and sodomized by other inmates at the penitentiary, as well as being the victim of verbal abuse. He was also scalded with boiling water. He began to spend up to twenty-three hours a day in his cell; he didn't want to leave his cell, go outside, or talk to anyone except a chaplain. Marshall was finally released in January 2003. His incarceration traumatized him and his mental state had deteriorated. After he was released, he was in a catatonic state. His mother, Manon Beaudoin, said, "He hears voices. He won't talk." He was hospitalized under psychiatric care.[3]

In the months subsequent to his release, a man wielding a knife forced a young woman to perform oral sex on him in an elevator at Place Laurier on July 25, 2003. While Marshall was undergoing treatment as an outpatient at Hôpital Robert-Gifford, a psychiatric hospital, he confided in a social worker. She recognized some of the information as being details about two recent assaults. The social worker picked up Marshall at his house and brought him to the police station. Once again, Marshall confessed to the two sexual assaults. He even told the police about the knife that was used during the elevator attack. He was arrested on August 8, 2003, on three more counts of sexual assault and jailed. The Crown requested that he be declared a dangerous offender.

But then his story began to unravel. The two victims who were involved in the elevator attack didn't recognize Marshall. The police had a DNA sample of the sperm from the elevator rapist. They sent it to the Laboratoire de sciences judiciaires et médecine légale to compare the 2003 rapist's DNA with that of Marshall. But on January 8, 2004, the lab discovered that it wasn't a match. Marshall hadn't committed the latest assaults to which he had confessed. That cast doubt on his earlier conviction in 1997.

In January 2004, Quebec City Police Chief Daniel Langlais asked the provincial police force, the Sûreté du Québec (SQ), to investigate. By then, the Sainte-Foy Police had amalgamated with the Quebec City force. Although the Sainte-Foy Police had conducted the original investigation that led to Marshall's conviction, Langlais wanted to ensure that members of his force weren't reviewing their own work. He wanted the SQ to review the original evidence from the 1995 and 1996 attacks. Investigators reviewed the original evidence and spoke to the victims. This led to the discovery that the original DNA had been collected but never tested.

On August 10, 2005, Police Chief Langlais announced that Marshall was not their man after all. He had spent more than five years behind bars for crimes he never committed. A review cleared him of the thirteen charges to which he had pleaded guilty in 1997. A test found that the sperm in the case of the seven-year-old girl didn't match Marshall's DNA. Marshall and his parents were pleased with the results of the investigation, but the ordeal had left its mark on Marshall. He was in a psychiatric hospital recovering from his incarceration when he learned the news.

Langlais turned the case over to Quebec's Justice and Public Security departments for review. What did the police learn from the case? According to Langlais, the police no longer closed investigations after getting a confession. They looked for other evidence to support it.

The Quebec government acted swiftly. Within two weeks, Quebec Justice Minister Yvon Marcoux announced that he would choose an independent arbitrator to decide upon the amount of compensation Marshall would receive. He also asked the Quebec Court of Appeal to overturn Marshall's convictions. The Quebec Court of Appeal quashed Marshall's convictions on September 23, 2005, after a twenty-minute hearing. The Crown admitted that Marshall's confessions were considered unreliable. The Court ruled that Marshall was a victim of a miscarriage of justice.

In September 2005, Marcoux appointed retired Quebec Court of Appeal judge Michel Proulx as independent arbitrator to determine compensation in the case. Proulx was a criminal lawyer and law professor at McGill University before he sat as an appellate judge from 1989 to 2004. Proulx used guidelines developed by the federal and provincial governments in 1988 to compensate victims of wrongful convictions. He would consider such factors as loss of liberty, physical and emotional suffering, loss of reputation, and loss of income. In December 2006, the province accepted the late Honourable Proulx and lawyer Pierre Cimon's recommendations. Marshall was awarded $2.3 million in compensation.

Lawyer Jean-Paul Michaud represented Marshall and his family in the negotiations. Marshall was the victim of sexual, physical, and verbal abuse from other inmates in prison. He "swam with the sharks and walked with the tigers," Michaud said. "It was a nightmare, a horror movie, that Simon Marshall and his parents went through."[4]

Public Security Minister Jacques Dupuis ordered Quebec's Police Ethics Commission to investigate the officers who handled the 1997 investigation that led to Marshall's convictions, and failed to test the DNA that would have exonerated him before the case went to trial. The committee is an administrative tribunal that does not establish guilt or innocence. It rules only on the conduct of officers and can issue sanctions ranging from a warning to dismissals.

The inquiry into the conduct of Police Lieutenant Luc Barrette and Detective-Sergeant Raymond Matte, who were both retired from the Sainte-Foy force, and Detective-Sergeant Hélène Turgeon, of the Quebec City force, opened in January 2007. The Police Ethics Commission was investigating them for abuse of authority, conducting incomplete investigations, and making false accusations. Commissioner Pierre Gagné presided over the hearings. Barrette and Matte were cited for their work in the investigation that preceded Marshall's 1997 conviction. Turgeon investigated a series of sexual assaults that occurred in 2003. Christiane Mathieu, a lawyer acting for the commission, said the officers didn't have victims of the assaults identify Marshall and failed to check on his whereabouts at the times that the attacks occurred. She also said that, had they talked to Marshall's parents, they would have been told that he was intellectually handicapped.

In April 2008, the Police Ethics Commission cleared two of the officers of allegations they had abused their authority and conducted incomplete investigations. However, Detective-Sergeant Matte was found guilty of making false accusations with respect to one of the victims. The charge related to the false accusation that was dropped before Marshall's trial started. But as Serge Goulet, the lawyer representing Marshall during the appeal that led to his exoneration pointed out, the ruling meant only that the police officers didn't breach their code of ethics during the investigation. "The commission didn't say anything about the quality of their work. You can botch your job and not go against your ethics code."[5]

The Quebec College of Physicians released a report by Dr. François Gauthier in March 2006 into the investigation of two physicians who had assessed whether Marshall was fit to stand trial and then assessed him before sentencing. They found that the psychiatrists had acted properly. There was no breach of their code of ethics.

In 2005, Quebec Bar president Madeleine Lemieux said that in light of Marshall's wrongful conviction the province should create a special Mental Health Court for people who are intellectually disabled or have mental health problems. According to the annual report of the Office of the Correctional Investigator of Canada released in November 2005, at least one in eight federal prisoners has a diagnosed mental illness — 1,500 of the 12,500 federal inmates. People with mental illness make easy targets for other prisoners.

In light of the Marshall case, in 2006, the Quebec Bar set up a committee to examine how the justice system deals with people with mental-health problems or intellectual disabilities. They released their report in March 2010. The nine-member committee's recommendations included a call for abolishing the use of video conferencing by justice officials when conducting a mental-health evaluation of someone involved in a criminal or civil case. The practice is confusing for people who suffer from such psychological problems as schizophrenia. "You try to explain to them that the judge is in the camera, in another city, and the prosecutor is in another city — it just exacerbates the symptoms [of paranoia]," explained lawyer and committee member Lucie Joncas.[6]

The committee also recommended that police videotape statements that are given by an accused person with mental health problems. This will help establish the person's state of mind. "Mental health can fluctuate over months and, at the time of a trial, it can be hard to prove what state the person was in at the time of an arrest," Joncas said.[7] They also found that it takes too long to determine whether an accused is fit to stand trial. The Criminal Code recommends that assessments take about five days, but the assessment often takes weeks to complete because of a lack of resources. The Quebec Bar planned to offer lawyers courses on representing people with mental health problems or intellectual disabilities. No one has been arrested in connection with the attacks for which Simon Marshall was wrongly convicted.

Chapter Five

Withholding Key Evidence: The Gary Staples Case

Gerald Burke handed his wife the $100 that remained of his final paycheque from Bermingham Construction after he had paid a few bills. "Here honey, keep this and we'll go out and do a little bit of Christmas shopping tomorrow," he said.

He kissed twenty-one-year-old Doreen goodbye and headed off to work. For the past two or three years, the twenty-four-year-old Burke had been driving taxis in between jobs to support Doreen and their two young sons, two-and-a-half-year-old Robert and eighteen-month-old Darrin.

Burke's shift at the Hamilton, Ontario, Kenilworth Kab Company began at 4:00 p.m. It was a busy evening for taxis on December 5, 1969, as he pulled up to the Greater Hamilton Shopping Centre filled with Christmas shoppers. A woman had phoned for a taxi and was waiting near the Laura Secord candy store. He reached for the radio in his cab as she climbed in. "Eighteen going to Division Street," he said, letting the dispatcher at Kenilworth Kabs know that his fare's destination was a five-minute ride. Eighteen was his radio number. It was approximately 7:30 p.m. as he pulled away from the curb. Burke didn't check in again for the rest of the evening, but it was so busy that the dispatcher didn't notice.

Police Constable Bayne Henderson was on a routine patrol of Hamilton's deserted north east-end industrial area at 2:37 a.m. when he spotted Burke's turquoise sedan. It was parked on industrial land between the Canadian National Railway tracks and the Hammant Car

Gerry Burke was last seen at the Greater Hamilton Shopping Centre. Photo: Tourism Hamilton

Engineering Company factory on Dunbar Avenue. When he approached the vehicle, he made a grisly discovery. Inside, the young cabbie was slumped behind the wheel. His wallet and identification were missing. The car's engine and two-way radio had been turned off. At about 9:00 p.m., just a few short hours after his shift had begun, Burke had been fatally shot twice in the head at close range. Police believed that he was robbed of $40.

Burke had no insurance and the $100 he'd given his wife earlier that evening was the only money he had left. Local taxi drivers began a fund for his family. In the aftermath of the killing, Burke's young widow suffered a debilitating emotional breakdown. She bundled up her two toddlers, abandoned her house, and fled from Hamilton and her old life. She wanted to forget. She remarried and her new husband raised her two boys as his own. Burke's sons, Robert and Darrin, grew up never knowing their father and his family. After Gerry Burke's death, they lost contact with their paternal grandparents and extended family.

For their part, police were having little luck with their investigation. Hamilton Police Detective-Sergeants Norm Thompson, James Williams, and James Campbell found few clues at the crime scene to help them find Burke's killer. They believed that robbery had been the motive for killing the amiable cabbie, but the investigators had no leads about possible suspects. They canvassed the neighbourhood and turned to the public for help. They also wanted to speak to the woman who was last seen climbing into Burke's cab at the shopping centre. Witnesses told police that three young men had been spotted causing trouble at various places near the scene of the murder before and after the killing. In the wee hours of the morning, after Burke's body had been discovered, three youths were seen at a lunch-counter-type of restaurant. Their behaviour was unusual, and they became visibly nervous and fled when the restaurant's customers began talking about the cabbie's murder.

Within twenty-four hours of the murder, Canadian National Railway railcar inspector Wayne Salisbury contacted police. He told them that while he was working the 6:00 p.m. to 2:00 a.m. shift on December 5, he drove his car to a laneway and spotted Burke's taxi at about 9:20 p.m. After watching it for several minutes, he saw three men in their late teens or early twenties run from the cab and head west. He said he thought that a fourth person might have joined them as they crossed the railway tracks. The next day, fourteen-year-old James Johnstone told police that he had seen only one person leave the taxi at about 8:45 p.m.

The two stories didn't add up; the timing wasn't quite right and neither was the number of people who had left the taxi at the scene of the crime. Investigating officers Thompson and Williams wanted to get to the bottom of the discrepancies. When they re-interviewed Salisbury on December 11, he said his wife was with him and that she, too, had seen three people running from the taxi. He hadn't told the police this when he was questioned earlier because it was against company regulations for her to be with him in his car while he was working. They spoke to his wife, who confirmed what she had seen. Unfortunately, this information didn't resolve inconsistencies between Johnstone's and the Salisburys' stories. Police were stumped and the investigation hit a dead end — until they got a phone call from the Ontario Provincial Police four months later.

The OPP had arrested Mary Conklin in connection with break-and-entry, robbery, and theft offences they were investigating. The young woman knew she was facing criminal charges; she needed to find something valuable that she could use to barter with police for favourable treatment. She told them that she could provide information into the unsolved murder of Gerry Burke in exchange for leniency on her own charges. The police agreed.

On April 24, 1970, the Hamilton Police detectives thought they had finally caught a break in the case. Conklin told them that she was at her Dunnville, Ontario, home with her cousin Ken Shellard on the evening of December 5, 1969. As they sat in her living room, her former boyfriend Gary Staples confessed that he had just robbed and murdered a taxi driver on his own. Staples was a lifelong resident of Dunnville. The police interviewed Ken Shellard, who was in prison at the time, but did not take a formal witness statement from him.

Little more than twenty-four hours after Conklin told them her story, the investigators made their move. Twenty-five-year-old Staples was asleep with his wife and son when police burst into his house in the middle of the night on April 26, 1970. Pointing a gun at him, they dragged him from his bed. Staples thought it was a joke until an officer waved an arrest warrant at him and claimed that he'd killed Burke. For months, Staples thought it was all a terrible mistake.

At the Dunnville police station, Staples was charged with non-capital murder. He steadfastly maintained that he had nothing to do with Gerry Burke's murder. But investigators Williams and Thompson were determined to extract a confession. They handcuffed Staples to a chair in the middle of the night and beat him during questioning. Unbowed, he continued to maintain his innocence.

Staples said that at the time of the murder, he was having his car repaired at a Dunnville garage, about fifty kilometres away from the scene of the crime. Between 8:00 p.m. and 8:30 p.m. that day he had been at a friend's house in Dunnville discussing the fact that his car needed repairs. Then he headed to a Canadian Tire to buy the part he needed for the car. He showed up at a service station at 8:30 p.m. and hung around until his vehicle was ready at 10:15 p.m. In ideal daylight driving conditions, the fifty-kilometre drive from the scene of the murder to the service station took at least half an hour one way. But the detectives didn't buy his alibi.

The young father was transferred to a police station in Hamilton and then brought to the Barton Street Jail downtown. Efforts to get him to confess to a murder he didn't commit continued. During his incarceration, while awaiting trial, Staples was removed from the jail's general population and segregated in solitary confinement. Prison guards told him that he would be allowed to rejoin the general population if he signed a confession admitting to Burke's murder. Staples refused. He spent sixty-seven days in solitary confinement and was held without bail until his preliminary hearing in the fall of 1970.

A hearing was held to determine whether there was enough evidence to bring Staples to trial. James Johnstone told the court that he had seen one man leave Burke's taxi. Conklin's cousin, Ken Shellard, was brought from the Burwash Jail in Sudbury to testify but he refused to corroborate Conklin's story. He denied that he had been present when Staples confessed to killing Gerry Burke. Staples was held over for trial without bail, but police investigators knew they had a problem. Conklin's story might not hold up at trial since Shellard couldn't corroborate it. They helped Conklin change her story.

On January 13, 1971, Staples's trial got underway before a judge and jury in what was then the Supreme Court of Ontario. Conklin told a story that was different from the one she had recounted during the preliminary hearing. She testified that her cousin was asleep when Staples arrived at her house during the evening of December 5. She and Staples were alone in the kitchen when he allegedly confessed to Burke's murder. The Crown also called fourteen-year-old James Johnstone, who testified that he saw one man flee Burke's taxicab at about 8:45 p.m.

Wayne Salisbury and his wife, who said they had seen three men fleeing the scene of the crime, were not called to the stand. In fact, police made no mention of them to the Crown, the court, or the defence. They had decided to withhold the information. Staples, himself a young father, was convicted of murder ten days later, on January 23, 1971. As the jury's verdict was about to be pronounced, Justice M.N. Lacourciere asked Staples if he had anything to say. "Yes, your honour. I haven't killed anyone," he replied. The judge's sentence was devastating. "I hereby sentence you to reformatory or penitentiary for the rest of your natural life."[1] He was sent to Kingston Penitentiary to serve out his sentence.

Inmates at the penitentiary were assigned jobs in the prison. A guard asked Staples if he would like to work in the kitchen. The bewildered prisoner said that he didn't know anything about cooking. He was told that he had the rest of his life to learn. Staples was nervous about the behaviour of other inmates and sometimes wondered if he would ever get out of that harsh place alive. "I worked in an environment where I was afraid for my own life," he later told the *Hamilton Spectator*. "I worked with twenty-four men who had committed murder."[2]

In April 1971, less than three months after finding himself at one of Canada's most notorious penitentiaries, Staples watched, but refused to participate, as a handful of prisoners rioted and took control of the Kingston Penitentiary for four days. Rioters brutally tortured and mutilated a number of prisoners. One man was clubbed to death. Staples and the other inmates lived in fear of being killed during the riots. In fact, he was nearly shot when authorities regained control of the prison. Although Staples hadn't participated in the uprising, prison guards beat him and other inmates in acts of vengeance.

The fight to free Staples wasn't over. Emma Staples knew that her son was innocent; she refused to believe he was a killer. He didn't belong behind bars. The answer, she believed, lay in finding people who could confirm his whereabouts in Dunnville the evening that Gerry Burke was murdered in Hamilton. She worked tirelessly to locate witnesses. Various members of Staples's family confirmed that he was in Dunnville continuously from 5:00 p.m. until after 11:00 p.m. on December 5, 1969. Emma found other witnesses who saw him at the service station while his car was being repaired. She also located a neighbour of Conklin's who heard Conklin and Staples having a loud argument the day after the murder over the fact that Staples hadn't visited the night before. This was new information that hadn't been available during the trial. Witnesses had been reluctant to become involved, and the Hamilton Police did not adequately investigate the alibi Staples gave them.

Armed with this new information, Staples appealed his conviction to what was then called the Court of Appeal of the Supreme Court of Ontario. The fresh evidence that Emma Staples had uncovered was presented. Affidavits were submitted from independent witnesses who supported Gary Staples's alibi and his whereabouts in Dunnville throughout the entire evening of December 5, 1969. A witness said that Conklin was not even home on the evening of Friday, December 5, when she alleged that Staples had confessed to her in her kitchen.

In a unanimous decision handed down on October 21, 1971, the Ontario Court of Appeal's three judges, led by then-Chief Justice of Ontario George Alexander Gale, set aside Staples's murder conviction and ordered a new trial. Staples was transferred from Kingston Penitentiary back to the Barton Street Jail in Hamilton to await his second trial. It opened on January 11, 1972, before a judge and jury. Defence lawyers Arthur Maloney and Walter Stayshyn represented Staples. Once again, the Crown called James Johnstone to the stand to testify. But this time the results were different. Staples was acquitted on February 3, 1972. The jury accepted that he couldn't have been involved in the murder since he was fifty kilometres away from the scene of the crime at the time. For the first time in twenty-two months, Staples was once again a free man. He was released after spending 649 days behind bars for a crime that someone else had committed.

The Crown wasted little time filing an appeal of the acquittal on February 16, 1972. Two months later, defence lawyers Maloney and Stayshyn heard a rumour about the existence of a possible material witness called Wayne Salisbury. Maloney wanted to know whether the Hamilton Police had obtained any information from Salisbury and his wife during their investigation. If so, had it had been given to the Crown prosecutor? Maloney wrote to the Hamilton police chief on April 28 to find out. The chief, in turn, asked the investigating officers about the Salisburys. Suddenly and inexplicably, the Crown dropped their appeal on November 6, 1972, before it had been heard. The Hamilton Police Services abandoned the investigation into Gerry Burke's murder, but it would take nearly thirty years to find out why.

Staples was relieved to be free again and looked forward to returning home to Dunnville to pick up the threads of his life. But his ordeal was far from over. His wife had taken their young son and left him, partly because she had learned during her husband's trial that he had been unfaithful. Many residents in his hometown believed that Staples was guilty of Burke's death and treated him like a murderer who "got away with it." Some crossed the street to avoid encountering him and his second wife,

Marie. Some businesses refused to serve him or members of his family. At coffee shops and restaurants, Gary and Marie were stared at and were the subject of finger pointing and hushed comments. He was sometimes refused employment and was fired from jobs he held because he had been falsely identified as a killer. "I knew people would be talking about me, but I thought in a couple of months it would blow over. In a couple of months it didn't blow over — it never did." He said, "I would never wish upon anybody the last 30 years of my life." But he refused to be driven from Dunnville. "I hadn't done anything wrong."[3] He said he even had to move from the centre of town because people would slow down in front of his house and point fingers as they drove by. "Most of the people I talk to think that I did it," he told a reporter. "Their kids feel the same way, who weren't even born then. They've grown up to believe I'm a murderer."[4]

Gerald Burke's two sons were told that Gary Staples had killed their father. They grew up believing he had returned to Dunnville and gotten away with it. Staples was traumatized by the idea that two small boys thought he was responsible for the death of their father, a man he had never laid eyes upon.

Staples appealed to the Minister of Justice, but his pleas for exoneration fell upon deaf ears. He wanted an apology from the police and recognition from the province that he had been the victim of a wrongful conviction. He wanted compensation and closure. He said that he was told he would either have to provide DNA evidence to back up his claim of a wrongful conviction, or produce Gerry Burke's killer. Publicity surrounding the wrongful convictions and exonerations of David Milgaard and Guy Paul Morin in the 1990s prompted Staples to continue his own fight.

In the summer of 1997, Staples turned to the newly formed Innocence Project at York University's Osgoode Hall Law School in Toronto for help. Law professors Alan Young and the late Dianne Martin founded the program that year. It was modelled after the original Innocence Project at the Cardozo School of Law in New York. The law students involved in the Innocence Project investigate cases where there is a claim of wrongful conviction.

Acting on behalf of Staples, the law students made an access to information request to the Hamilton Police in November 1997. They wanted to see the files relating to the Burke murder investigation. The

Hamilton Police replied on February 16, 1998, that their files in the case no longer existed and the case was closed. The response also indicated that the records had been "purged" and the court exhibits "destroyed" in accordance with the "records retention by-law" of the Hamilton Police. Undeterred, the students continued their efforts to clear Staples's name throughout 1998 and 1999. After reviewing the evidence they had, the students concluded that it was impossible for Staples to have shot Burke. They submitted an application on his behalf to the Attorney General for Ontario in accordance with the federal and provincial guidelines on wrongful convictions. The application and a supplemental brief filed in the fall of 1999 requesting reconsideration were both denied.

In the meantime, Burke's son Darrin had married Juliana Lutz and moved to St. Catharines, where they had three children. Robert, a truck driver and volunteer firefighter, married Cherylynn Denison and lived in Smithville with their children. Now in their early thirties, the two young men and their wives contacted the Innocence Project in the summer of 2000 looking for answers about their father's death. They told Dianne Martin they wanted to know more about their father's murder and that the Hamilton Police had indicated they were willing to give them access to police records.

In early October 2000, Robert Denison, Darrin Burke, and their spouses met with Colleen Robertshaw and Dean Ring, the law students who were investigating the case on behalf of the Innocence Project. Robertshaw had previously been a court reporter and a case manager for the Crown attorney's office. Ring had worked as a forensic analyst with the Ontario Provincial Police. Arrangements were made with the Hamilton Police Service for the Burke family and the law students to go to a Hamilton police station to see the files on the Burke murder investigation. It became clear that the files had, in fact, not been destroyed as the police had claimed two years earlier. No explanation for the discrepancy was given.

On October 30, Robertshaw, Ring, and members of the Burke family spent seven hours reading through the police files, that included papers, memos, and reports. It was an emotionally draining day. Burke's two sons had never seen photographs of the father they never had a chance to know. The first photos that Denison saw of his father were autopsy pictures. The students and family members were not allowed to make photocopies of the documents they found in the police files. Instead, they took lengthy and detailed notes of the information they collected. Unable to finish their review by the end of the day, the law students agreed with Detective Peter Bracci, the police officer responsible for arranging and supervising their access to the file, that they would return at a later date to finish. This was confirmed by Hamilton Police Chief Ken Robertson on December 7, 2000.

As the day was winding down at 5:00 p.m., Robertshaw stumbled upon a memo that made a stunning revelation. Her hands began to shake. She signalled to Ring to keep chatting with their clients and Detective Bracci. Since they weren't allowed to make photocopies of any of the documents, Robertshaw transcribed the memo as quickly as she could. "You can see my handwriting, see where the pen is pushing so hard it went through the page," she recalled in an interview with a York University newspaper.

The memo, from one of the investigating officers to his superiors, was dated May 7, 1972. It revealed why the Crown had dropped its appeal of Staples's acquittal nearly thirty years earlier. The chief of police had asked whether or not information obtained from Wayne Salisbury and his wife had been divulged to the Crown and defence lawyers. The officer was reluctant to even reply to the chief's inquiry in writing, but a question from the chief could not be ignored. In the memo, titled "The Damned Salisburys," the officer explained that evidence about the Salisburys, and what they had seen the night of Burke's murder, was not disclosed to the Crown and defence. At the time, the investigating officers came to the conclusion that the Salisburys' testimony was immaterial and irrelevant and that it would confuse a jury so much that they would acquit Staples, because of the confusion. The officer admitted that the decision was based on inconsistencies between the stories Johnstone and the Salisburys told police. He also wondered how defence lawyers found out about the Salisburys in the first place.

Police investigators had deliberately suppressed evidence from the Crown and defence that was inconsistent with their theory and could lead to an acquittal. They never admitted to Staples's defence lawyer the existence of the Salisburys' information — even when the case was dropped in November 1972. The students and family members also found handwritten notes and entries indicating that the investigating officers, or other members of the Hamilton Police, had helped Mary Conklin tailor her story to take into account evidence that emerged during the police investigation, preliminary hearing, and trial. Following the lead investigator's admission, the Hamilton Police had written to the Crown prosecutor on July 11, 1972, explaining why the evidence had been suppressed. For the first time in nearly thirty years, it was finally clear why the Crown's appeal of Staples's acquittal was dropped abruptly.

Gerry Burke's sons now knew that Gary Staples had not killed their father. After reading information in the police's file, Darrin Burke couldn't understand how Staples had ever been arrested in the first place. But the brothers' quest for answers had only raised more questions. Since Gary Staples didn't kill their father, who did? "Somewhere out there is a guy who thinks he got away with murder," an emotional Robert Denison later said at a news conference. Denison and Burke wanted to know the truth and to find justice for the father they never knew.

The law students and the Burke family phoned and emailed the Hamilton Police to arrange further access to the file in January 2001. On January 31, Detective Bracci advised the Innocence Project that the decision had been made to deny them access to the file because it was inactive but "officially" open. However, Police Chief Robertson confirmed a week later, on February 5, 2001, that no investigator had been assigned to work on the case. This contradicted their response to a previous access to information request three years earlier indicating the file into Burke's murder was closed. It appeared that Burke's two sons would never find the answers they were looking for.

Perhaps it was time for Gerry Burke's sons to meet Gary Staples. In a poignant meeting hosted by the Innocence Project, members of the Burke and Denison families met Gary and Marie Staples at Osgoode Hall Law School on March 9, 2001. The three families wanted answers that the police appeared unprepared to give. In an unusual move, they decided to join forces to try to get to the truth. They wanted the Police Services Board to conduct a thorough investigation and to admit that Staples was innocent.

On April 26, 2001, Toronto lawyer Sean Dewart filed a $6.1 million lawsuit against the Hamilton Police Services Board on behalf of Staples, Denison, and Burke. Also named in the suit were Police Chief Kenneth D. Robertson, Deputy Police Chief Bruce Elwood, Detective Peter Bracci, who had denied access to the murder file, and investigating officers James Williams, James Campbell, and Norman Thompson. According to the lawsuit's statement of claim, "Members of the Hamilton Police suppressed exculpatory evidence because they knew it would lead to an acquittal." They also knew that Mary Conklin, their only witness against Staples, was highly unreliable and had a motive to fabricate evidence. Yet, they didn't investigate further after taking her statement and before laying charges against Staples.

The police also ignored, suppressed, and failed to act on evidence that Staples was innocent and didn't investigate his alibi once they became aware of it. In an attempt to get Staples to confess, the statement said, the police assaulted him and arranged to have him unlawfully held in solitary confinement. Tunnel vision, an unreliable witness, and suppression of evidence had led to the wrongful conviction of Gary Staples. The lawsuit called for Staples to be awarded damages for negligence, malicious prosecution, misfeasance in public office, conspiracy, and assault and battery for the beating the police administered when they interrogated him.

During an emotional news conference on June 5, 2001, in Hamilton, Robert Denison said he wanted the police investigation to be reopened. He wanted to find out the truth about what happened that December night. "Gary Staples didn't murder my father, somebody else did and I'd like to know who. If it was your father, I'm sure you'd like to know," he said.[5] Staples had suffered the embarrassment, humiliation, stigma, pain, and suffering of being wrongly convicted of murder. Staples wanted an apology and to bring closure to this chapter of his life. "I'm very tired and I want an end to this," he said. "I want someone to say they're sorry, because I haven't killed Gerald Burke."[6] The amiable cabbie's two sons stood by his side. "What better way to have people believe you didn't do it than having the victim's sons sitting beside you?" Darrin Burke said.[7]

Police Chief Robertson said that he was frustrated that his police service was being held accountable for an investigation that was carried out thirty-one years prior. There have been major changes in the law covering disclosure of evidence since then, he said. In 1991, twenty years after Staples was brought to trial, the Supreme Court of Canada had ruled, in the Stinchombe case, that the Crown is required to disclose its evidence to the defence, regardless of whether or not it exonerates the accused. Lawyer Dewart said the passage of time doesn't mean police shouldn't still be held accountable. "The simple fact that police misconduct was not uncovered for thirty years does not relieve police of the obligation of dealing with police misconduct," he commented.[8] "The system needs checks and balances. And the police have to be accountable."[9] There was a lack of oversight of the investigating officers who had arrested and detained Staples.

The Hamilton Police finally exonerated Staples and apologized publicly on December 5, 2002. The lawsuit was settled out of court for an undisclosed amount exactly thirty-three years after Burke was shot to death. Although two Hamilton Police officers attended the news conference announcing the settlement, they refused to speak to Staples

Text of the apology of the Hamilton Police Service

In 1972 Gary Staples was unjustly convicted of a murder he had not committed. The wrongful conviction was caused at least in part by the substandard conduct of certain members of the Police Department in 1969 to 1972. Gary Staples spent 22 months in prison for the crime and unfairly carries the stigma of wrongful conviction to this day. The Hamilton Police Service apologies to Mr. Staples and his family for this miscarriage of justice. In addition, the Hamilton Police Service acknowledges that the investigation of the murder of Gerald Burke, in part, did not meet the accepted standards for police in 1969-1972. It apologizes to the late Mr. Burke's sons Darrin Burke and Robert Denison and to the late Mr. Burke's family for the problems in this investigation of the matter. The Hamilton Police Service has made significant improvements in the standards of investigations in the intervening years and the foregoing is no reflection on the current police service.

Signed by Kenneth D. Robertson Chief of Police

http://go.to/networkforjustice.com/

to offer the apology on behalf of the police department. In a statement read by Staples's lawyer, the police promised to turn over the murder file for re-investigation by the Ontario Provincial Police. Bob Denison made a public plea on his own and his brother's behalf for information that could finally close the case into their father's murder. "Someone alive today knows who killed our father and we are asking whomever that is to call the Hamilton Police or the OPP and let them in on the secret. Both of us and Gary deserve to know who the killer or killers are."

For Denison and Burke, a desire to learn more about their father did lead them to find family members with whom they had not had contact throughout their lives. They included aunts, uncles, and cousins. "The best part about this is that we finally got to meet a lot of family we never knew," Denison said. "Now we have pictures of my brother and I with my father and things that we never had before." Unfortunately, their paternal grandmother passed away without seeing her grandsons.

The murder of Gerry Burke remains unsolved. As Dewart noted, "To this day, Gerald Burke's sons, who were toddlers when their father was murdered, don't know who is responsible for the crime." Somewhere, whoever killed him for $40 remains free.

PART II

Forensic Investigation: Nailing the Evidence

Chapter Six

Jailhouse Informants and Faulty Forensics: The Guy Paul Morin Case

Queensville was a small, quiet community surrounded by rolling farmland nearly 60 kilometres north of Toronto. Robert and Janet Jessop had moved to the area of about 700 people from nearby Richmond Hill because they thought it would be a safer place to raise their children. No one was home when nine-year-old Christine Jessop climbed off the school bus from Queensville Public School at about 3:50 p.m. on the afternoon of Wednesday October 3, 1984. Her fourteen-year-old brother, Ken, had gone to the dentist in Newmarket with their mother, Janet.

Christine grabbed her bicycle, rode to the nearby Queensville General Store, about 500 metres from the house, and bought some bubble gum. People saw the grade four student that afternoon, but Christine never showed up at a nearby park to meet her friend Leslie at 4:00 p.m. Nobody answered when Leslie phoned the Jessops soon after to check on Christine. When Ken and Janet returned home, sometime between 4:10 p.m. and 4:30 p.m., Christine wasn't there. But her bicycle was in the garage, her school bag was on the counter, and the newspapers and mail had been brought inside, as was Christine's usual routine. Oddly, her bicycle was lying on its side instead of being in its usual upright position. When she was last seen, she was wearing a blue sweater with a zipper on the front, blue corduroy pants, and blue-grey running shoes.

Janet went looking for her daughter in the cemetery behind their home, at the park, and the variety store. Then she went back to the house and made dinner. When Christine still hadn't returned home, Janet Jessop telephoned the York Regional Police to report her missing. About fifteen police cars and emergency vehicles, as well as seventeen police officers, went to the Jessops over the next seven hours. About fifteen or twenty civilians also arrived to join the search. The police searched the Jessops' home but made no effort to preserve possible evidence or protect the house from being contaminated by people coming and going. They didn't cordon off the area around Christine's bicycle in an effort to preserve any fingerprints that could be on it. Nor did they dust the house, including Christine's bedroom and anything she may have touched, to preserve her fingerprints or determine if other fingerprints were present. They did not consider the possibility that this missing person case could become a major crime investigation.

The police set up a mobile command post at the Queensville fire hall. For the next few days, officers and hundreds of volunteers searched fields, woods, ponds, and ravines as far as 16 kilometres from the Jessops' home. The police also interviewed neighbours and nearby residents, but they didn't record any information such as who was in each home the day that Christine disappeared, their activities and whereabouts, a complete description of their vehicles, or whether they had noticed anything suspicious. Christine's father, Robert, was three weeks into serving an eighteen-month sentence on fraud charges when he was granted a temporary release from the Toronto East Detention Centre on October 5 to help search for his daughter.

Christine's disappearance sent shock waves through the small community. Many parents started to meet their children after school and refused to let them play in the park. Holding out hope their daughter would be found, Christine's parents left her bedroom the way it was the day she disappeared. For weeks after her disappearance, Janet Jessop consulted a Montreal spiritualist who told her that Christine was alive and safe.

Police checked on known sex offenders and reports of suspicious people in the area. However, the York Regional Police lacked a systematic approach to following up on possible leads in a timely manner. Consequently, a couple's report that they saw a man in a dirty, dark green or blue Buick who appeared to be forcibly holding a small child wasn't investigated until some twelve days later. By then, the couple could no longer remember if they had seen the man on the afternoon of Christine's disappearance or the day before.

Queensville was a quiet community north of Toronto surrounded by farmland.
Photo: Milan Chvostek

On Monday December 31, 1984, Frederick Patterson and his two young daughters were walking along a tractor path near their home shortly before noon looking for their dog. Suddenly, they spotted something just off the trail in a clump of cedars in a wooded area. It was the badly decomposed remains of Christine Jessop. She was lying on her back with her knees spread apart in an unnatural position. A sweater had been pulled over her head. Her blouse had been pulled off with such force that all the buttons except one were ripped off. Her underwear and blue corduroy pants were at her feet. A recorder with her name taped to it was found nearby. This was near the town of Sunderland in Durham Region, about 56 kilometres east of Queensville. Patterson called the Durham Regional Police.

Inspector Robert Brown, head of Durham's Crimes Against Persons Squad, led the investigation. Sergeant Michael Michalowsky arrived at 2:10 p.m. As chief identification officer, he was responsible for collecting and preserving the evidence found at the scene. The police cordoned off the area and officers got down on their hands and knees to search for clues. They found a cigarette butt, a milk carton, and a gas station credit card receipt. But they didn't create a grid pattern to conduct a more methodical and thorough search, nor did they finish by the time it got dark. That night, a storm blew in.

That day, New Year's Eve, Robert and Janet Jessop were sitting at their dinner table with their son Kenneth discussing what more they could do to find Christine. She was listed with the Child Find program for missing children and they'd planned to hire a private detective the following week. That's when homicide detectives pulled up to their home and told them they were almost certain that they had found Christine's remains. They told the Jessops that they had located what appeared to be some of her clothes and the recorder she had received from her music teacher the day of her disappearance.

Police returned the next day with family friend Reverend Bev Hall of St. Mary's Anglican Church in nearby Richmond Hill. The Jessops were told that dental records had confirmed the remains were those of Christine. Hundreds of mourners turned up for the little girl's funeral on Monday January 7, 1985. Police officers took pictures of passing cars and made a note of licence plates in case anyone suspicious turned up. Christine was buried in the snow-covered cemetery where she used to play behind her house. It was there that she had once tended the grave of an eight-year-old boy who died a few years before she was born. For the Jessops, it was the end of a three-month nightmare of not knowing what had happened to their daughter. But it raised a new question: who killed Christine? Her murder spread fear among the small community, as parents kept a closer eye on their children.

Pathologist Dr. John Hilsdon-Smith performed an autopsy on January 2, 1985. Christine's remains were badly decomposed, but nicks on the bones indicated that she had been stabbed repeatedly, at least five times in the chest and back. One of the blows was so strong that it broke one of her ribs. Her legs had been pulled apart violently. Although her body was too decomposed to determine if she had been sexually assaulted, there were traces of semen in her underwear and her clothes were soaked in blood. However, they were too deteriorated for forensic analysts to determine a blood type. Some hairs were found embedded in

Guy Paul Morin. Photo: Rick Eglinton/Toronto Star/GetStock

the decomposed flesh stuck to the silver chain she wore around her neck. Some hairs belonged to Christine but others didn't. Did they belong to her killer? That was a question the police would try to answer.

The Durham Police continued to search for clues that would lead them to Christine's killer. They interviewed Queensville residents, but memories of events surrounding Christine's disappearance had begun to fade. During an interview with the Jessops on February 14, 1985, Ken and Janet Jessop described next-door neighbour Guy Paul Morin, as a "weird-type guy" who played the clarinet. On February 22, detectives Bernie Fitzpatrick and John Shephard spoke to Morin for more than ninety minutes while seated in a cruiser outside his parents' home. During the secretly tape-recorded conversation, Morin repeatedly asked the police how close they were to finding her killer. He described Christine as "a sweetheart," then added, "Little girls are sweet and beautiful, but they grow up to be corrupt."[1] Since a portion of the conversation was not taped, the context surrounding the comment was not clear. Morin also described Christine as "a very, very innocent kid. She wasn't aware that there was anything bad out there."[2] Seemingly out of the blue, he also uttered the phrase "Otherwise I'm innocent."

Morin told police that he finished work at a furniture factory in northwest Toronto and then arrived home at about 4:30 p.m. the day Christine disappeared. As Morin sat in a police cruiser, he told them that "Normally I would have seen it.... If I was there that day, I guarantee you I could even tell you the licence plate, everything, because I'm really suspicious of anyone who stops in front of here. So that's why I'm really pissed off at myself at not being there. Shopping screwed me up that day."[3] Shephard became suspicious when Morin said that Christine's body had been found near Ravenshoe Road, correcting a piece of incorrect information that was mentioned in the media. That road was a direct route between the Jessop home and where Christine's body was found. Shephard noted that Morin was familiar with the area.

The police's attention had shifted toward Morin as a potential suspect, but they needed more than a hunch to tie him to the murder. They wanted to get a lock of his hair to compare with the one found on Christine's necklace. They sent an undercover policewoman pretending to be a hairdressing student to one of Morin's band practices. She told the band members that she needed hair samples to perform dyeing tests. Samples of Morin's hair were brought to Stephanie Nyznyk, a hair and fibre analyst at Toronto's Centre of Forensic Sciences, on April 11. She conducted a preliminary comparison with the hair found in Christine's necklace and told Detectives Shephard and Fitzpatrick that the hairs were consistent with having come from the same source. This information strengthened their case against Morin.

Although the police had a suspect, they enlisted the help of Federal Bureau of Investigation profiler John Douglas. He was an agent from the National Centre of the Analysis of Violent Crimes located at the FBI Academy's Behavioral Science Unit in Quantico, Virginia. Douglas spent a few days in Queensville and Sunderland interviewing police, the Jessops and neighbours. According to the profile Douglas submitted to Durham Regional Police, portions of which they released to the public on April 17, 1985, Jessop's killer was a white male between the ages of nineteen and twenty-six who lived in Queensville, was intelligent, a sloppy dresser, a manual labourer, familiar with the Sunderland area, had recent family problems, and knew Christine personally.

Four days later, on April 22, 1985, Durham Regional Police arrested twenty-five-year-old Guy Paul Morin. The Jessops' next-door neighbour was from a family of six children, unemployed, and living with his parents. Police officers surrounded his home in Queensville, while fourteen more sealed off the area where he was arrested. Durham Regional Police Detectives John Shephard and Bernard Fitzpatrick pulled him over and arrested him on Highway 48 at 7:45 p.m.; he was on his way to band practice in nearby Stouffville with the Whitechurch-Stouffville Concert Band. His family's home was searched, and his Honda Accord was towed to Toronto's Centre of Forensic Sciences for examination. Fibres taken from the car and from his home were compared with fibres taken from Christine Jessop's clothing and recorder bag. Nyznyk said she found that several fibres from Morin and Christine were similar and could have come from the same source.

During Morin's six-hour interrogation at the police station he provided hair, saliva, and blood samples, but he refused their request for a polygraph examination. He was charged with first-degree murder in Christine's death, remanded to Whitby Jail, and denied bail. At a news conference announcing Morin's arrest, Durham Regional Police Superintendent Douglas Bullock said that Morin fit the widely publicized profile that Douglas had prepared of Christine's killer.

A preliminary hearing opened on June 24, 1985, in Oshawa Provincial Court. After a three-day hearing, Judge Norman Edmondson ruled there was enough evidence against Morin to have him stand trial on a charge of first-degree murder. Defence lawyer Bruce Affleck applied in Ontario Supreme Court to have the trial moved from Whitby because of the negative impact that publicity about the case could have on Morin's ability to have a fair trial. Affleck pointed to details from the FBI's psychological profile, which police officers had released at a news conference on April 16, 1985, and subsequent comments following Morin's arrest that he matched the profile. The fact that the profile had been prepared by an FBI analyst could lead potential jurors to give it more scientific weight than it ought to be accorded, even though it wouldn't be introduced at trial due to its inadmissibility as evidence. Police officials made another comment that Morin's lawyer believed could prejudice the case. When Morin was arrested, a police official stated that, "I think there is a great sense of relief there now.… People will be able to get back to living their normal lives."[4] This suggested Christine's killer had been found — despite that Morin hadn't yet been tried. Following a hearing on October 7, 1985, Supreme Court Justice John Osler ordered that Morin's trial was to be moved from Whitby to London, Ontario.

A year after Christine Jessop was buried, Morin pleaded not guilty to first-degree murder. His trial got underway on January 7, 1986, before Justice McLeod A. Craig. He sat calmly in the prisoner's box wearing a grey tweed jacket, light blue shirt, and blue tie. He was less than fifteen feet from Robert and Janet Jessop, who had taken a front-row seat in the courtroom. Lead Crown prosecutor John Scott and Morin's new defence lawyer Clayton Ruby interviewed fifty-eight potential jurors before choosing six men and six women within three hours. Since the case had received widespread publicity, Ruby wanted to know whether potential jurors had read any of the media coverage of the case and if it would make it difficult for them to make an impartial decision. After the jury was selected, but before they had a chance to hear any evidence, one juror was excused due to illness in her family. A new juror was chosen to replace her.

Police and prosecutors have been using informants for years to help them bolster their cases, particularly when they're relying on circumstantial evidence. Until 1982, a conviction could be overturned if the judge didn't warn a jury about the dangers of accepting the uncorroborated testimony of an informant. Then the Supreme Court of Canada ruled that a judge didn't have to warn a jury, particularly if the judge decided that the informant was credible.

The seven-man, five-woman jury heard that Morin had allegedly confessed to the killing to jailhouse informants. Robert Dean May, who was serving a sentence for forgery and fraud-related charges, claimed that he was sharing a cell with Morin at the Whitby Jail when Morin became upset on the night of June 30 or July 1, 1985. According to May, Morin began to cry as he said "Oh why did I do it? I did it. I killed that little girl."[5] Then he changed the subject. May also claimed that, earlier that day, Morin said it took forty to fifty minutes to drive from his house to his job in Toronto. During their discussion, Morin initially said that he went straight home from work and arrived at his house at 4:15 p.m. or 4:30 p.m. Later, he said it was 5:45 p.m. because he went shopping before heading home. May immediately went to police and asked for a deal on his own criminal charges in exchange for his statement implicating Morin. Crown prosecutor Scott apparently told May that he would be "looked after" on two of the three criminal charges he was facing.

Another man, who is identified in official records as Mr. X because of a publication ban, was serving a sixty-day sentence for sexual assault at the Whitby Jail. He was in an adjoining cell when he claimed that he heard Morin confess to May about Christine's murder. "Those are words I'll never forget," he testified. "I didn't know what to do."[6] He said he covered his head with pillows and then got up and smoked a cigarette to calm down. He said that Morin's cellmate, Richard May, confirmed the next day that Morin had confessed. Mr. X said he also discussed with Morin the possibility of pleading insanity in an attempt to be sent to the psychiatric hospital in Penetanguishene instead of being incarcerated at the Kingston penitentiary "where the inmates would just have a heyday with him. He'd probably never get out of that place alive."[7]

Defence lawyer Clayton Ruby accused Mr. X of making up the story about Morin in order to get out of prison. During a meeting with police officials, Mr. X had insisted that he would cooperate if he were transferred to a halfway house that would allow him to see his wife and keep his job. According to excerpts of a transcript that Ruby read in court, Mr. X was desperate to get out of jail. "You get me out of here … and I'll give you a statement, signed, I'll appear in court, I'll give you anything. I've got to get out of here. My nerves are shot,"[8] he told police and prison officials. In court, Mr. X denied he received any concessions in his own case in exchange for his testimony. May denied that he and Mr. X had collaborated to create a story implicating Morin. Morin later testified that he was depressed the day of the alleged confession because of being wrongly accused; he never confessed to a crime he didn't commit. "If you're in jail for something you haven't done, then you're bound to feel that way," he testified.[9]

Undercover police officer Sergeant Gordon Hobbs of the Metro Toronto Police also testified for the prosecution. He was posing as a child killer named Jeffrey Rickertt when he was placed in Morin's cell for nearly four days in May 1985. Morin told him that the best way to deal with frustrations was to "redrum the innocent."[10] The word "redrum" comes from the 1980 horror film *The Shining*, in which actor Jack Nicholson plays an insane author. Hobbs asked Morin what he meant by "redrum." Morin replied: "What's redrum spell if you put it in a mirror? M-u-r-d-e-r."[11] Morin also told Hobbs that he had a mind like a monk and kept "unpleasant problems" from bothering him by storing things "in the back." Hobbs said that Morin made stabbing motions toward his chest to indicate how Christine Jessop had died, but he didn't admit that he'd killed her.

Nineteen-year-old Mandy Paterson played clarinet beside Morin in the Whitchurch-Stouffville Community Band. She testified that she talked to Morin at a band practice on April 15, 1985. He seemed to be familiar with many details of Christine Jessop's death and showed little emotion when he talked about the case. She recounted that she told Morin "Whoever did it must be a really sick person." He had replied: "Things like that happen. What can you do?" Paterson said she was shocked at his response. "The way he said it, it was like it was something that happened every day, something that you couldn't do anything about," she said in court.[12]

In an effort to tie Morin to the crime, the prosecutor used hair and fibre evidence recovered from the crime scene, Morin, his home, and car. The Crown's theory was that Morin's Honda had been used to transport Christine to the place where her body was found. Forensic expert Stephanie Nyznyk testified that she "found no differentiation" between a dark brown, 8.6-centimetre-long hair attached to a silver chain on Christine's decomposed body and a hair sample surreptitiously taken from Morin during band practice. There were also no differences, she said, between Christine Jessop's hair and three hairs found in the backseat of Morin's Honda. Nyznyk's testimony suggested that the similarities between the fibres were evidence of direct contact between Christine Jessop and Morin.

The defence pointed out that Christine's hair could have found its way into Morin's car if his parents had spent time at the Jessops offering their condolences after her body was found. According to Janet Jessop, the Morins did visit at that time, and Morin's father may have been brought to Christine's room. Under cross-examination, Nyznyk agreed that samples of Morin's hair were not an exact match for the one found on Christine Jessop's necklace. Nor could it be concluded that the hairs in his car were Christine's. Investigators also found five fibres in the Morin family's home and car that were similar to some that were found on Christine's clothes. Nyznyk admitted that "the possibility does exist for cross-transfers" of fibres between the families through visits or by the wind.[13]

Royal Canadian Mounted Police forensic expert Barry Gaudette headed the hair and fibre section of the RCMP's Ottawa forensic laboratory. He testified that two hairs at a time are placed under a powerful microscope to compare them and assess whether they are from the same person. He admitted, however, that a suspect cannot be identified conclusively from a hair sample. "Fingerprints are unique to an individual ... hair is not necessarily unique to an individual," he said under cross-examination.[14] Despite this, Nyznyk's testimony proved to play a significant role in the Crown's case.

Morin took to the stand in his own defence. He testified that he left work at 3:30 p.m. on the day Christine Jessop disappeared. His parents said that he didn't get home until about two hours later, carrying two bags of groceries. The prosecution claimed they were mistaken about the day. Morin said he didn't help search for Christine after she went missing because he worked all day and he was busy helping his father do major home renovations in the evening.

In an unexpected moment during the trial, defence lawyer Clayton Ruby argued that Morin was mentally ill. If he did kill Christine Jessop — and he wasn't saying that he had — Morin's psychological state was such that he would not know whether or not he killed her. Clinical psychologist Graham Turrall testified that after more than ten hours of interviews and tests, he was convinced that Morin suffered from schizophrenia and had a "very tenuous hold on reality." He said that if Morin did kill Christine, he might have been able to block it from his memory. "In Mr. Morin's mind, the act of stabbing could have represented a magic wand, and he was touching her and giving her life ... preserving her innocence in some strange, illogical way."[15] Dr. Basil Orchard, senior staff psychiatrist of the Clarke Institute of Psychiatry's forensic service, also said that Morin was suffering from schizophrenia and might not be aware if he did, in fact, fatally stab Christine Jessop.

Ruby cautioned the jury not to see the testimony of these experts as an admission of guilt, "not to confuse craziness with guilt."[16] Morin continued to maintain that he didn't kill Christine Jessop. In his closing arguments, Ruby referred to his client as "a quiet Queensville musician, on the evidence, who happens to be quietly schizophrenic," he said. "What happened here? Have [police] got the right man or merely the crazy neighbor?"[17] He said that Morin's discussion with an undercover police officer in his cell could simply be the ramblings of a mentally ill man.

The defence's argument that Morin was mentally ill left the jury with five possible verdicts: guilty, not guilty, not guilty by reason of insanity, guilty of second-degree murder, or guilty of manslaughter. If Morin were found not guilty by reason of insanity, he would be sent to a maximum-security psychiatric institution for an indefinite period of time, until he was deemed to no longer pose a risk to society. Following a five-week trial in which evidence was heard from more than fifty witnesses, Judge Craig delivered his instructions to the jury before they retired to deliberate. He told them they must first look at the facts of the case to decide if Morin killed Christine Jessop. If they believed Morin had killed her, they could then consider whether or not an insanity defence applied. He also cautioned them about the limitations of the hair and fibre evidence that the prosecution said established a connection between Morin and Christine Jessop. He noted that the hair and fibre evidence was not conclusive in the same way that fingerprints could be. "The evidence does not go beyond proving that Christine Jessop *could have been* in the Honda, and that the accused *could have been* at the scene of the crime," he said.[18]

The jury deliberated for fourteen hours. Morin was acquitted on February 7, 1986. After the verdict, Ruby pointed out that much of the evidence against Morin had been obtained after he was arrested. In such circumstances, he said, "one can never be sure whether police are really finding out who committed the crime," or simply demonstrating that "if you put someone under enough of a microscope, enough of a spotlight, you can find evidence that looks like something, even though it's not very convincing."[19]

Morin had spent ten months behind bars, never far from the knowledge that inmates are not kind to prisoners who have been accused of crimes of a sexual nature. "All night I'd hear the other inmates yelling, 'Morin, you baby-killer, you're going down. We're going to slit your throat. You're dead," he recounted in an interview with the *Toronto Star*. "I've been through a lot," Morin said. "And it was all for something I haven't done. In those circumstances, that's when hell comes to earth."[20] He returned to his home next door to the Jessops, but his ordeal was not over. As his father Alphonse said in an interview with the *Toronto Star*, "He was tried before he ever got to court, he was convicted in the courts of public opinion."[21]

Despite his acquittal, a cloud of suspicion hung over Morin. "I'm not the one who did it. I can say that all my life — and it doesn't matter," he said. "The only thing that would totally clear me is for the real killer to be caught."[22]

The Crown filed an appeal of the verdict in the Ontario Court of Appeal on March 4, 1986. They raised questions with respect to the judge's instructions to the jury about hair and fibre evidence and the psychiatric evidence the defence had introduced. The Crown contended that Judge Craig was incorrect when he told jurors to weigh pieces of evidence individually to assess whether they proved guilt beyond a reasonable doubt. The Crown believed the evidence should have been weighed in its entirety. They also took issue with the judge's instructions that the psychiatric evidence about Morin could only be used to determine his sanity, not his guilt.

The Court of Appeal overturned the verdict on June 5, 1987, and ordered a new trial. Morin appealed. In the Supreme Court of Canada's decision on November 17, 1988, they agreed with the trial judge's ruling that the psychiatric evidence that had been presented at trial was not admissible as proof Morin killed Christine Jessop. However, it upheld the lower court's ruling ordering a new trial.

In March 1990, while preparing for Morin's second trial, the Crown discovered that Durham Police Sergeant Michael Michalowsky had created a second notebook about the Jessop murder after he testified at the preliminary inquiry. The OPP conducted an investigation and learned that a number of entries in the second notebook gave different information than what was included in his first. For example, the second notebook included the time that Michalowsky arrived at the area where the body was found, as well as more details about the location.

Michalowsky had used the second notebook to refresh his memory during Morin's first trial but incorrectly stated to the judge that the notes were made at the time of the events depicted in his notebook. During that same trial, he also falsely claimed that a cigarette butt provided as an exhibit was the same one that was found near Christine Jessop's body. The Crown's position was that it belonged to a police officer that had smoked at the site. However, the police officer later determined that it wasn't his because it was the wrong brand and searchers had found it before he arrived at the scene. In late summer 1990, Michalowsky was charged with perjury and related offences in connection with his testimony about the notebook and the cigarette butt. The charges were stayed in 1991 due to his ill health.

Morin's defence team, led by criminal lawyer Jack Pinkofsky, filed a number of pre-trial motions. They claimed the Crown had suppressed evidence that could strengthen Morin's defence. For example, prosecutors had not disclosed that hair samples were taken from Christine Jessop's classmates in May 1985. Hair from two of them were microscopically similar to the one found on her necklace. Also not disclosed was the result of a test that showed fibres could have been transferred between the Morins and Jessops via the laundromat they both used. The trial judge ruled that the defence needed to be specific about the type of materials it was after when it made disclosure requests to the Crown. A general request asking for anything that would help the defence was deemed too vague. The trial judge's ruling came before the Supreme Court of Canada's 1991 landmark judgment in the Stinchcombe case, which requires the Crown to provide the defence with any and all evidence that could be relevant to a case.

After repeated delays, Morin's second trial got underway with the Crown's opening address on November 13, 1991. Leo McGuigan was the lead Crown prosecutor, he was assisted by Susan MacLean who'd worked with John Scott on Morin's first trial. The Crown's theory was that Morin had abducted Christine and then sexually assaulted and killed her. The two jailhouse informants who had claimed that Morin had confessed to them testified again, as did hair and fibre expert Stephanie Nyznyk. They were among 120 witnesses to be called to the stand during the nearly nine-month trial.

Morin's defence lawyers Jack Pinkofsky, Elizabeth Widner, and Joanne McLean discarded the first trial's insanity defence. They argued that Morin didn't have an opportunity to kill Christine; the police had arrested the wrong person. The jury began deliberations on July 23, 1992. A week later, they returned with a unanimous guilty verdict. Morin was sentenced to life imprisonment and kept in the general population at Kingston Penitentiary instead of being in protective custody. Morin appealed the conviction on August 22, 1992, based on 181 points, including the reliability of Robert Dean May as a witness and the significance of the hair and fibre evidence the Crown had presented at trial. He was granted bail on February 9, 1993.

In the meantime, a grassroots group of volunteers who believed in Morin's innocence had come together to support him. In 1993, the Justice for Guy Paul Morin Committee became the Association in Defence of the Wrongly Convicted. Since then, volunteers of the Toronto organization have reviewed hundreds of cases and contributed to the exoneration of about fifteen people, often with the help of advances in DNA testing.

Efforts to perform DNA tests between 1988 and 1991 on the blood and semen found on Christine Jessop's blouse and underwear were inconclusive. This was due to deterioration from exposure before her body was found, and the state of forensic science at the time. New advances prompted another DNA test while Morin waited for his appeal to be heard. A report issued on January 20, 1995, concluded that DNA typing on the sperm from Christine's underwear had been successfully completed. It was not a match with Morin's DNA. The report was submitted to the Court of Appeal as fresh evidence. On January 23, 1995, Morin was acquitted. Almost ten years after he was first arrested, and after having spent eighteen months behind bars, he was finally free. Morin filed a $17-million lawsuit against police and the Ontario Crown for malicious prosecution.

On June 26, 1996, Ontario Attorney General Charles Harnick announced that the provincial government would hold a public inquiry. The Commission on Proceedings Involving Guy Paul Morin was headed by Justice Fred Kaufman, a former judge of the Quebec Court of Appeal. The Commission would examine the investigation into the death of Christine Jessop, how the Centre of Forensic Sciences handled evidence, and the criminal proceedings against Morin. The Commission was also directed to make recommendations about the administration of criminal justice in Ontario. As Harnick noted, "An inquiry cannot wipe away the years of pain and turmoil Mr. Morin suffered, but it can examine the complex circumstances surrounding the case, and allow us to learn from it and prevent any future miscarriage of justice."[23]

Public hearings opened on February 10, 1997. During the inquiry, Justice Kaufman found that the Centre of Forensic Sciences overstated the importance of the hair and fibre analysis used to convict Morin. Analyst Stephanie Nyznyk failed to properly communicate to police investigators and prosecutors the limitations of the results of her findings. This turned Morin into the prime suspect, contributed to his arrest and incarceration, and formed a significant part of the prosecution's case. In fact, it was of little value in connecting Morin to Christine Jessop. As Justice Kaufman noted in his final report, "Had the limitations on Ms. Nyznyk's early findings been adequately communicated by her, Mr. Morin may not have been arrested when he was — if, indeed, ever."[24]

The hearings also learned that the fibre evidence was contaminated while it was under the care of the Centre of Forensic Sciences. The two analysts, who were aware of the contamination prior to Morin's first trial, did not divulge the information to the police. The inquiry's hearings revealed that the crime scene may have been contaminated, evidence was not handled properly, some evidence in the case was lost, jailhouse informants committed perjury when they testified against Morin, and police and prosecutors suppressed exculpatory evidence (although not malevolently) that could have eliminated Morin as a suspect.

After 146 days of hearings and 120 witnesses, Justice Kaufman issued a two-volume report of nearly 1,400 pages. Released in April 1998, it contained 119 recommendations. He noted that jailhouse informants are unreliable witnesses; their testimony is tainted by self-interest. "The systemic evidence emanating from Canada, Great Britain, Australia and the United States demonstrated that the dangers associated with jailhouse informants were not unique to the Morin case. Indeed, a number of miscarriages of justice throughout the world are likely explained, at least in part, by the false, self-serving evidence given by such informants," he said.[25]

Justice Fred Kaufman. Photo: James Knowler, The Independent Weekly *(Australia)*

Kaufman recommended that the provincial government establish a policy limiting the use of in-custody informants and the benefits they could receive for their cooperation. Juries should also be given strong warnings regarding the reliability of such testimony, and informants should be prosecuted for making false statements. Kaufman suggested that "tunnel vision" had focused the police and the Crown's attention on Morin as a prime suspect instead of keeping an open mind for other possible suspects. However, errors that were made in the case were the product of poor judgement rather than a deliberate attempt to put an innocent man behind bars, he determined.

Kaufman declared Morin innocent "beyond a shadow of a doubt." By then, Morin had dropped his lawsuit against the police and the Crown for the role they had played in his wrongful conviction. In January 1997, more than a year before the inquiry issued its report, the Ontario government apologized to Morin and awarded him $1.25 million in compensation. The report and compensation brought that chapter of Morin's life to an end. Christine Jessop's killer has never been found. For her family, there was no closure. Perhaps there never will be.

Chapter Seven

Deadly Cereal: The Ronald Dalton Case

CIBC bank manager Ronald Dalton returned home from work at about 8:15 p.m. on August 15, 1988. He and his wife Brenda put their three young children to bed. Then they sat on the couch together in the television room of their house in Gander, a small community in central Newfoundland, reading and talking. Brenda snacked on a package of raisins at about 10:30 p.m. About forty-five minutes later, she began eating a small bowl of cereal as she and her husband watched the news. They were talking about the children, and she expressed her frustration at how they'd misbehaved that day.

Suddenly, at about 11:30 p.m., Brenda began to cough uncontrollably. Dalton slapped her on the back two or three times to try to dislodge whatever was choking her. He went to the kitchen and returned with a glass of water. By then, Brenda (who was wearing shorts) was on her knees. He rushed to her side and tried to get her to stand up to take a drink of water. A panic-stricken Brenda was swinging her arms and clawing at her throat. He couldn't get her to stand up and struggled to try and grab her arms so that he could get her to take a sip of water to clear her throat. He finally managed to pin her arms but she continued to move her head around. By then, her face was quite red. While Dalton tried to force her mouth open, Brenda lost consciousness. Dalton tried CPR to revive her and used a spoon to try to clear her throat, to no avail. He couldn't get her breathing again. At 11:55 p.m., he left her lying on the floor and rushed to the phone to call an ambulance.

Stuttering and upset, he told emergency nurse Mildred Guzzwell that he thought his wife was dead. When she asked what happened, he said that he had just arrived home from work at 11:30 p.m. and found her lying on the floor unconscious and not breathing. Guzzwell paged the ambulance attendants, who told her to notify the RCMP. She did. As Dalton waited for the ambulance to arrive, he tried again to clear her throat of the cereal that was choking his wife.

When the ambulance arrived five minutes after Dalton's call, the driver, Claude Elliott, found Brenda lying on the floor next to a pool table while her husband knelt by her head giving her mouth-to-mouth. Her lips were blue, she wasn't breathing, and had no pulse. Dalton told Elliott that Brenda wasn't breathing and he thought she was dead. "Get her breathing, get her breathing," Dalton said. Elliott couldn't find a pulse, but he told Dalton that he had. He didn't want to upset the man any further.

Dalton was crying as the ambulance attendant, Viola Summers, performed CPR on his wife. "Make her breathe," he kept saying. While breathing air into Brenda's airways during mouth-to-mouth resuscitation, she could hear a "rattly sound" as thought something was in Brenda's airway. She looked inside Brenda's mouth for a possible obstruction. She didn't see anything, but Brenda's breath had a distinctly fruity scent. Guzzwell and Elliott both noticed marks on Brenda's knees and another on her foot.

Summers was a registered nursing assistant who had only been an ambulance attendant for a month. It was the first time she had performed CPR in an emergency situation. There was pure oxygen in the ambulance, but it couldn't be used on Brenda because Summers didn't have the appropriate training to administer it. Then Elliott phoned Guzzwell back and told her to have the emergency resuscitation team ready at the hospital, where she was on duty, because Brenda Dalton was non-responsive.

Just after midnight, an RCMP officer knocked on the door of next-door neighbour Jim Hill and told him there had been an accident at the Dalton home. Hill came over to look after the children. He checked on them. Then he walked into the TV room and noticed crumbs on the couch and floor. He brushed them together in a pile on the floor. Then he put them inside a small dessert bowl that was near the couch. The crumbs were very fine, like cereal crumbs.

When the ambulance arrived at the James Paton Memorial Hospital in Gander, Guzzwell believed the thirty-one-year-old patient was dead. Brenda was unconscious, her face was blue, she wasn't talking or moving. There was no sign of life. Guzzwell cut off Brenda's sweater and bra so that staff could try to revive her. Dr. Michael Griffin, a recent medical school graduate, noted that Brenda Dalton's face was swollen and blue, she was very cold, her pupils were fixed and large, she wasn't breathing, and there were no sounds to indicate that her heart was beating. Her white limbs were signs that no blood was circulating. A heart scan showed that there was no activity, but the medical team tried to resuscitate her with drugs and CPR. In an effort to open an airway, Dr. Griffin inserted a trachea tube down her throat. But he lost sight of the larynx and her vocal chords. He removed the tube, repositioned her head, and tried again. But he accidentally placed the tube in her esophagus instead of her trachea.

Following their efforts, the heart monitor showed that Brenda had a heartbeat. She had a weak pulse, but it only lasted about twenty seconds. Her heart had begun beating in response to the resuscitation efforts. CPR was administered again, but it became clear that Brenda Dalton could not be revived. More than an hour after they began their efforts just after midnight, the doctor pronounced Brenda Dalton dead at close to 2:00 a.m. on August 16, 1988. Her husband saw her before her body was brought to the morgue to be autopsied.

Ronald Dalton was brought into an office, where he sat down at a desk. He covered his face and rocked back and forth as he cried. When Dalton returned home, he immediately went to see his children. Hill had to help the upset and stressed Dalton up and down the stairs. Dalton and his children stayed at Hill's home later that day while the RCMP investigated.

Meanwhile, RCMP Constable Shelly Thomas went to the Dalton home after being called about a sudden death there. Nothing seemed out of place in the house. A bowl of cereal was sitting on the pool table near the spot where Brenda had been lying. It occurred to Thomas that perhaps Brenda had choked. In the emergency room, she had only noted a small scratch on Brenda's nose. She didn't suspect foul play until another officer raised his own suspicions.

Hospital pathologist Dr. Hermanildo Alinsangan conducted an external examination of Brenda's body and became suspicious when he noticed bruises on her arms, legs, neck, and a few cuts on her nose and forehead. He and the RCMP officers suspected foul play. They called in the province's chief of forensic pathology, Dr. Charles Hutton, to perform the autopsy. He flew in from St. John's and arrived in Gander at about 4:30 p.m. He went to the Dalton home to see where Brenda choked. The RCMP told him that they suspected foul play because they found a lot of marks on her body. After being briefed on the case by the RCMP, Hutton was suspicious about Brenda Dalton's death even before he had started performing her autopsy. He thought it was odd that Dalton had taken twenty-five minutes to call an ambulance after he said he had arrived home at 11:30 p.m. to find his wife lying on the floor unconscious.

Hutton went to the hospital and autopsied Brenda's body as RCMP officers waited for the results. He found spots in her neck where she had hemorrhaged. He dissected her bruised larynx and concluded that the injuries stemmed from having been strangled by someone who used their right hand. Given the bruises and scratches on her body, he concluded that she had been assaulted before being strangled. He drew these conclusions prior to completing the autopsy.

The Gander RCMP investigation into the sudden death became a homicide investigation. Hutton told RCMP officers to look for scratches on a suspect's face, hands, elbows, and arms — common places to have injuries when strangling someone. Subsequently, a 1989 forensic report found that the only DNA under or on Brenda Dalton's fingernails was her own. If there were signs of a struggle, one would expect to find her assailant's DNA under her nails, as she tried to fend him off. None was found. But this didn't alter the course of the investigation against Ronald Dalton.

RCMP officers returned to the Dalton home on August 17 to look for signs of a struggle, but they found none. There were also no signs that anyone broke into the house. Neither of the two doors had been forced open. However, two brown stains they found on a wall were later found to be blood. Photographs were taken of the scene and Brenda Dalton's autopsy.

On August 16, just twenty-four hours after Brenda began choking, Ronald Dalton went to the RCMP detachment. He gave RCMP Staff Sergeant Greg Morrow a ten-page statement that he returned home for supper at about 7:15 p.m. the day before. When he left to go back to work after 8 p.m., his wife was sitting on the end of the couch closest to the pool table. He told them that he arrived at the bank at about 8:30 p.m and didn't see anyone while he worked, although he said that he did get a phone call from an account manager from St. John's just after he arrived. Dalton said he found Brenda lying unconscious next to the pool table when he returned home at 11:30 p.m. He said that she was lying on her left side and there was nothing unusual about her clothing. He claimed that he then turned her onto her back and called her name. There was no response. He couldn't find a pulse. He tried mouth-to-mouth resuscitation, blowing into her mouth eight or ten times. He called for an ambulance and continued to administer CPR while he waited for it to arrive. He said, in his statement, that his wife had not shown signs of choking nor sustained injuries. Dalton spent more than two hours preparing his statement, but he stayed at the police station for more than four hours. Dalton lied to the police about the sequence of events, but it wasn't immediately clear why.

Dalton was arrested at about 5:00 a.m. the next morning, on August 17. He was charged with first-degree murder and read his rights. A forensic identification officer photographed Dalton. He found two scratches on his right hand, four marks on his left hand, and a small cut on his ear. Hutton had completed his autopsy less than seven hours earlier.

RCMP investigators questioned Dalton repeatedly over nearly a week following his wife's death. They believed there were discrepancies in his police statement. RCMP Sergeant Michael Doyle, who was in charge of Gander's general investigation section, concluded that Dalton had lied about his whereabouts the night of his wife's death. In an attempt to gain more information, two undercover police officers posing as criminals were placed in his cell after he was charged with murder. Nothing came of it and Dalton was released. The RCMP also used wiretaps and bugging devices. It was unusual to authorize them after someone is charged, but the request was granted. Dalton's home was bugged and he was followed. Police watched Dalton and Beverly Ladouceur, a woman with whom he had been having an affair. They wiretapped the phone lines between Dalton and Ladouceur for thirty days, but neither of them made an effort to contact each other. According to defence lawyer Jerome Kennedy, RCMP officers went to Brenda Dalton's graveside three times to watch Dalton. None of the techniques led to new evidence against him.

RCMP Staff-Sergeant Ronald Fraser visited Brenda Dalton's family and asked them to set up a meeting with Dalton to try to elicit information about what really happened the night Brenda died. The family, which had not received information from Dalton about what happened, was reluctant until Fraser told them Dalton had a girlfriend. Brenda's brother, Ken Caissie, and her sister, Erma, met with Dalton a month after Brenda's death. Dalton told them his lawyer instructed him not to discuss it. He didn't want his wife's relatives to get involved in the case and be forced to testify in court as a result. The story he told them was the same as his police statement after his wife's death.

Days after Brenda died, Dalton had told his lawyer David Eaton that his wife had choked to death on cereal. More than a month later, Dalton hand wrote a 160-page letter to Eaton finally admitting that he was actually at home when his wife choked to death. The letter was dated September 12, 1988, and September 27, 1988. He admitted that he had lied in his first statement to police because he didn't want anyone to know that he had been having an affair. He was also distraught and panicked over his wife's sudden death. An RCMP investigation discovered that he was not working at the bank the night Brenda died, contrary to his police statement.

Dalton's affair with former bank employee Beverly Ladouceur began on June 13, 1988, after she quit her job, and lasted until June 29. It ended when he went on summer holidays with his family to his native Prince Edward Island and she prepared to move outside the province. However, they continued to trade love letters and phone calls until the day of Brenda's death. It was understood from the outset that neither one of them would leave their spouses. The affair was intended to be short.

On August 15, just a few hours before Brenda died, Dalton left work at about 5:50 p.m. and went to a pay phone at the Gander airport. There, he spoke to Ladouceur on the phone in Greenwood, Nova Scotia for nearly half an hour. There was no argument, nor did they talk about leaving their spouses to be together. After the call ended, he went back to work until about 8:00 p.m. then went home. Ladouceur didn't hear about Brenda's death until August 18.

Dalton was tried in Newfoundland Supreme Court in Gander in 1989 before Justice Kevin Barry. Dr. Hutton testified that Brenda Dalton had been strangled. Dr. Walter Hofman, a forensic pathologist from New Jersey, testified for the defence that Brenda Dalton's injuries were due to medical intervention during prolonged efforts to revive her. Nevertheless, Dalton was convicted on December 15, 1989, of second-degree murder and sentenced to life in prison with no eligibility for parole for ten years.

Twelve days later, on December 27, Dalton filed an appeal. Then he waited. He was incarcerated at the Atlantic Institution in Renous, New Brunswick. His sister, Linda Gallant of Prince Edward Island, took in Dalton's three children and raised them alongside her own three. He applied for day parole, but the National Parole Board denied his request in November 1996. He was not considered to be a security threat, but denying that he killed his wife was clearly a concern. "You deny the offence and state that she choked on a bowl of cereal and you tried to assist her but to no avail. Police believe you have difficulty accepting guilt and the consequences of your guilt," the parole board decision said. It also stated that Dalton refused to deal with the institution's psychologist because he denied killing his wife. He also wasn't adapting to prison life. He was a loner and an angry individual who was abrupt and sometimes rude to staff. He would be eligible for full parole in 1999.

Dalton was still sitting in a prison cell when St. John's lawyer Jerome Kennedy became involved with the case on April 3, 1997. In his appeal, Kennedy argued that the Crown's case against Dalton was based on false statements he made to police about his whereabouts the night his wife died, his extramarital affair, and speculation by Crown forensic pathologist, Dr. Hutton. He also pointed out that the trial judge's charge to the jury indicated that he thought Dalton was guilty. In his appeal, Kennedy argued that there was compelling evidence that Brenda Dalton had choked accidentally. Her injuries were consistent with having being sustained during resuscitation and there was no history of family violence, or that Brenda Dalton knew of her husband's affair.

In early December 1997, Kennedy told judges of the Newfoundland Supreme Court of Appeal that he had new evidence that would prove that Brenda Dalton was not strangled to death. Two pathologists said she wasn't strangled: she choked to death on food. He filed an application with the Court of Appeal to hear the new evidence and make a ruling on whether Dalton's conviction should be overturned or if a new trial should be ordered. "In this case the doctors look at what's not present — no bruising, no damage to the thyroid. It's more consistent with resuscitation attempts. How do you strangle someone and not leave marks, not break the bones or cartilage?'" Kennedy asked the judges.[1] Crown prosecutor Wayne Gorman argued that Dalton's conviction was not entirely based on Hutton's testimony. He also pointed out that Dalton had initially lied about his whereabouts the night Brenda died and failed to mention that she had choked on cereal.

In an eighty-four-page decision on May 29, 1998, the Newfoundland Court of Appeal overturned the conviction and ordered a new trial. It also expressed concerns about how it was that Dalton spent eight years in prison before his appeal was heard. "The resolution of this appeal leaves unanswered the deeply troubling question of how this man could have passed eight years of his life in jail before substantial grounds challenging the integrity of his conviction were brought on for hearing," the decision read.[2]

Dalton was released on $10,000 bail the following month and spent time with his family in PEI, including his children, ages eleven, sixteen, and nineteen. It was the first time he had seen his children in three years. He was pleased that his case was finally moving forward, but it didn't erase the years he lost with his children while he waited behind bars for his appeal to be heard.

The provincial Department of Justice filed leave to appeal the decision to the Supreme Court of Canada. In the meantime, Dalton's long and winding road to justice took another turn. He wanted lawyer Jerome Kennedy, who had successfully argued his appeal before the Newfoundland Court of Appeal, to represent him at trial. Kennedy and his law partner Bob Simmons filed an application to be appointed Dalton's counsel. But an amendment to the province's Legal Aid Act in 1996 restricted people charged with offences that could lead to life imprisonment to using legal aid lawyers. This limited their ability to choose a publicly funded lawyer of their own choice. Newfoundland's Legal Aid Commission refused to provide legal aid so that Dalton could hire Kennedy. Dalton went to court to appeal the Legal Aid Commission's decision. The commission reversed its decision and agreed to fund Dalton for his trial.

In November 1998, the Supreme Court of Canada refused to hear the Crown's appeal overturning Dalton's conviction and calling for a new trial. That paved the way for Dalton to be retried for murder more than nine years after he was first convicted. Dalton's trial began on March 1, 1999, with jury selection. It took three days to find twelve impartial jurors from among Gander's less than 10,000 residents. Among the forty-two people challenged, fourteen had established an opinion on the case before opening arguments had even begun. Other prospective jurors said they knew about the case but that they could, nonetheless, be impartial. Once a jury was selected, the case got under way.

After five days of testimony, from only one witness, in April 1999, Dalton's case hit yet another snag. Justice Gordon Easton informed the jury that he had to withdraw from the case for medical reasons. This forced Newfoundland Supreme Court Justice Raymond Halley to declare a mistrial. A new trial — Dalton's third — was postponed until mid-September 1999. The wheels of justice had ground to a halt for Dalton yet again.

Defence lawyer Jerome Kennedy argued before Justice Raymond Halley that Dalton's trial should be moved from Gander to St. John's — a city of more than 100,000 people — to ensure a fair trial. He argued that the RCMP had spread rumours and innuendo about the case throughout the small community of Gander. That, coupled with Dalton's prior conviction, would make it difficult to find an impartial jury in Gander. On June 28, 1999, Newfoundland Supreme Court Justice Halley agreed that Dalton would be more likely to receive a fair trial in St. John's. "Their opinions about the trial were such that one third of the potential jurors were deemed to be partial. I find that to be an extremely high percentage which will probably increase because of the mistrial and the new trial scheduled for September," he wrote in his judgment. "The public interest in the trial arises from the fact that Dalton was a bank manager and a well-known member of the community. Murder trials in Gander also are very rare. There has also been a considerable amount of publicity arising out of the Court of Appeal's decision to order a new trial."[3]

Dalton's retrial finally got under way in December 1999, before Newfoundland Supreme Court Justice Raymond Halley and a jury of seven women and five men. Kennedy told them that the RCMP called in Dr. Hutton when they saw marks on Brenda's body and suspected she had been murdered. However, the marks they saw were consistent with prolonged and aggressive efforts to resuscitate her. He argued that Hutton was wrong and inexperienced when he concluded in 1988 that Brenda Dalton was assaulted and strangled, citing her bruised larynx as evidence of strangulation. Hutton had been appointed as chief of forensic pathology for the province shortly before Brenda Dalton's death. He had seen a case of manual strangulation only once before in his career.

Unlike in other jurisdictions such as the United States and Britain, Canada's Royal College of Physicians and Surgeons had not yet recognized forensic pathology as a subspecialty within the field of pathology. There were also no training programs in Canada. Consequently, few Canadian pathologists who practiced forensic pathology possessed the specialized training they needed. Formal recognition for forensic pathology in Canada would only come in 2003, after a number of men and women had been wrongly convicted following testimony from under-trained forensic pathologists.

Dr. Vincent Di Maio, chief medical examiner for Bexar County, Texas, agreed with Hutton's assessment that Brenda Dalton had been murdered — but not how she died. Testifying for the Crown, he believed the nature of her scratches showed that she was smothered to death when someone sat on her chest, pinned her arms to the floor, and then covered her nose and mouth. He ruled out accidental choking.

However, three experts called upon by the defence disagreed that Brenda Dalton was either strangled or smothered. Dr. Rex Ferris, former chief medical examiner of British Columbia, said two small bruises on either side of her jaw were not in the right position for her to have been strangled. He would also expect to see more injuries around her neck if she had been strangled. Injuries to her larynx most likely occurred when medical staff performed life-saving techniques to try to revive her. Ferris believed that Brenda Dalton had choked on food.

Dr. Bill Hunt, a leading forensic pathologist in the United Kingdom, testified that a victim of strangulation would likely have bruises around the Adam's apple — not just two tiny bruises. There was also no evidence that anyone had sat on her chest and smothered her. Otherwise, the inside of her lips would have more cuts and bruises from pressing against her teeth. He agreed that Brenda Dalton's injuries were more likely sustained during resuscitation efforts.

Dr. Walter Hofman, a forensic pathologist from New Jersey who testified at Dalton's original trial, stood by his initial conclusion that Brenda Dalton was not strangled. He pointed out that in more than 80 percent of cases of strangulation, victims have external neck injuries. He admitted that he was not asked at the first trial whether it was possible that she had choked to death on food; but he believed that she had. The cereal had irritated her windpipe and caused it to narrow, he explained, decreasing the amount of oxygen she could breathe, then killing her.

The breathing tube that was inserted at the hospital to help Brenda breathe was placed in her esophagus instead of her trachea. That's where Hutton found it during his autopsy. Dr. Harry Emson, who was educated in England but lived in Saskatchewan, agreed with the other pathologists testifying for the defence. "There's no damage to the voice box. The injuries found in the neck area internally are caused from the inside out. Such as inserting the tube, which was found in the wrong place," Emson said.[4]

It wasn't the first time that other pathologists had contradicted Hutton's opinion. In the 1993 Nova Scotia case of Clayton Johnson, who was accused of the death of his wife, Hutton testified that Janice Johnson had been beaten to death. Johnson was convicted. He was subsequently exonerated after an international team of experts exhumed and examined the victim's body and found she had died after a freak accident in which she fell down the basement stairs in the family's home. As lawyer James Lockyer commented at the time, "Dr. Hutton has a modus operandi, by his own admission, which is to approach a case by 'thinking dirty,'" he said. "What he did to Mr. Dalton was, he thought dirty, found dirt that didn't exist and Mr. Dalton spent eight years in jail."[5] However, Hutton stood by his conclusions in the case. "Pathologists in our business have to think dirty," he said. "You find a woman, healthy as a horse, who is suddenly full of bruises — thinking dirty is how you have to approach a suspicious death."[6]

The jury in Dalton's case began deliberations on the afternoon of Wednesday June 21, 2000, following a five-month trial during which they heard testimony from more than fifty witnesses. On June 24, 2000, the Newfoundland Supreme Court jury found Ronald Dalton not guilty of murdering his wife. Spectators burst into a round of applause after hearing the verdict. Dalton's long road to exoneration was finally over. Nearly twelve years after he was arrested, and eight-and-a-half years behind bars, he had been acquitted. Dalton was accompanied by his sons — twenty-one-year-old Adam and thirteen-year-old David — mother Mary, sister Linda Gallant, and friend Jacinta Edwards. Then he headed home to Miscouche near Summerside, Prince Edward Island to attend the high school graduation of his eighteen-year-old daughter Allison.

In March 2003, following three wrongful convictions in the province within about six years, the Newfoundland government agreed to hold an inquiry to examine the circumstances that led to the convictions of two of the men. Former Supreme Court of Canada Chief Justice Antonio Lamer was named to head the inquiry into the wrongful convictions of Gregory Parsons, Ronald Dalton, and Randy Druken. In each case, the Newfoundland Court of Appeal had found that there were enough errors to warrant a new trial. Lamer was tasked with examining the circumstances surrounding the cases of Druken and Parsons, from the initial investigations to the final verdicts. He would also look at why it took eight years before Dalton's appeal received a hearing. Lamer could recommend changes to the justice system and compensation for Dalton and Druken. Parsons had already received compensation from the province.

Parsons was convicted in the 1991 murder of his mother, Catherine Carroll, on the basis of hearsay and the lyrics of a song he once wrote that included the words "Kill your parents." He was exonerated using DNA evidence in 1998. A former friend was subsequently convicted of the murder. Druken was convicted in 1995 of killing his girlfriend, Brenda Marie Young. He was jailed for five years largely based on the testimony of a jailhouse informant, who later admitted that he lied. Subsequently, DNA tests exonerated him. The provincial government apologized to Parsons and awarded him $650,000 in compensation in 2002.

Dalton was pleased about the inquiry, but, he said, it could never repay time away from his children. "My sister and her husband raised our three children while I was in prison. I was still away from them for 10 years. You don't get back that kind of time."[7] Dalton was the first to testify when the inquiry opened on September 23, 2003. Dressed in a suit and tie, he testified about his difficulties with lawyers, legal aid officials, and prison officials during his incarceration in a maximum-security penitentiary outside the province. Dalton seldom had access to a telephone in prison and was too far away to meet with lawyers in person. He also didn't receive all of his mail. He and his family spent $100,000 in his defence at his first trial, which depleted their entire savings. Legal aid initially turned down funding for an appeal. When they overturned their decision, the Legal Aid Commission told his lawyer, David Eaton, but not Dalton himself that he was eligible for funding. Eaton never told Dalton, nor did he answer the commission's offer of funding. Eaton wrote to Dalton fifteen months later, in August 1992, to tell him that he didn't have time to handle Dalton's appeal.

Dalton's second lawyer, David Day, took the case from 1993 until October 1997. He researched the case and his junior partner Sandra Burke gave Day a draft document in August 1994. It was not filed with the court. When Dalton's letters to his lawyer went unanswered, he got frustrated and filed the draft himself in October 1996. Burke told the inquiry she was "absolutely horrified."[8] In January 1997, she contacted Dalton and told him to get another lawyer. Then she contacted Jerome Kennedy and asked him to take Dalton's case. Legal aid issues were finally resolved in 1997, and Dalton's appeal finally proceeded in 1998. Newman Petten, who was the provincial director of the Legal Aid Commission, said one of the commission's lawyers questioned why Dalton needed a forensic expert, even though two forensic experts had testified that Brenda Dalton was strangled to death.

Justice Lamer's 400-page report was released in June 2006. In it, he slammed a Crown "culture" that accepted police theories without question and aggressively pursued legal victories instead of viewing evidence objectively. That approach played a key role behind the wrongful convictions of Dalton, Druken, and Parsons. "Any system that depends on human beings is, by virtue of that very feature, fallible," Lamer said.

"This helps explain why tunnel vision is seldom the result of personal malice, and why wrongful convictions are not aberrations, but are rooted in systemic problems."[9]

Lamer also criticized the provincial government for underfunding its justice system. He made forty-five recommendations, including calling for an independent review of the office of the Director of Public Prosecutions. Newfoundland Justice Minister Tom Marshall immediately appointed retired Newfoundland Supreme Court Judge William Marshall to examine the resources, training, morale, and the systemic issues that Lamer's report identified. Other recommendations included appointing more judges with criminal law expertise, videotaping and audio-taping all police interviews in major criminal investigations, and that Crown prosecutors critically assess evidence in a case at each major stage during a prosecution. Parsons received an additional $650,000 in compensation for a total of $1.3 million for his wrongful conviction, while Druken was given $2 million by the province.

Newfoundland Justice Minister Tom Marshall apologized to the three wrongly convicted men on June 21, 2006, and encouraged them to negotiate compensation. Clyde Wells, chief justice of the province's Court of Appeal, wrote a letter of apology to Dalton the following day. He said that Lamer's criticism was justified. On October 26, 2007, the provincial government agreed to pay Dalton $750,000 in compensation. The money was an *ex gratia* payment, which meant the government was giving the money without acknowledging any liability or legal obligation. Dalton was relieved to have the issue of compensation addressed, but no amount of money could make up for the lost years. "It's not a lot of money in terms of the 8½ years I spent in a federal maximum-security prison. It's not a lot of money in terms of my three children being orphaned," he said. "It's certainly not much money by today's standards. My loss of income over that period alone is well in excess of that amount."[10] Dalton's daughter Allison was just entering grade one when her father was jailed. He attended her high school graduation two days after he was acquitted. Nothing could make up for those lost years.

Chapter Eight

Down the Stairs: The Clayton Johnson Case

Shelburne is a lovely seaside town of fewer than 5,000 people on Nova Scotia's southwestern shore, where historic buildings line the waterfront. Clayton, forty-three, and Janice, thirty-six, had been married for thirteen years and had two young daughters, Dawn, eight, and Darla, eleven. The devout and devoted couple was very involved in the local Pentecostal community. The morning of February 20, 1989, was shaping up to be a busy one in the Johnson household.

Janice Faye Johnson, a stay-at-home mom, was supposed to look after three-year-old neighbour Brittany Malloy that day. Janice's brother was planning to drop off some clothes around 8:00 a.m. At Janice's request, her husband Clayton phoned their neighbour, Robert Malloy, at 7:00 a.m. to ask that he drop off Brittany by 8:00 a.m. Janice wanted to take the little girl to a local carnival that morning. Clayton packed a lunch for his two daughters and carried a load of laundry downstairs for his wife.

At 7:40 a.m., next-door neighbour Clare Thompson watched the two Johnson girls climb onto the school bus. She picked up the phone and called Janice, and the two women chatted for about ten minutes. While they were on the phone, Janice paused to say goodbye to her husband. "See you later, hon," she said.

Clayton kissed his wife Janice goodbye and drove to a high school 27 kilometres away where he was an industrial arts teacher. He stopped for gas and drove slowly for the last 10 kilometres, stuck behind a school bus.

Shelburne is a quiet Nova Scotia community. Photo: Sandra Phinney

Janice and Clare ended their conversation and hung up just before 7:50 a.m. Robert Malloy arrived at the Johnson home with his daughter Brittany in tow moments later. When they stepped inside the unlocked basement door, the washing machine was running, and Janice was lying on her back in a pool of blood at the bottom of the wooden basement stairs. She was alone, unconscious, struggling for breath. One foot was resting on the bottom step and she was clutching her car keys. A high-heeled shoe was lying nearby under the stairs. It looked as though she had tripped and fallen while running up the steep stairs. There was blood on the steps and the wall. Malloy rushed next door and called an ambulance at 7:54 a.m. Ambulance attendants moved blood-soaked equipment around the basement as they tried to stabilize Janice.

When Clayton arrived at work at 8:11 a.m., the school secretary told him to make his way to the hospital. The distraught family man watched as doctors tried to save his wife, but she died four hours later. As he sat by her side, alone with her body for fifteen minutes, he held her hand and kept asking, "Why, God?"

Mary Hartley and Mary Davis were friends with Janice and attended the same church. At their pastor's suggestion, they went to the Johnson home and cleaned up as much of the blood in the basement as they could. Clayton told his daughters about their mother's deadly fall. The three of them went to live with Janice's parents for a few weeks.

Chief Medical Examiner Dr. Roland Perry examined her injuries. Both sides of her skull were severely crushed and she had a linear mark on her left calf. In his report, dated April 26, 1989, he concluded that Janice Johnson had tripped and fallen face-first down the basement stairs. As she tumbled, her head got wedged into a fourteen-centimetre gap between the steps and a concrete wall before she landed at the bottom of the stairs. Perry ruled that Janice's death was the result of an accidental fall.

Three months later, Clayton Johnson began dating Tina Weybret, a twenty-two-year-old member of his Pentecostal congregation. The devoted family man was worried that he wouldn't be able to raise his two daughters on his own. "I think he wanted to fill a void," Weybret told *The Globe and Mail.* "He needed a mother for his girls."[1] They got married a year later. The community was abuzz as tongues wagged about Johnson marrying a much younger woman so soon after his wife died. Some even speculated that perhaps he had been carrying on an affair with Weybret and had killed Janice.

RCMP Corporal Brian Oldford, who wasn't involved in the police investigation that cleared Clayton Johnson, heard the gossip and became suspicious. Sparked by the small town's rumours and innuendos, he reopened the case — twenty-one months after Janice died. He could find no evidence that Johnson and Weybret had been carrying on an affair before Janice's death. As he nosed around, he learned that Johnson had collected $125,000 on an insurance policy on his wife. During his investigation, Oldford once showed Weybret autopsy photos of Janice Johnson and told her that her husband would probably kill her, too.

Oldford interviewed the two women who had cleaned up Janice's blood. During their first statements to police during the initial investigation, they said they only saw blood around Janice Johnson's body. Suddenly, they "remembered" seeing blood spatters in other parts of the basement besides the stairs. It's said that Oldford had shown them gruesome autopsy photos. Police officers who searched the basement just after Janice was found, as well as the ambulance attendants, didn't remember seeing the blood stains to which the women referred.

Oldford thought the blood spatters were an indication of a struggle between Janice Johnson and her purported assailant, who had beaten her to death. Two RCMP forensic analysts disagreed. Inspector Herb LeRoy wrote a report on September 10, 1992, that also confirmed the earlier findings of his colleague Sergeant Vic Gorman. Both officers said that the changing stories of the women who cleaned up the blood after Johnson's fall were not reliable. There were other plausible explanations for the possible existence of other bloodstains. Using a device that detects tiny traces of blood, one analyst was unable to find any traces of blood in the parts of the basement where the two women had claimed to have seen blood spatters. The reports were sent to Corporal Oldford.

Nonetheless, Oldford asked Newfoundland pathologist Dr. Charles Hutton and Hamilton, Ontario, pathologist Dr. David King to weigh in. The two men weren't shown the reports that the RCMP forensic analysts had submitted. Based on the alleged presence of bloodstains, both pathologists agreed that Janice Johnson had likely been murdered. They suggested that while she had been beaten with a two-by-four her head got trapped between the stairs and the wall. Then she was struck a few more times while she was lying on the floor. No weapon was ever found. Oldford informed the Nova Scotia coroner, Dr. Perry, who changed his conclusions to match those of the two outside pathologists.

Johnson was charged with first-degree murder in April 1992. He turned down the Crown's offer to plead guilty to a reduced charge of manslaughter. In May 1993, he was tried in Nova Scotia Supreme Court before Justice Jamie Saunders in his hometown of Shelbourne. Small-town gossip about whether Johnson had been having an affair with Weybret and Janice's $125,000 insurance policy played a role at his trial. The defence, led by top Halifax lawyer Joel Pink, argued that Johnson knew that his brother-in-law and Malloy were expected to stop by the house before 8:00 a.m. That would have given him fewer than ten minutes to assault his wife, make the scene look like an accident, and then change his clothes before heading to work. There was no real opportunity to commit a murder.

Nonetheless, Crown prosecutor Jamie Burrill convinced a jury that Johnson had beaten his wife to death with an unidentified weapon before leaving for work. They never heard that RCMP bloodstain experts raised questions about the bloodstains and murder theory; neither did the three pathologists who testified that Johnson had likely been bludgeoned to death. The 1992 RCMP report stating that it "would be dangerous" to view bloodstains as proof that she was murdered was also never disclosed to the defence. As for the insurance policy, 40 percent of the province's teachers were part of the insurance plan, and Johnson testified that he didn't realize his wife was covered until after she died.

After a three-week trial, Justice Saunders gave a charge to the jury that pointed out weaknesses in the Crown's case, which relied on circumstantial evidence. He said that if bloodstains did exist, they could have come from other sources, such as from the equipment that ambulance attendants used to try to stabilize Janice Johnson at the scene or the family dog shaking blood off its fur. He also pointed out that Clayton Johnson would likely have been caught in the act of beating his wife, given that people were expected to drop by the house any minute. He also said that no wood fragments were found in the victim's wounds, nor were any blood spatters found on the ceiling.

The jury, most of whom were acquainted with Johnson, deliberated for eight hours before concluding that he was guilty of first-degree murder. Despite a weak case against him, he was convicted on May 4, 1993. "I had thought for sure I was going home," he recalled. "It came as a total shock to me."[2] He had been convicted by a jury of people whom he had known all his life, and eleven for whom he had done work. They had been swayed by disapproval over his relationship with a younger woman. Johnson's knees went weak when he heard the verdict. "Let God be my witness, I had nothing to do with it whatsoever," were his last words to the jury.[3] Then he was taken into another room to see his family before being led off to prison.

Four years after his wife died, Johnson was sentenced to life in prison with no chance of parole for twenty-five years. The Nova Scotia Court of Appeal dismissed his appeal in March 1994. In 1995, the Supreme Court of Canada refused to hear the case. Weybret spent two years travelling to the maximum-security Atlantic Institution in Renous, New Brunswick, to visit Johnson, then lost hope. She divorced him, left Nova Scotia, and remarried. "I got tired of saying goodbye all the time," she said. "I had lost faith in the justice system. I have always been 100-per-cent certain he didn't do it, but I felt no matter what we did, we were going to lose."[4] Relatives raised Johnson's two young daughters.

James Lockyer was one of the lawyers who helped exonerate Clayton Johnson. Photo: Grant Martin Photography

Less than two years after Johnson was convicted, the province forced Nova Scotia's chief medical examiner, Dr. Roland Perry, into retirement by making it mandatory for someone in his position to be a pathologist. Medical examiners perform autopsies to determine the cause of death. Perry, a physician, had investigated more than 6,000 deaths and conducted 2,500 autopsies during his ten years as chief medical examiner. The law was changed after members of the legal community complained about Perry's qualifications. His initial conclusions about Janice Johnson's death sparked some of the complaints. He was succeeded by Dr. John Butt, who was Alberta's chief medical examiner for a number of years.

Having exhausted the legal avenues to have his conviction overturned, Johnson sent a three-page handwritten letter to the Association in Defence of the Wrongly Convicted (AIDWYC) in 1995. The Toronto-based non-profit group advocates on behalf of people who have been wrongly convicted. Lawyers volunteer their time to review files, re-interview witnesses, analyze court transcripts, and look for any information that may have been overlooked previously and could cast doubt on a conviction. They were instrumental in clearing David Milgaard and Guy Paul Morin, among others. Lawyer James Lockyer reviewed the case and concluded that Johnson was innocent. Who phones their brother-in-law and neighbour to ask them to come over for the very time that they're planning to kill their wife? "The most ... striking thing for me is that the time that the Crown theorized he was killing her, he knew there were three people about to come to the door," he said. "Clayton was long gone when she was still alive."[5]

Lockyer needed an explanation for the wounds that Janice Johnson had suffered. He asked Dallas, Texas, forensic pathologist Dr. Linda Norton to review the case. She reviewed the forensic evidence and the sequence of events the morning of Janice Johnson's death. She concluded that the two previous experts, Dr. King and Dr. Hutton, who believed a murder had occurred, assumed that Johnson had fallen face first as she walked down the basement steps. Dr. Norton found that Janice Johnson's injuries were consistent with losing her balance and falling backwards from the top of the stairs. She had a linear bruise on the back of her left calf, as though her leg had hit the edge of a step. There was little blood on the wall and the third step; there would have been a lot of bloodstains from a head wound if she had been hit and fallen there. There were also no defensive wounds on her hands or other signs of a struggle. A murder weapon was never found and there was no blood on her husband or his vehicle.

Herbert McDonell, director of the Laboratory of Forensic Science in Corning, New York, came to the same conclusion as Dr. Norton. While he was reviewing the case, McDonell built a stairwell that was identical to the one found in the Johnson home. Then he used a model in safety straps to re-enact the fall. He concluded that Johnson's death was the result of an accident — not a homicide.

Lockyer and his co-counsel, Phil Campbell, believed that Johnson was the victim of a wrongful conviction. He had been convicted following a police investigation plagued by tunnel vision (the single-minded pursuit of one suspect), prosecuted based on circumstantial evidence, and tried in a community where emotions about the case ran high. The defence had focused on trying to prove that Johnson wasn't the killer, not whether or not a murder had even taken place.

Lockyer met Johnson at the Renous prison in November 1997. For the next hour, he shared Norton's conclusions and outlined his plans to apply for a new hearing under Section 690 of the Criminal Code, as well as request bail for Johnson. His client stared at him stoically. Curious about his client's lack of emotion, Lockyer asked Johnson, "Are you still religious after all you've been through?" he said. "I thought you might have renounced your God."

Johnson replied that he hadn't. "God has helped me to bear all of this."

Lockyer explained that he was asking because he had laid out what he thought would happen, but Johnson hadn't shown any emotion. Johnson then began to weep. "He'd been holding it in for years," Lockyer recounted at a conference on wrongful convictions. "The poor abandoned man thought that was the thing to do, to be stoic. It's what can happen to these innocent guys."[6]

In March 1998, AIDWYC lawyers petitioned then-federal Justice Minister Anne McLellan to reopen the case and order a new trial. Under Section 690 of the Criminal Code, the minister could examine questionable convictions once the person has exhausted the appeals process. The minister cannot overturn a conviction, but other options that are available are to order a new trial or refer the case to an appeal court if the minister believes that fresh evidence could have affected the verdict if it had been available at the time of the trial.

In their 250-page submission, Johnson's lawyers argued that the RCMP withheld vital information from the two pathologists who assessed Janice Johnson's death and concluded that she had been murdered. "Clayton Johnson is serving a life sentence, not for a crime he didn't commit, but for a crime that never happened," James Lockyer told a news conference in Halifax. "It is the ultimate tragedy. His daughters lost their mother to a tragic accident, and then they lost their father to a miscarriage of justice."[7]

Upon learning that they had not been shown the RCMP reports before Johnson's trial, the three pathologists who testified against him wavered about their conclusions that Janice Johnson was murdered.

Canadian forensic pathologist Dr. James Ferris agreed with Norton and McDonell's conclusions that Janice Johnson had sustained her fatal injuries after falling backward down the stairs, instead of face forward.

Her injuries were inconsistent with those of someone who had fallen face front down the stairs, which is what prompted the other pathologists to theorize that she had been murdered.

In April 1998, the federal justice department hired Halifax criminal lawyer John Briggs to review Johnson's case and determine if he was wrongfully convicted. Briggs was director of research for the inquiry into Donald Marshall's wrongful murder conviction. The RCMP examined the conduct of Sergeant Brian Oldford and determined that he had done nothing wrong in his investigation that led to Johnson's murder conviction.

As Johnson's lawyers waited for the federal justice department's verdict on their application for a review of his case, Dr. Hutton's work in another case was called into question. He had concluded that Brenda Dalton had been strangled to death in 1988. Her husband Ronald had been found guilty and sent to prison. But in 1998, two other Canadian pathologists said that Hutton was wrong. Brenda Dalton's injuries were consistent with having choked on a piece of cereal and subsequent efforts to resuscitate her. In court testimony at Johnson's trial, Hutton had admitted that he tries to "think dirty," by starting autopsies with the assumption that a person was murdered. He had also presented the jury with slides and autopsy photos of Janice Johnson.

Briggs studied the file that AIDWYC had submitted to the federal justice department and submitted his report on July 30, 1998. In September, Justice Minister McLellan asked the Nova Scotia Court of Appeal to re-examine Johnson's case to determine whether the forensic evidence that his lawyers had submitted constituted fresh evidence. The two forensic experts consulted, Manitoba chief medical examiner Dr. Peter Markesteyn and University of Manitoba physics professor Dr. Norman Davison, agreed that Janice Johnson's death was more consistent with an accidental fall down the basement stairs. The judges could choose to hear the appeal on the basis of fresh evidence that was not presented at trial, order a new trial, or acquit Johnson.

After waiting behind bars for five years, a handcuffed Johnson walked into a courtroom packed with friends and family at the Nova Scotia Court of Appeal. Following a one-and-a-half day hearing, Justice Gerald Freeman released him on bail on September 25, 1998, pending a review of his case by the Nova Scotia Appeal Court to determine if evidence that his lawyers presented constituted grounds for an appeal. Johnson wiped away tears with a blue handkerchief. Relatives and friends crowded around to hug him when he left court. It was the first time that some of them had seen him since he was convicted more than five years earlier. His two daughters, Darla and Dawn, stood by his side, each clutching one of his arms. "What happened to me could happen to anybody. Any of you that have a husband or wife ... you could leave in the morning, something happens. If you're the last one, you're a suspect."[8] Johnson returned to Shelburne and went to live with his parents and younger daughter, Dawn. While he waited for a final decision on his case, the former industrial arts teacher kept busy building furniture and doing home renovations.

Manitoba's chief medical examiner, Dr. Peter Markesteyn, said that Janice Johnson's head injuries were more similar to what one would expect to find from someone who had fallen backward down the stairs than a person who had been beaten. His report to Halifax lawyer John Briggs, who had consulted him while investigating Clayton Johnson's case on behalf of federal Justice Minister McLellan, said that he would feel more comfortable giving an opinion if he could examine the body. The decision was made to exhume the body and perform a second autopsy in an effort to assess whether she was beaten to death or her fatal injuries were the result of an accident.

On December 9, 1998, a large green tent in the East Green Harbour Cemetery shielded workers as they spent almost two hours removing Janice Johnson's metal coffin from its resting place. It was just down the road from her family's home. The coffin was placed in a van and taken to the Victoria General pathology laboratories in Halifax, where Dr. Markesteyn and an international team of eight pathologists from three countries examined the injuries to her skull to determine how she really died. A model that replicated the basement staircase in the Johnson home stood in the hospital morgue. Dr. Norton lay backwards on the staircase and demonstrated her theory to the four skeptical pathologists, who were holding her legs. When they began to let go of her, Norton's legs started to flip over her head. Johnson had probably tumbled to the bottom of the stairs rather than sliding. After also reviewing the case file, the pathologists were expected to submit a report of their findings to the Crown in early January 1999.

Bob Hagell, the prosecutor assigned to the case, said the exhumation was the only way to unearth new evidence about the cause of Janice Johnson's injuries. But the decision to exhume the body was difficult for the family, daughter Darla told *The Globe and Mail*. "I was always brought up to think you are supposed to respect the dead. The way my sister and I have to look at it is, this is the way Mom would have wanted it. It is the last thing she can do to bring our family back together."[9] Darla hoped the exhumation would help resolve the case. "I want this to be over, and I really do believe this is going to be it," she said. "I think this is going to bring closure and finally let us get on with living a normal life again."[10] As Clayton Johnson noted, "Her family says they have lost a daughter, but they don't seem to realize that I lost a wife and loving companion, and the girls lost a mother."[11] The day after the exhumation, Janice Faye Johnson's remains were returned to the quiet graveyard where she was first buried nearly ten years earlier. She was reburied following a quiet ceremony.

Johnson's next court date was put off repeatedly while lawyers waited for all of the pathologists to submit their reports following the second autopsy on Janice Johnson. On February 18, 2002, almost thirteen years to the day that his wife died, Johnson finally received the news he had been waiting almost a decade to hear. The Nova Scotia Court of Appeal quashed his 1993 conviction for first-degree murder in connection with his wife's death and opened the door to a new trial. He left the Halifax court surrounded by his parents, two daughters, and a team of lawyers.

Five hours later, the Crown announced before the Nova Scotia Supreme Court that it wouldn't pursue a new trial in the case. They had consulted twenty-two forensic experts, including pathologists, engineers, biomechanics, and physicists. Overwhelming forensic evidence indicated that Janice Johnson had fallen backwards down the basement stairs of her home after accidentally slipping. This was consistent with the initial assessment of Nova Scotia Chief Coroner Dr. Perry. Johnson had been convicted of a crime that never even occurred. "Science, unfortunately, took us further and further away from the truth — until finally after five years, science managed to yank us closer to the truth again," Philip Campbell, one of Johnson's lawyers commented.[12]

Johnson's lawyer, James Lockyer, filed a ten-page brief requesting that his client be issued a formal apology and asked that court records indicate that Johnson had been acquitted. Chief Justice Joe Kennedy responded, "Mr. Johnson leaves court today an innocent man."[13] For Johnson, "This not only brings justice for me, but for Janice, too," he said. "Now she can rest in peace."[14]

Bad pathology had convicted Johnson. Dr. Norton pointed out in a newspaper interview that medical examiners often work closely with police officers and the Crown. This makes it more difficult for medical examiners and pathologists to remain neutral during their investigations, and to keep an open mind to different explanations for a death. As the late Dianne Martin, a law professor at Osgoode Hall in Toronto, put it, "Once it was decided there was something suspicious about Mr. Johnson and that he killed his wife, you then go looking for information that would support that conclusion. You build a case. You justify a conclusion you've already reached."[15] At a weekend conference of the Association in Defence of the Wrongly Convicted, the late Quebec Court of Appeal judge Mr. Justice Michel Proulx pointed out the challenges of having the prosecution and the defence use experts at trial. "Fundamentally, experts and lawyers are enmeshed in an insidious relationship," he commented. Experts become loyal to those who have hired them, instead of offering maximum objectivity. "Expert evidence is a powerful weapon."[16]

On March 5, 2002, Johnson sent a letter to Nova Scotia Attorney General Michael Baker seeking compensation from the Nova Scotia government. He had incurred more than $500,000 in legal fees while spending nine years trying to clear his name. His wrongful conviction cost Johnson his job as a teacher, his home, reputation, freedom, and more than five years of watching his two daughters grow up. The following August, he sued the Nova Scotia government, the RCMP, and the province's Public Prosecution Service for wrongful arrest, prosecution, conviction, and imprisonment, malicious prosecution, and negligence. "As far as I'm concerned, no compensation can bring back the years I lost with my girls," he said.[17] He agreed to drop his lawsuit if the government agreed to compensation. He said that as part of the negotiations, the Nova Scotia government asked for proof that he suffered during his incarceration. In June 2004, the Nova Scotia government finally agreed to award Johnson $2.5 million to cover legal fees, compensation, and other expenses such as loss of his home.

Throughout his incarceration in cell 1B7, the soft-spoken Johnson tried to keep himself busy using his carpentry skills in the prison wood shop and working as a cleaner. He began going to the prison chapel on Thursday evenings and Sundays. He relied on his religious faith to sustain him. "I always say the Lord doesn't give you more than you can stand," he said. "My faith gets me by."[18] He never lost hope. "I know the truth is out there, it's just a matter of them trying to find it," he told the *Saint John Telegraph-Journal* in an interview at the federal penitentiary in Renous, New Brunswick.[19]

Now Johnson is free at last, but it will never erase the years that he missed watching his daughters grow up — and that they missed with their father. "I think of her often. I love my wife," he says. "We have two lovely girls. I missed a lot of their years growing up. My oldest, Darla, is 21. I missed her graduation. My youngest, Dawn, will be 18 this September. I'm hoping to see her graduate."[20] By the time Johnson was released from prison, he was about to become a grandfather.

Chapter Nine

Natural Causes: The William Mullins-Johnson Case

William Mullins-Johnson woke up at about noon on Saturday June 26, 1993. The twenty-two-year-old was raised by his Ojibwa mother in the Batchewana First Nation. For the past three months, he had been staying with his brother, Paul Johnson, and sister-in-law, Kim Lariviere, in Sault Ste. Marie. The couple had three children, ages three, four, and six. As Lariviere prepared to go to a baseball tournament with her family, she asked Mullins-Johnson to make supper later that evening and babysit the children for a few hours afterward. He often looked after the children.

Mullins-Johnson sat down on the couch after supper and watched cartoons with the children. Four-year-old Valin had been ill with a fever for two days. She was tired and already wearing her one-piece white pajamas with a teddy-bear print when she went off to bed. "She gave me a kiss and a hug the way she always did, told … told me she loved me and I told her I loved her and she went off to bed herself, and left me and [her brother] John downstairs," he later testified. When Mullins-Johnson checked on her at 8:00 p.m., she was sleeping with her head resting on her arm.

Lariviere returned home at 9:30 p.m., while Paul Johnson stayed out with friends for another few hours. Lariviere didn't check on her daughter until 7:00 a.m. the next morning. When she did, she found Valin lying on her stomach with her knees pulled up towards her chest and her rear raised up off the bed. Her pajama was still done up. There was vomit on her, the bed, and the floor. When Lariviere turned her daughter over, she saw that Valin's face was purple, and the little girl was cold and stiff. Lariviere rushed from her daughter's bedroom and ran downstairs yelling "Valin's dead! Valin's dead!" While Lariviere dialed 911, Johnson ran into his daughter's bedroom with Mullins-Johnson and performed cardiopulmonary resuscitation, to no avail. Ambulance attendants Nancy Scott and Robert Weir, who arrived moments later, couldn't find a pulse. Valin was dead. Her parents believed that she had choked to death.

Sault Ste Marie Police Sergeant Robert Welton and Constable Jane Martynuck arrived at the house and took statements from Johnson and Mullins-Johnson. Valin's body was taken to the hospital for an autopsy. Dr. Bhubendra Rasaiah, the director of pathology at Sault Ste. Marie General Hospital, began conducting an autopsy at noon. He noticed a large opening in the rectum and some bruising around Valin's vagina. He called a doctor at Toronto's Hospital for Sick Children and was told that it appeared to be a sign of chronic sexual abuse.

Dr. Rasaiah called in local obstetrician and gynecologist Dr. Patricia Zehr, whom he considered an expert in childhood sexual abuse. Neither physician had experience in forensics, but Zehr concluded that Valin was the victim of chronic sexual abuse — the worst she had ever seen. Dr. Rasaiah used a body temperature analysis to conclude that Valin had died between 8:00 p.m. and 10:00 p.m. the night before. A bruise on her neck and marks on her chest and face led him to conclude that she had probably been strangled or smothered. He listed her cause of death as "homicidal asphyxia." Suspicion fell on Mullins-Johnson, who had been looking after Valin when she died. Police told Lariviere that her daughter was the victim of chronic sexual abuse. She was stunned. She told police that her children loved staying with their uncle; there had been no sign of physical or sexual abuse.

At 6:30 that evening, about an hour after the autopsy was completed, Lariviere, Johnson, and Mullins-Johnson were sitting in their living room when police officers arrived at the front door. They announced that they were arresting Mullins-Johnson and he was being charged with first-degree murder and aggravated sexual assault. "And next thing I could feel is two officers, one on each side, grab my arms, put them behind my back," he later testified. "And my life got sucked right out of me. I went into hysterics. Paulie and Kim were in total shock. I looked at Paul and he said that he'd call ma. And I said don't call ma. Get me a

Dr. Charles Smith. Photo: Dale Brazao/Toronto Star/GetStock

lawyer. So out they took me I wasn't even in my shoes. They didn't even let me put my shoes on, just dragged me out of the house."[1] Mullins-Johnson sobbed and protested his innocence as he was arrested and charged. His family was stunned.

In an interrogation that Mullins-Johnson described as surreal, the police claimed to have evidence that Mullins-Johnson had hurt his niece. He repeatedly denied the allegations. The six-foot-five-inch, 260-pound Mullins-Johnson was placed in protective segregation at the Sault Ste. Marie jail within days of his arrest. He was so devastated by Valin's death and the accusations against him that he was unable to eat. "I had guys in other cells pounding on the wall beside me saying 'You're going to f---ing die. We're going to cut your f---ing head off,'" he recalled. "If anybody would have got to me I wasn't in a position to defend myself. That's how much out of it I was."[2]

Dr. Charles Smith, who headed the Pediatric Forensic Pathology Unit at the Hospital for Sick Children in Toronto, was consulted on the case. He was considered Ontario's expert on pediatric forensics. Four other specialists were also consulted. Smith reviewed autopsy photographs and performed microscopic examinations of tissue samples. His report on August 6, 1993, was the only one to state that Valin had died while being sodomized. However, no semen was found on Valin or her pajamas. The only evidence investigators had was entirely circumstantial, but they pressed ahead.

Mullins-Johnson refused the prosecutor's offer to plead guilty to a lesser charge of manslaughter, an offence that doesn't have a mandatory life sentence. He insisted that he was innocent. His trial began on September 6, 1994, in Sault Ste. Marie. The Crown argued that he had raped and murdered Valin, despite the lack of physical evidence of semen or other bodily substances. The jury was shown graphic autopsy photos including one of Valin in her pajamas with dark red marks on her chest. Dr. Rasaiah said the marks were consistent with being slowly asphyxiated.

Dr. Zehr testified that Valin showed evidence of chronic sexual abuse and having been sodomized repeatedly. She didn't have folds around her anus; perhaps that was from "wearing away." The head of forensic pathology at a British Columbia hospital, along with another expert, also testified that they saw evidence of sexual assault. Dr. Smith testified as an expert witness, telling jurors that, "I probably do a little bit more of this kind of work than anyone else in the country."[3] He told the court that he saw a laceration inside Valin's rectum, which he said was evidence that she had been sodomized just before she died. One of the photographs showed her buttocks slightly raised up. That indicated she was being raped when she died, he claimed. However, experts couldn't agree on exactly when Valin died. Five medical experts testified at the trial, but Smith was the only one to say that Valin had died while being sexually assaulted. He had reached his conclusion based on photographs and tissue samples.

The defence said that Valin had a history of vomiting in bed and that it was possible she had died of natural causes after choking on her own vomit. Her mother, Kim Lariviere, testified that expert findings were a surprise to her, since she had seen no signs of abuse. Testifying in his own defence, Mullins-Johnson denied that he had sexually assaulted or murdered his niece. He said he babysat until his sister-in-law returned home at 9:30 p.m.

Prosecutor Glen Wasyliniuk's final words in his address to the jury were, "she died when there were fresh bruises that indicated sexual assault, and she was killed by that man right there." Though there was no physical evidence linking Mullins-Johnson to his niece's death, the so-called scientific evidence of the girl's time of death, the cause of death, and whether she had been assaulted made an impression on the jury. The judge also indicated that he had no doubt Valin had been sexually abused.

At the end of the two-and-a-half-week trial, the jury of six men and six women deliberated for only six hours before finding Mullins-Johnson guilty of first-degree murder. In order to do so, they needed to believe that Valin had died during the commission of another crime — a sexual assault. He was convicted largely on the weight of Smith's testimony. Mullins-Johnson, now twenty-four, was shaken by the verdict. He wept as family members sobbed in the courtroom. On September 21, 1994, he was sentenced to life in prison with no chance of parole for twenty-five years.

Mullins-Johnson was incarcerated at Joyceville Institution near Kingston, Ontario. Inmates are not kind to sex offender; he worried about having his throat slashed by other inmates. He had himself placed in solitary confinement for four months after other inmates threatened to kill him. He was sent to Warkworth Institution in 1995, a jail 150 kilometres northeast of Toronto that serves as protective custody for sex offenders. He was confined to a cell with a desk, chair, bed, sink, toilet, and a steel door. Prison officials noted that he was reluctant to participate in programs for sex offenders.

Throughout his incarceration, he would phone his mother, Laureena Hill, at least once a week to let her know that he was still alive. She would write him lengthy letters every week sharing details of her life, such as local weather and gossip. Meanwhile, Mullins-Johnson spent his time behind bars reading, taking correspondence courses, and learning about Aboriginal culture. The conviction tore his family apart. He had no contact with his brothers, including Valin's father. Other family members shunned his mother for sticking by her son and fighting for his release. "What gave me hope was mom. She would not let me give up," he said. "There were times when I literally wanted to slash my wrists and be done with this."[4]

Mullins-Johnson appealed the verdict to the Ontario Court of Appeal, which upheld the conviction in a two-to-one decision just before Christmas 1996. The late Justice Stephen Borins disagreed with his colleagues. In a dissenting judgment, he ruled that there was no evidence that Mullins-Johnson had abused Valin physically or sexually, nor was there any proven motive. He said Mullins-Johnson should receive a new trial. He noted that even the Crown admitted that it didn't have "an overwhelming case." In fact, their case was almost completely based on circumstantial evidence. Justice Borins criticized the trial judge's instructions to the jury. On May 26, 1998, the Supreme Court of Canada dismissed Mullins-Johnson's appeal.

Mullins-Johnson turned to Toronto's Association in Defence of the Wrongly Convicted for help on June 18, 1998. "I am asking for help because nobody is going to listen to a native convict convicted of a murder with sexual overtones in the case," he wrote. "I honestly believe I will not win in this fight all by myself."[5] Toronto lawyer David Bayliss took the case on behalf of AIDWYC. They had heard that Dr. Smith's testimony in other murder cases was being questioned. In December 2001, he asked the Office of the Chief Coroner for Ontario to review the work that Dr. Smith had conducted. There was no response.

On February 27, 2003, Bayliss asked the Crown's lawyers to produce the forensic materials from Valin's autopsy. He wanted to have them independently tested by other experts to determine whether a crime had, in fact, occurred. The tissue samples could exonerate Mullins-Johnson. Dr. Rasaiah confirmed that he had sent the samples to Dr. Smith in 1994. They were never returned. Smith didn't respond to letters requesting that he produce them.

By then, Smith's career as a pediatric forensic pathologist had begun to unravel. He had performed more than a thousand autopsies for the Ontario Chief Coroner's Office as the province's main pediatric forensic pathologist from 1981 to 2001, and was the head of the pediatric forensic pathology unit of the Hospital for Sick Children since it was established in 1991. But in 2002, a panel of the Ontario College of Physicians and Surgeons reprimanded him for deficiencies in his approach to three cases. This included a case where his forensic opinion about the time of death of a two-year-old girl led to the mother being charged with

Dr. Michael Pollanen. Photo: Ontario Forensic Pathology Service — Government of Ontario

murdering her daughter, until she was freed when other pathologists offered different conclusions. He had also collected a pubic-like hair during the child's autopsy and kept it in a drawer until giving it to police as possible evidence more than five years later.

Charges that had been laid against other mothers who were accused of murdering their children were either stayed or withdrawn when questions were raised about Smith's findings. In one particular 1997 case, a mother was accused of killing her seven-year-old daughter when Smith said the little girl had been stabbed more than eighty times with a knife or pair of scissors. Other experts determined that she had been mauled to death by the family's pit bull. The charges were dropped, and the coroner's office reviewed Smith's work investigating children's deaths in Ontario. In late 2002, a senior Crown official asked prosecutors to look through their files for previous cases where Dr. Smith's credibility or reliability were questioned. Prosecutors identified twenty-five cases. He was removed from the pediatric forensic pathology team but continued to work in the pathology division at the Hospital for Sick Children.

In November 2004, a few days after the Office of the Chief Coroner for Ontario had a meeting with Smith, the pathologist's assistant found twenty of the slides from Valin's autopsy on a shelf in Smith's office. The coroner's office sent them and autopsy photographs to forensic pathologist Dr. Michael Pollanen, the medical director of the Toronto Forensic Pathology Unit of the coroner's office. Dr. Pollanen examined them and concluded there was no evidence that Valin had been sexually assaulted or murdered. The little girl had died a natural death. His report was forwarded to AIDWYC in February 2005.

The following month, Ontario Chief Coroner Barry McLellan admitted that Smith couldn't find all the tissue samples (known as "tissue blocks") that had been sent to him by the pathologist who performed Valin's autopsy. Dr. Glenn Taylor, head of the Hospital for Sick Children's pathology division, revealed to the *Toronto Star* that the hospital's five-person pediatric forensic pathology unit, which conducts autopsies for the coroner's office, didn't have a system to keep track of "medical legal" exhibits sent to them for testing until December 2004.[6]

McLellan ordered the review of all the exhibits from autopsies involving homicides and suspicious deaths of children that were conducted at the hospital since 1991 to ensure that they were accounted for. He and Dr. Taylor conducted the review. The three-month audit checked whether the hospital had properly kept and stored thousands of slides from these cases. They reviewed seventy cases. In a small number of them, the tissue slides were misplaced or could not be found. However, in each case they did find tissue blocks that could be used to create new slides, if needed.

In May 2005, the remaining materials from Valin's autopsy were finally found in Dr. Smith's office. His office was so disorganized that staff had to search the office in its entirety. In August, Welsh pathologist Dr. Bernard Knight submitted a report on Valin's death: he agreed with Dr. Pollanen's assessment. No semen was found on Valin or her pajamas, and her DNA was not found on Mullins-Johnson's clothing. Vomit was found on her pajamas, which, according to Pollanen, suggested that she was wearing them when she threw up. The enlarged anus that Zehr had interpreted as a sign of repeated penetration was, in fact, a natural occurrence when the muscles relax after death. A 1996 peer-reviewed study found that the lack of folds around a child's rectum is normal post-mortem. The marks and bruises on her throat and chest were consistent with blood collecting to those areas after she died, since blood tends to collect around the lowest parts of the body. The tear to Valin's anus that Dr. Smith attributed to penetration most likely occurred when her temperature was taken post-mortem.

As for two or three bruises on Valin's thighs and buttocks, Pollanen said there could be a number of explanations including learning to ride a bicycle. He said it was not possible to ascertain the cause of death. In addition, pathologist Dr. Rasaiah, who conducted the original autopsy, had no professional qualifications in forensic pathology. He had erred when he concluded that Valin was murdered between 8:00 p.m. and 10:00 p.m. the previous night. According to Dr. Knight, Valin may have died between 10:00 p.m. and 5:00 a.m., although it's more likely she died later in that period of time.

Armed with the new information that Valin had not been sexually assaulted or murdered, Mullins-Johnson's lawyers filed an application on September 8, 2005. They asked then federal Justice Minister Irwin Cotler to review the case as a miscarriage of justice and quash Mullins-Johnson's conviction. They noted that inaccurate testimony from medical professionals including Dr. Smith had played a key role in Mullins-Johnson's conviction. Lawyer James Lockyer said that medical experts had rushed to judgment in the case and then looked for evidence to support their views, instead of focusing on trying to determine how Valin died.

Smith had misinterpreted autopsy findings and over-stated or misstated findings of other experts. It was part of a pattern he had developed of finding a murder where one hadn't occurred. Under Section 696.1 of the Criminal Code, Cotler could nullify the conviction and either send the case to the Ontario Court of Appeal or order a new trial. This marked only the second time an application to the minister was made based on the non-occurrence of a murder. The minister appointed University of Ottawa law professor David Paciocco to conduct the review.

While awaiting the ministerial review, Mullins-Johnson was released on $125,000 bail on September 21, 2005 — exactly eleven years to the day since he had been convicted. He woke up that morning in a segregation cell at the West Detention Centre and put on a navy suit with a new tie. He entered a University Avenue courtroom in handcuffs and sat down in the prisoner's dock before Superior Court Justice David Watt. He walked in a prisoner, but left the courtroom for his first taste of freedom in more than twelve years. His lawyers, his mother, and other family members accompanied him out of the building. They walked to a downtown steakhouse for lunch, where he ordered a New York strip steak, mashed potatoes, fresh creamed spinach, sauteed mushrooms, and asparagus with Hollandaise sauce. He had cheesecake with fresh fruit for dessert, marking the first time in twelve years that he had ordered from a menu. The day ended at a College Street fundraiser for AIDWYC that evening. "I'm just grateful that somebody started up an organization like this," Mullins-Johnson said. "It gives guys hope."[7]

He returned to Warkworth Penitentiary near Campbellford, Ontario, with his mother on September 26, 2005, to collect his belongings. The possessions he had accumulated over more than twelve years behind bars fit into two metal footlockers, along with a burned-out television set and $105 in cash. As Warkworth disappeared into the distance, Mullins-Johnson looked back just once — at the spot where a teepee once stood. It was used for Native programs and ceremonies.

Difficulties locating the tissue samples that could exonerate Mullins-Johnson and the results of Pollanen's review in the case led Ontario's chief coroner to launch a 2005 review of Smith's work on all the suspicious deaths he handled since 1991. Judges and medical experts began casting doubts on the work of the man who had been considered Ontario's leading expert on child deaths for twenty years. Under McLellan's review, an international panel of experts would review Smith's work in forty-five cases of homicide or criminally suspicious deaths between 1991 and 2002 to assess whether his conclusions were correct. They began by looking at ten cases in which someone was in custody, or had their freedom restricted through bail or parole conditions. Reviewers would be able to use all of the materials, including tissue samples, photos, and police reports, on which Smith based his conclusions. Examining his courtroom testimony would allow them to see how he presented scientific evidence and whether it was consistent with his findings. The panel was comprised of Nova Scotia forensic medicine consultant Dr. John Butt and three pathologists from Britain: Christopher Milroy, Helen Whitwell, and Jack Crane. The review was expected to take a year to complete.

Smith resigned on July 9, 2005, only weeks after McLellan launched his review. Two months later, he found a new job working at Saskatoon City Hospital on a one-year contract analyzing slides for signs of disease. He would not be doing autopsies. But the Saskatoon Health Region Board voted to revoke his hiring three months later, in December 2005.

Louise Reynolds, the woman whose daughter was mauled to death by the family pit bull, launched a $7-million lawsuit against Smith for negligence, bad faith, and misfeasance of public office, but his lawyers contended that he couldn't be sued. A centuries-old legal doctrine, called witness immunity, says that Crown witnesses cannot be sued over testimony they provide in court under any circumstances, even if it's alleged that it was given with malice or in bad faith. The rule allows witnesses to appear in court without fear of being sued. Reynolds alleged in a statement of claim, which contained allegations that hadn't yet been proven in court, that Smith displayed "a reckless disregard for the truth," and was motivated by "improper purposes" such as "assisting the police in securing the respondent's conviction, self-aggrandizement, and to avoid professional embarrassment in having to reverse his prior report."[8]

In 2007, the Kingston, Ontario, mother won the right to sue Smith over his findings. This opened up a new avenue of redress and could help rein in overzealous experts. Brenda Waulby, who was falsely accused of killing her two-year-old daughter also following a report by Smith, told the *Toronto Star*, "Pathologists have enormous power because their opinion will determine if a person is to be charged with the most serious crimes," she said. "They have to be accountable. Why should the law shield officials who may have abused their powers?"[9]

In April 2007, Ontario's Chief Coroner announced the results of the eighteen-month review of Smith's work. Of the forty-five cases reviewed, where Smith either performed an autopsy or was consulted for an opinion, the team of international experts found that the one-time star pediatric forensic pathologist likely made mistakes in twenty cases — in either his reports or court testimony or both — in which criminal charges were filed. In thirteen of those cases, people were convicted for offences including homicide, criminal negligence leading to death, and aggravated assault. One person was still in jail, three others were out on bail or parole, while others had completed their sentences. Some of the errors that Smith made ranged from minor to potentially more serious. The reviewers felt that in a number of cases, Smith provided an opinion that wasn't supported by the materials available for review.

In wake of the findings, McLellan announced that the coroner's office would review cases that Smith handled from the time he was hired in 1981 to 1991. By then, the coroner's office had made changes, which included creating committees to carefully review child deaths, new sets of guidelines, and an audit process in criminally suspicious cases. The Association in Defence of the Wrongly Convicted adopted nine of the thirteen cases as possible miscarriages of justice.

In April 2007, following the investigation by the chief coroner's office, Ontario's Attorney General Michael Bryant announced that a public inquiry would be held into how faulty forensic pathology evidence used by prosecutors had led to as many as thirteen people being convicted of killing children. Ontario Court of Appeal Justice Stephen Goudge would lead the inquiry, with the assistance of an expert panel of scientists and medical professionals chaired by Senator Larry Campbell, the former chief coroner of British Columbia and a twelve-year veteran of the RCMP who inspired the Canadian television series *Da Vinci's Inquest*. "Charles Smith was the go-to guy" in the coroner's office when there was a suspicious death of a child in the 1990s, according to Mullins-Johnson lawyer David Bayliss. But, Bayliss suggested, Smith's attitude was common in the coroner's office at that time. "There was a tendency to see abuse everywhere."[10]

Justice Stephen Goudge. Photo: Court of Appeal for Ontario

Mullins-Johnson completed the transitional-year program at the University of Toronto and was chosen by his classmates to be valedictorian in June 2007. Just over a month later, in July 2007, federal

Justice Minister Rob Nicholson said there was reason to conclude that a miscarriage of justice had occurred and he referred the case to the Ontario Court of Appeal. Crown prosecutor Michal Fairburn agreed that Mullins-Johnson should be acquitted.

Mullins-Johnson's lawyers, James Lockyer and David Bayliss, urged the Ontario Court of Appeal to go a step further and declare him "factually innocent" for a crime that never even happened. Besides exonerating him, this could affect compensation in the wrongful-conviction case. However, lawyers for Ontario's attorney general disagreed. They argued that going beyond verdicts of "guilty" and "not guilty," and allowing official findings of "factual innocence," could create a three-tier system of verdicts. This would leave people found "not guilty" with a tarnished and devalued status.

On October 15, 2007, Mullins-Johnson walked out of an Osgoode Hall courtroom a free man. Dr. Michael Pollanen, Ontario's chief forensic pathologist, had testified that there was no evidence that Valin had been sexually assaulted and killed. Her cause of death was "unascertainable." "A pathologist should resist speculation," he said in reference to the findings of Dr. Smith.[11] Justice Fred Kaufman, who had headed the inquiry into the wrongful conviction of Guy Paul Morin less than ten years earlier, pointed out that scientists need to be objective, independent, and accurate in their findings. They also need to be perceived as being independent by participants in the criminal justice system. As Lockyer told the court, Smith's work led to an "extraordinary rush to judgment" despite a lack of any physical evidence that Valin had been sexually assaulted. "There was no stopping the train," he said. "It had left the station."[12]

During the hearing, Mullins-Johnson testified about his reaction to findings that Smith had erred in his conclusions about Valin's death. "It was the first time I saw not only the light at the end of the tunnel but the end of the tunnel. All those years I was wondering who [killed Valin]. I now know that nobody violated her. I am happy for that."[13]

Fourteen years after being charged with first-degree murder in a homicide that never was, Mullins-Johnson was finally acquitted. "It is regrettable that as a result of the flawed pathological evidence you were wrongfully convicted and you spent so long in custody," Associate Chief Justice Dennis O'Connor said on behalf of the panel that included

Justices Marc Rosenberg and Robert Sharpe. Crown prosecutor Michal Fairburn rose in court and offered Mullins-Johnson an apology:

> On behalf of the Attorney-General of Ontario, I wish to extend our sincere, our profound and our deepest apologies to Mr. Mullins-Johnson and to his family for the miscarriage of justice that has occurred in this case and all that he has had to endure as a result. There can be no doubt this miscarriage of justice has exacted an incredible toll on Mr. Mullins-Johnson, on his mother, Mrs. Laureena Hill and his entire family. For this we are truly, we are profoundly, sorry.[14]

The appeal court panel agreed with the Crown's argument against finding him factually innocent. In a written statement, the court said, "There are not in Canadian law two kinds of acquittals." The court explained that declarations of factual innocence could "degrade" the meaning of the not guilty verdict. However, there was no evidence that Valin was murdered and the panel was critical of the work of the two Sault Ste. Marie doctors who were involved in the original autopsy, as well as Dr. Smith. "It is now clear that there is not and never was any reliable pathological evidence that Valin was sexually assaulted or otherwise abused during her short life and certainly not on the evening of her death," the court statement said. "While the cause of Valin Johnson's death remains undetermined, there is now no evidence to suggest it was the result of any crime. That Mr. Mullins-Johnson was arrested, convicted of first-degree murder and spent twelve years in prison because of flawed pathology evidence is a terrible miscarriage of justice."[15]

The commission of inquiry, led by Ontario Court of Appeal Judge Stephen Goudge, got under way in downtown Toronto in November 2007. It placed Ontario's pediatric forensic pathology field under the microscope. The mandate of the Inquiry into Forensic Pathology in Ontario was to examine how suspicious child deaths were handled by the coroner's office and in the province's criminal justice system since 1981. It looked at systemic problems that allowed Dr. Smith to flourish throughout the 1990s.

Former Ontario Chief Coroner Barry McLellan and the province's chief forensic pathologist, Michael Pollanen, were the first to testify. They said that, in 1995, the Chief Coroner's Office issued a directive that examiners, including pathologists, must "think dirty." That is, they should assume that foul play was involved until proven otherwise. However, that directive was retracted in recent years. "The advice we give now is not to think dirty," Dr. Pollanen said. "It is to search for the truth and think objectively."[16] Dr. Pollanen, who had trained in England, said poor pay made it difficult to recruit qualified provincial forensic pathologists. They were paid $1,000 per autopsy, and a $300 bonus for complex cases. Dr. McLellan said very few of the more than 300 coroners across the province had any training in pathology. This made it more difficult for them to adequately evaluate the opinions of pathologists reporting on suspicious deaths or probable homicides.

Signs of potential problems with Dr. Smith's work began during a trial in Timmins in 1991. A twelve-year-old babysitter, who was a good student and had taken the Red Cross babysitting course, was looking after sixteen-month-old Amber on the afternoon of July 28, 1988. Amber pulled away from the babysitter when they walked toward a flight of five steps and tumbled down the stairs. She died two days later at the Hospital for Sick Children. Smith testified at the trial that the baby died of shaken baby syndrome. Justice Patrick Dunn found the defence experts more credible than Smith. He acquitted the twelve-year-old girl of manslaughter, convinced that the baby had died of an accidental head injury. In his seventy-five-page judgment, Dunn criticized Smith for refusing to consider the possibility that the toddler had died from a fall. He also noted that Smith incorrectly stated that an autopsy was not needed in order to confirm a diagnosis of shaken baby syndrome; he was not aware of the latest research in the field and he kept changing the definition of shaken baby syndrome. Dr. James Young, chief coroner from 1990 to 2004, only read Dunn's judgment sixteen years later, before testifying at the Goudge inquiry.

Photographs showed that Smith's office was a mess: there were files and mail piled on his desk, papers and books on his chair, slides and papers on the floor, as well as boxes and papers on the windowsill. Maxine Johnson, administrative coordinator in the pathology division of the hospital, testified that she found "dried-out" pieces of human tissue and bones when she searched his office for autopsy slides from criminal cases in June 2005. She found missing tissue samples and slides from the Mullins-Johnson case in Smith's office in November 2004, after he claimed that he didn't have them.

The inquiry also learned that Smith was educated in pediatric pathology, which gave him the knowledge to diagnose disease and conduct autopsies within a hospital. He had no training in forensic pathology to perform autopsies in cases of criminally suspicious deaths or homicides — a field that requires vastly different skills. However, the Royal College of Physicians and Surgeons of Canada only began recognizing forensic pathology as a sub-specialty in 2003. In this regard, Canada lagged behind Britain and the United States. The American Board of Pathology recognized forensic pathology in 1959.

When Dr. Smith took to the witness stand on January 28, 2008, he described his "profound ignorance" of pediatric forensic pathology and admitted that he was unqualified to do the work. As a courtroom full of victims of his errors listened, Dr. Smith said that he had erroneously believed that his job was to help the Crown mount a case. "I honestly believed that it was my role to support the Crown attorney. I was there to make a case look good. This is very blunt, but we shared the same kind of attitude. I think it caused me to become more fixed in my opinions."[17]

In an unexpected moment, Dr. Smith apologized to Mullins-Johnson, who was sitting in the public gallery. Mullins-Johnson told Smith about the impact of his wrongful conviction for the sexual assault and murder of a child. "You put me in an environment where every day I could have been killed any day for something that never happened. I didn't do it, I didn't do anything," he said. "You destroyed my family. My brother's relationship with me, and my niece that's still living and my nephew that's still living, they hate me because of what you did to me.... I'll never forget that but for my own healing, I must forgive you." Smith replied, "That is kind of you, thank you."[18]

After hearing from more than ninety-four witnesses during sixty-three days of hearings, Justice Goudge released his 1,000-page report in October 2008. He pointed to Smith's lack of expertise and training in forensic pathology, and characterized Smith as an arrogant and unqualified forensic pathologist who provided biased and unprofessional testimony in criminal cases. "Dr. Smith was adamant that his failings were never intentional," Justice Goudge said. "I simply cannot accept such a sweeping attempt to escape moral responsibility."[19]

Goudge criticized former Chief Coroner James Young and his deputy, Jim Cairns, for lack of oversight and for ignoring signs of mounting problems with Smith's work, and then trying to protect him. Young initially argued that the College of Physicians and Surgeons had no jurisdiction to investigate complaints involving Smith or any other doctor working for the coroner's office. But, in 2000, the Health Professions Appeal and Review Board ruled that the College did have the authority to investigate complaints. When Dr. Young finally did attempt to rein Smith in, Goudge said, "It was to protect the reputation of the office, and not out of concern that individuals and the public interest may already have been harmed."[20]

Justice Goudge made 169 recommendations to improve Ontario's pediatric forensic pathology system. The Royal College of Physicians and Surgeons of Canada officially recognized forensic pathology as a subspecialty in 2003, but no accredited training programs were offered. In 2009, the University of Toronto began offering a one-year residency-training program in forensic pathology. The program was accredited by the Royal College of Physicians and Surgeons of Canada and marked the first time that forensic pathologists were trained and certified in Canada. Following the $8.3-million inquiry, the province agreed to develop a process for compensating victims of wrongful convictions.

In October 2008, Mullins-Johnson launched a $13-million lawsuit against Dr. Smith, Dr. Young, and Dr. Cairns. In May 2010, the College of Physicians and Surgeons of Ontario dropped investigations into Young and Cairns in exchange for their pledge not to reapply for a licence to practise medicine. In August 2010, the Ontario government announced up to $250,000 in compensation for Smith's victims but left the door open for civil claims. In October 2010, the Ontario government agreed to pay Mullins-Johnson $4.25 million in exchange for dropping his lawsuit. But as his lawyer David Robins told the *Windsor Star*, "No amount of money can turn back the hands of time and give him those twelve years back and erase this ordeal from his mind."[21]

PART III

Before the Court: Pleading the Case

Chapter Ten

Prosecutorial Misconduct: The Thomas Sophonow Case

Sixteen-year-old Barbara Stoppel arrived at the Ideal Donut Shop in St. Boniface, Manitoba, at 3:30 p.m. to begin her waitressing shift. It was December 23, 1981, and the grade eleven student was excited about having won the lead role in the school play. The café's owner, Vlademir Ududec, came to the shop that evening and took money from the till. He left $33. When a customer departed at about 8:10 p.m., the shop was empty. Stoppel picked up the telephone and called a friend. They chatted for a few minutes.

When Lorraine Janower arrived at the doughnut shop at about 8:20 p.m. for coffee, she saw a man lock the door of the shop from the inside and walk toward the washroom at the rear of the store. She thought it was odd, so she returned to the nearby drugstore where she worked and tried, unsuccessfully, to phone Ududec. The door of the doughnut shop was locked when John Doerksen went there at about 8:35 p.m. He had been selling Christmas trees at a nearby lot. Norman Janower joined him outside the Ideal Donut Shop about five minutes later. A man inside the shop walked out of the women's washroom, picked up a box, changed the sign to "closed," unlocked the front door, and left. On his way out, he told Janower and Doerksen that the store was closed.

Janower went inside. When he called out and received no response, he went to the back of the store and into the women's washroom. He found Stoppel lying on the floor. She had been strangled with a piece of twine that was wrapped tightly around her neck twice. The washroom showed signs of a struggle. There were bloodstains on the floor, on one wall, and the sink. The wastepaper basket had been knocked over and the contents were strewn around. While the Janowers called police, Doerksen stopped at a local gas station to pick up a baseball bat and then followed the man they had seen leaving the shop. When he caught up to him on the Norwood Bridge, the man was throwing items into the river. Doerksen confronted him but backed off when the man pulled a knife. Then Doerksen headed home where he consumed approximately five beers. It wasn't until hours later that he spoke with police.

The dying Stoppel was rushed to St. Boniface Hospital. According to witnesses, the man they had seen leaving the shop was in his twenties, scruffy looking with brown hair, a longish mustache, slim, just over six-feet tall, and weighed 145–185 pounds. He wore glasses, a black or dark-coloured cowboy hat, a dark waist-length coat, blue jeans, and round-toed or cowboy boots. A police artist created a composite sketch, which led to more than 700 tips.

When the police searched the riverbank near the bridge, they found a cardboard box and five pieces of green and yellow braided nylon rope that were identical to the ones that had been used to strangle Stoppel. They also recovered a pair of woven gloves that had the same type of green and yellow twine.

The Winnipeg Police were tipped off about Terry Arnold after he went to the St. Boniface Hospital on December 28 to find out about Stoppel's condition. He told her mother that he had come to know Barbara because he was a customer at the Ideal Donut Shop. The Winnipeg Police interviewed him the next day. He also resembled the man depicted in the composite sketch, and lived in an apartment building near the doughnut shop. A friend of his called police and said that Arnold often wore cowboy hats and cowboy boots. Arnold didn't appear to have an alibi for his whereabouts when Stoppel was murdered.

Winnipeg Police interviewed him again on January 17, 1982. Arnold admitted that he had a crush on Stoppel. Police had Arnold's fingerprints on file, but they never compared them to prints found at the doughnut shop. No single police officer was heading the investigation into Stoppel's murder; further investigation of Arnold as a possible suspect fell through the cracks.

Stoppel was taken off life support and died on December 29, 1981, six days after she was found lying on the floor of the women's washroom at the Ideal Donut Shop. Six hundred people attended her funeral on December 31. The Winnipeg Police Commission offered a $2,000 reward for information leading to the arrest of her attacker, and a local firm added another $5,000.

The piece of twine that was used to strangle Stoppel proved to be the only piece of physical evidence the police had in the case. The piece that was found under the bridge contained fibres from Stoppel's sweater. The police determined that the twine had likely been manufactured by one of two companies in North America. Samples of the twine were sent to Powers Twines Inc. in Washington State and the Berkley Company, which had a plant in Portage la Prairie, Manitoba. After examining the twine, officials from Berkley Canada said that it didn't appear to be theirs, but they did offer to test it — for $100 — to see whether it contained a chemical tracer element that would conclusively indicate if they were the manufacturer. The police decided not to order the test. Powers Twines said the twine appeared to be theirs. The police didn't have it tested to confirm the manufacturer; they assumed the American company had made the twine, which was sold to BC Hydro and available at construction sites in British Columbia. The Winnipeg Police concluded they were looking for a suspect who had a connection to British Columbia.

Enter twenty-eight-year-old Thomas Sophonow. The Vancouver doorman was in Winnipeg on December 23, 1981, to visit his two-year-old daughter, but his estranged wife didn't allow the visit. That evening, he went to the Canadian Tire on Pembina Highway to have his car's brakes fixed. While he waited, he shared half a sandwich with the daughter of a woman who was also having her vehicle repaired. He made two trips to a nearby Safeway store to buy Christmas stockings for children in Winnipeg hospitals. He called his mother in Vancouver from 7:52 to 7:56 p.m. When his car was fixed, Sophonow drove away as Canadian Tire employees mopped the garage. His vehicle was the last one to be repaired that evening. Then he delivered Christmas stockings to a few Winnipeg hospitals. While he was at Victoria General Hospital, he chatted for a few minutes with a Filipina nurse who said she had a five-year-old son named Phillip. Then he drove back to Vancouver.

In early 1982, he pulled into Ryan's Restaurant in Hope, British Columbia, for chicken pot-pie. While he was there, he noticed a poster on the wall for a missing person who looked like the former babysitter of a friend's child in Winnipeg. Sophonow phoned the RCMP, who came to take his statement; they passed along the information to the Winnipeg Police. With the Stoppel murder investigation still under way, a sergeant asked the RCMP what Sophonow looked like. The description they provided was similar to the one that eyewitnesses had given of the man who had been seen leaving the doughnut shop moments before Stoppel was discovered.

The Winnipeg Police also learned that Sophonow had been in the city at the time of the murder. Although no vehicle bearing British Columbia license plates was found in the doughnut shop parking lot after Stoppel's assailant fled on foot, police decided to pursue the lead because the twine used in the murder was readily available in British Columbia. At their request, Vancouver Police Detective Michael Barnard interviewed Sophonow on March 3, 1982. The tone of the meeting was casual, Sophonow was cooperative and apparently indicated that he was willing to provide hair and blood samples. Barnard made notes as the two chatted, but none were a word-for-word record of what was said. According to his notes, Sophonow said, "I could have been in Ideal Donut Shop 49 Goulet." However, the detective did not read back his notes to Sophonow nor have him sign them to confirm their accuracy. Barnard told the Winnipeg Police that Sophonow was cooperative, but that he should be investigated further because of the reference to the doughnut shop.

Two days after Sophonow celebrated his twenty-ninth birthday, Sergeants Wade Wawryk and Ed Paulishyn from the Winnipeg Police flew to Vancouver. They interviewed him on March 12, 1982, for four hours, starting at 1:30 p.m. They took turns questioning him, but didn't record verbatim his responses to their questions about the Ideal Donut Shop. Nor did they show him their notes to confirm accuracy. Although they considered him their prime suspect, they didn't caution him that his comments could be used against him.

Although the detectives had no evidence implicating Sophonow in the murder, they told him that witnesses had seen him leave the doughnut shop. When he denied any involvement, they accused him of lying. After a portion of the interview had been conducted, the detectives strip-searched

Sophonow, even though there was no threat to their safety. The interview and the way in which it was conducted continued to haunt Sophonow for years. When the interview was over, he was placed in detention and charged with Stoppel's murder. He was flown to Winnipeg the next day.

John Doerksen, who had seen the man leave the doughnut shop and then chased him along a bridge, viewed a police line-up on March 13, 1982. He was not able to positively identify Sophonow as the man he saw that night. Doerksen was at the police station two days later to pay a fine for a traffic violation when he saw Sophonow as the two men passed each other in the hall of the cells area on the fourth floor of the Public Safety Building. After seeing Sophonow in lockup, in court on March 24, and his picture in a Winnipeg newspaper, Doerksen told Sergeants Wawryk and Paulishyn that he was now "ninety percent sure" that Thomas Sophonow was the man he had seen exiting the doughnut shop.

Lorraine Janower, another witness, was shown a photo line-up in which the background of Sophonow's picture looked different than the others. It had a border around it and appeared to be the only one that had been taken outside. After looking at the photos, she said that, "If anything he's like this. There's something about this guy, of all of them he'd be the closest." She couldn't say for certain that it was Sophonow she had seen inside the Ideal Donut Shop, only that he most closely resembled the man she had seen. Norman Janower tentatively identified Sophonow in a physical line-up on March 15 in which the six-foot-five-inch Sophonow stood out because of his height. About forty-five minutes after seeing the line-up, Sergeant Ken Biener confirmed that Janower had picked out the police's suspect in the case.

During their investigation, police checked Sophonow's alibi. Although they found people at Canadian Tire and Safeway who remembered seeing a man who looked like Sophonow, the police discounted the information. It took between fourteen and nineteen minutes to drive from the garage to the doughnut shop. If he left Canadian Tire at 8:00 p.m., it would have been difficult — but not impossible — to arrive at the doughnut shop at the time that witnesses say they saw a man inside. However, Sophonow's car was never found in the store's parking lot, and the amount of time needed to walk to a parking spot in a nearby street would make it impossible for him to reach the Ideal Donut Shop at the time a man had been seen inside.

Nonetheless, the Crown prepared to try Sophonow for second-degree murder. At a preliminary hearing on May 17, 1982, the judge found that there was enough evidence to commit him to stand trial. The twine and its British Columbia origins would be at the centre of the case against him. Crown attorney Gregg Lawlor would assist senior Crown counsel George Dangerfield. The night before Sophonow's trial got under way on October 18, 1982, in the Court of Queen's Bench of Manitoba, Lawlor met with Melvin Williamson. The witness from BC Hydro planned to testify that the type of twine used to kill Stoppel was often found on construction sites throughout British Columbia. During the meeting, Williamson told Lawlor that a company in Portage la Prairie also made the same type of twine. Lawlor didn't inform Sophonow's defence lawyer Robert Pollack of this information, which could cast doubt on a key piece of evidence in the Crown's case. Nor did he ask Williamson during the trial about the Manitoba manufacturer. Pollack was also not aware that it was possible to test the twine for a trace element that would confirm whether it was made in Manitoba or British Columbia.

Although Doerksen and the Janowers had trouble positively identifying Sophonow during police line-ups more than six months earlier, they testified at trial that he was the man they had seen at the Ideal Donut Shop. Robert Pollack was never told that the witnesses were initially uncertain about the identification. The jury also heard a female friend of Sophonow's say that she had seen BC Hydro twine in the backseat of his car. Sophonow testified that he had been delivering candy-filled Christmas stockings to children at local hospitals when Stoppel was attacked. In Justice Louis Deniset's instructions to the jury, he questioned why Sophonow didn't provide an alibi when police first interviewed him in Vancouver. However, there was enough doubt in the minds of the jury about Sophonow's guilt that they couldn't agree. On November 6, Justice Deniset declared a mistrial when the jury was unable to reach a unanimous verdict after a day and a half of deliberations.

Sophonow hired well-known criminal lawyer Greg Brodsky to defend him at his second trial, which began before Justice John Scollin on February 21, 1983. Brodsky assumed that the twine had been tested to confirm which company had manufactured it. He agreed to allow evidence about the twine being made near British Columbia entered into the record. During the second week of the trial, the Crown called jailhouse informant Thomas Cheng to the stand. He had faced a number of charges including passing more than $6,000 in bad cheques, unlawful possession of a car and various licence plates, fraudulently obtaining about $500 in food and lodgings, and impersonation.

He claimed that Sophonow had confessed to Stoppel's murder the previous month while the two men were in the recreation area of Winnipeg's Public Safety Building jail. According to the Hong Kong immigrant, Sophonow said he tried to rob a doughnut shop, that he was friends with Stoppel, and that she would tell him where the rest of the shop's money was hidden. When she didn't, he got angry, brought her to the washroom, and killed her. During Brodsky's cross-examination, it was revealed the Crown had dropped more than two dozen criminal charges against him a few days after he made a statement implicating Sophonow in the murder.

Another witness, a nurse, testified that she'd met a tall man fifteen minutes from the doughnut shop when he delivered stockings to the hospital where she worked. Brodsky had found her when he went around to hospitals to determine if there was any substance to Sophonow's alibi. In his instructions to the jury, Justice Scollin told jurors to be wary of Sophonow's alibi, since he didn't share it with the Crown until eight months after he was arrested. The trial lasted twenty-five days and heard from sixty witnesses.

The jury returned to the courtroom after lunch on March 16, 1983, and announced that they found Sophonow guilty of Stoppel's murder. People in the courtroom gasped. He was sentenced to ten years in prison without the possibility of parole. The lanky, soft-spoken Sophonow, wearing wire-rimmed glasses, protested his innocence as he was led away. "I didn't do it, I didn't do it, I'm the only one who told the truth." He appealed his conviction to the Manitoba Court of Appeal on twenty-six grounds. They included the way in which the trial judge had dismissed the testimony of a hospital ward clerk that supported his alibi. In a two-to-one ruling handed down on March 13, 1984, the Court of Appeal agreed and ordered a new trial. The Crown sought leave to appeal the decision to the Supreme Court of Canada but was refused on December 10, 1984.

In Crown counsel Stuart Whitley's application to the Supreme Court of Canada, he had said the type of twine used in the killing was rare and that the police could not find another manufacturer for it outside of Washington State. He wasn't aware that Williamson had told Lawlor that the twine could have been made by a Manitoba company. Sophonow's lawyer had also accepted the Crown's assertion that the twine was from British Columbia. Had they been aware of the Manitoba company, the twine would likely have been tested and the one piece of evidence that linked Sophonow to the murder could have been eliminated.

Sophonow spent a portion of his incarceration, waiting for another trial, at the medium security Saskatchewan Penitentiary in Prince Albert, where cells only had toilets and cots. He refused to sign a document that could give him telephone and visiting privileges because it meant admitting guilt for a crime he didn't commit. He was forced to transfer there from Manitoba's Stony Mountain Penitentiary when Stoppel's family, who operated a bus service that brought inmates' relatives to Stony Mountain, stopped the service. They said they would resume if he were transferred elsewhere. Sophonow was sent to the federal institution in Prince Albert.

Sophonow's third trial got under way on February 4, 1985, before Justice Benjamin Hewak of Manitoba Court of Queen's Bench. Whitley led for the Crown and Brodsky was the defence counsel. Potential jurors were asked whether the widespread publicity surrounding Sophonow's previous trials influenced their perceptions as to his guilt or innocence. Three prospective jurors were dismissed after they said they believed Sophonow was guilty and another said he was probably not guilty. It took four hours to select a six-man, six-woman jury.

During the trial, jailhouse informant Adrian McQuade, who had a lengthy criminal record, testified that he had met Sophonow when the two men were being held at Winnipeg Police headquarters in March 1982. He claimed that Sophonow confessed to him that he had murdered Stoppel. McQuade denied that he invented the story in order to make a deal with authorities on his own charges. However, Sophonow later learned that McQuade had been offered $10,000 in cash and that a rape charge against him was dropped. Douglas Martin, another jailhouse informant, also testified. He was nicknamed "Father Confessor" by lawyers and inmates because of his repeated claims that other prisoners had confessed to him.

Joan Barrett, a maternity ward clerk at Winnipeg's Grace Hospital, testified that a tall, slim man in his late twenties arrived between 8:10 p.m. and 8:30 p.m. the night Stoppel was strangled. She said he told her that he was from out of town and wanted to give two bags of stockings to children. Since the hospital didn't have a children's ward, she gave him directions to three other area hospitals. Employees at other hospitals confirmed that they had received Christmas stockings from a man fitting the description Barrett provided, but none could confirm whether the man was Sophonow. The judge did not allow the hospital employees to testify.

More than sixty witnesses testified at the six-week trial. The jury deliberated for fifty-two hours before reaching a guilty verdict on March 16, 1985. However, it didn't come without a bit of last-minute drama. Two hours before the verdict was presented, the jury was deadlocked; one woman stood firm that Sophonow wasn't guilty. The foreman sent judge Hewak a note that read, "We have a juror who speaks of psychic powers and special gifts. We are unable to reach a unanimous decision." It explained that the rest of the jury believed the person was "mentally unable to deal with arguments or discussion … or with the evidence that is before us."[1]

Provisions in the Criminal Code allow jurors to be excused for illness or another reasonable cause. A jury that renders a verdict must have a minimum of ten jurors. After a closed hearing with the judge and foreman, the juror was dismissed. The jury returned shortly afterward and pronounced Sophonow guilty. He held his face in his hands when the verdict, along with a life sentence with no possibility of parole for ten years, was read out. He had been convicted largely on questionable eyewitness testimony and jailhouse informants. As Sophonow climbed into the sheriff's van to be taken to prison, he remained determined to continue fighting to clear his name. "I'll be back for the fourth time around," he said. "That's not a court, that's a joke."[2]

Sophonow appealed the verdict on thirty-eight points, including the holdout juror's dismissal. His lawyer argued that medical evidence was not presented to support the judge's finding that she was ill. After a two-day hearing, the three judges of the Court of Appeal of Manitoba unanimously overturned the conviction on December 12,

1985. Justices Joseph O'Sullivan, Kerr Twaddle, and Charles Huband agreed there were grounds for a new trial. They cited the fact that alibi witnesses, who would have testified that Sophonow was delivering Christmas stockings at the time of the murder, were excluded. They also found the trial judge erred in his instructions to the jury with respect to the testimony of witnesses.

The judges also noted the witnesses' identification of Sophonow was unreliable and the opportunity and motive for the killing was weak. As Justice Twaddle said in a written judgment released in February 1986, "If a thousand persons had seen a tall, thin man with a cowboy hat flee the doughnut shop on Dec. 23, 1981, it would not advance the case against Sophonow, for the evidence of such persons would not address the vital issue: was the tall, thin man with the cowboy hat Thomas Sophonow?"

Sophonow had already spent three years and nine months in custody without bail since he had been arrested. There seemed no point in ordering a fourth trial. On December 12, 1985, the Manitoba Court of Appeal acquitted Sophonow. He went home to Vancouver later that month to spend his first Christmas as a free man in nearly four years.

The Crown sought leave to appeal the acquittal, but the Supreme Court of Canada dismissed the request on April 22, 1986. Sophonow took a polygraph test for an episode of the CTV Television investigative show *W5* about his case. Polygraph specialist Ben Silverberg, who taught polygraph use at the Canadian Police College, administered the test. He concluded with 95 percent certainty that Sophonow was telling the truth when he said he was not involved in Stoppel's murder.

In February 1986, Sophonow hired lawyer Terence Robertson to seek compensation for his wrongful prosecution and imprisonment. They also asked Manitoba Attorney General Roland Penner to set up an inquiry into how the case was handled. In July of that year, Penner announced that the province planned to compensate people who have been wrongly convicted and imprisoned. Compensation could include money for lost income, property, or future earning ability. Awards for less tangible effects, such as loss of dignity, would be limited to $100,000. However, a person would be required to prove their innocence conclusively before any compensation would be paid. Penner indicated that this would exclude Sophonow from receiving compensation because he was acquitted — not found innocent.

He also ruled out an inquiry into Sophonow's conviction. As Sophonow pointed out at the time, the only way that he could conclusively prove his innocence was if Stoppel's killer confessed.

Sophonow returned to Vancouver, married, and had three children. But a cloud of suspicion that he was guilty and had somehow managed to "beat the system" hung over him. His name was mentioned in news reports after White Rock resident Melanie Carpenter was murdered, before her killer was found. Sophonow's house was firebombed in 1995, which resulted in $50,000 in damage. The perpetrator of the firebombing was not found. On another occasion, he bought a lot and planned to have a house moved there. But a neighbour confronted him, telling him, "We know who you are." The house mysteriously burned down two weeks later. Letters telling him to go back to Winnipeg were slipped under his door. He and his family were shunned.

Sophonow continued to call for forensic testing on the pair of gloves that were found under the Norwood Bridge and for a public inquiry into the circumstances surrounding his case. Lawyers with Toronto's Association in Defence of the Wrongly Convicted worked to reopen the investigation into Stoppel's murder in an effort to clear Sophonow's name. The Winnipeg Police's major crimes unit reopened the Stoppel case in 1998.

Sophonow still remembers the exact moment when he was finally told that he had been exonerated. He received the news at 12:38 p.m. on December 18, 1999, more than ten months after the Winnipeg Police sent some of the items from the crime scene for DNA testing at an RCMP lab. But he needed to keep the news under wraps to avoid jeopardizing the police investigation into a new suspect.

On June 8, 2000, more than eighteen years after his arrest, Winnipeg Police Chief Jack Ewatski announced that Sophonow had been cleared in the Stoppel murder. He also apologized to him. "It's never too late to do the right thing," Ewatski said. "There have been lingering questions about this case that never went away. New evidence came to light that was not available at the time. The investigation has determined that Thomas Sophonow was not responsible for this crime and the seven-person investigating team has identified another suspect."[3] Although the results of DNA testing had played a role in reopening the investigation, police said it wasn't what led to Sophonow's exoneration.

The province of Manitoba also apologized for his wrongful arrest and conviction, and promised compensation. Provincial Justice Minister Gord Mackintosh announced that retired Supreme Court of Canada justice Peter Cory had been chosen to head a public inquiry into the circumstances surrounding Sophonow's wrongful conviction and to decide on appropriate compensation. "On a personal level I cannot even begin to understand the feelings that Mr. Sophonow must have had when he was arrested and imprisoned," Mackintosh said.[4]

The government promised an interim payment of $75,000 to cover some of the legal costs Sophonow incurred in defending himself. Sophonow was relieved, but he knew that reliving his ordeal during the inquiry wouldn't be easy for anyone who had been affected by the Stoppel murder. "I feel sincerely, sincerely sorry for the Stoppel family," he said. "I know this inquiry is going to bring a great deal of pain and memories but this is something that has to be done. When I take that stand and spill my guts, that will be a great day for me."[5] But he also knew that being cleared created unanswered questions for Stoppel's family. "We all sort of seem to overlook the fact there was a girl murdered and there is a family in Winnipeg that have believed for 18 years that I killed her and now they have to say, 'Well, who did?'" [6]

Police had a new suspect in the case: convicted serial rapist Terry Samuel Arnold. He had spent six-and-a-half years in a Newfoundland jail for sexual assaults against four girls ages ten to sixteen. In 1999, he was convicted of first-degree murder in the 1991 killing of fifteen-year-old Christine Marie Browne from Kelowna. He was implicated in the slaying in 1997, after bringing undercover RCMP officers to the spot where he allegedly raped and killed Browne near Penticton. The British Columbia Court of Appeal ordered a new trial after it learned that the Crown had failed to disclose three forensic reports and two witness statements to the defence. Without explanation, the Crown stayed the charges in March 2001. Arnold was also a suspect in the 1987 murder of seventeen-year-old Denise Lapierre, whose body was found less than a block from Arnold's home in Calgary. He was never charged in Stoppel's murder. He committed suicide in 2005, leaving a three-page note in which he denied killing Stoppel.

In the wake of the role that jailhouse informants played in Sophonow's conviction, Manitoba Justice Minister Gord Mackintosh announced new rules in July 2000 governing the use of jailhouse informants at criminal

Justice Peter Cory. Photo: Rick Madonik/Toronto Star/GetStock

trials. That province became the fifth to impose new measures, after Ontario, British Columbia, Alberta, and Newfoundland. According to Manitoba's policy, Crown prosecutors who wanted to use evidence from a prison informant now had to bring their request to a five-member committee comprised of senior justice department officials, including the director of prosecutions and the assistant deputy minister. The committee would then assess the informant's credibility based on his criminal record, history as an informant, demeanor, and the extent to which the evidence they give is corroborated. Prisoners would not be allowed to testify if they had a conviction for perjury, unless their evidence was corroborated independently. Informants would be charged with obstruction of justice if they were caught lying.

The public inquiry led by former Supreme Court of Canada Justice Peter Cory opened in October 2000. It examined the circumstances surrounding Sophonow's arrest, conviction, his fight to clear his name, and the amount of compensation he would receive. Sophonow testified that his interrogation by two Winnipeg Police detectives in Vancouver in March 1982 was so devastating that by the end of it he began to believe he had killed Stoppel. Police told him that he couldn't remember committing the crime because he had blacked out or had a psychological problem. They said that five witnesses saw him at the doughnut shop and his fingerprints were found at the scene. In fact, neither claim was true. Sophonow subsequently suffered from recurring nightmares.

During the inquiry, the Winnipeg Police said that interviews with suspects are now videotaped or, at least, audiotaped to ensure more accurate records of interrogations. A senior officer is also placed in charge of each serious criminal investigation to ensure that leads, such as those relating to Terry Arnold, are pursued. Mrs. Janower testified that a photo of Arnold she saw in a Winnipeg newspaper looked more like the person she saw at the Ideal Donut Shop than did Sophonow.

During the inquiry, it also came to light that the Crown had failed to disclose evidence to the defence on a number of occasions. For instance, they did not share a witness's statement that the twine used to strangle Stoppel could have been manufactured in Manitoba as well as in Washington State. They also should have disclosed information that would have allowed the defence to cross-examine the credibility and reliability of jailhouse informants. With regard to Thomas Cheng, the judge and jury may have been led to believe that Cheng was testifying with the best of motives. In fact, he received concessions from the Crown on his own criminal charges in exchange for his testimony.

Adrian McQuade, who testified at Sophonow's third trial, was an informant for the Winnipeg Police on at least several matters. He was arrested on March 27, 1982, on charges of break and entering, theft, and possession of stolen goods. He knew Sophonow and had offered to be placed in a cell with him to try to elicit a confession. Two days later, he told a police constable that he had talked to Sophonow four times but that none of their discussions were about the murder. The constable wrote up a report, which was later submitted to the Crown as part of the file of information to assess McQuade's credibility before he testified at Sophonow's third trial.

By the time Sophonow's third trial rolled around, McQuade claimed that Sophonow had, in fact, confessed that weekend. Police had apparently threatened to expose him as a police informant if he didn't. McQuade's contradictory statements were never disclosed. This made it impossible for the defence to question McQuade on his two statements. Sophonow's lawyer was told that McQuade's statement was taken on January 30, 1985, for the first time. As for jailhouse informant Douglas Martin, Justice Cory described him in the inquiry report as "a prime example of the convincing mendacity of jailhouse informants. He seems to have heard more confessions than many dedicated priests. He has testified as a jailhouse informant in at least nine cases in Canada."

Justice Cory's report was issued on September 2001 and contained forty-three recommendations. He noted that jailhouse informants can deceive even experienced observers.

> Jailhouse informants comprise the most deceitful and deceptive group of witnesses known to frequent the courts. ... They rush like vultures to rotting flesh or sharks to blood. They are smooth and convincing liars. Whether they seek favours from the authorities, attention or notoriety, they are in every instance completely unreliable.... Usually their presence as witnesses signals the end of any hope of providing a fair trial.[7]

That's because juries tend to accord the same weight to an alleged confession regardless of whether it has been made to another inmate or a police officer. The greater the number of jailhouse informants who testify at a trial about an alleged confession, the greater the impact on a jury. Therefore, alleged confessions will have more impact if three jailhouse informants testify rather than just one.

Jailhouse informants are unreliable, yet their testimony has devastating consequences. Justice Cory recommended that jailhouse informants should only be used in the most rare of circumstances. Peter Neufeld, an American lawyer and the co-founder of the Innocence Project at the Benjamin Cardozo School of Law, found that prosecutors used jailhouse informants in about 20 percent of the cases that were later determined to be wrongful convictions. A number of provinces, including Ontario, Alberta, and Manitoba, have created special guidelines governing the use of jailhouse informants. In some provinces, committees evaluate the credibility of informants to decide whether or not to allow them to testify.

Cory also noted the Crown had an ethical duty to disclose information about the informants to the defence. "This failure to disclose," Cory stated in his report, "constituted a very serious error. They demonstrate that there was not a fair disclosure made based on the standards of 1982. Those failures further indicate that there could not have been a fair trial based on the standards of that time."[8]

The Canadian Charter of Rights and Freedoms, which was passed in 1981, guarantees that a person has a right to know the evidence against them in order to mount a proper defence, as well as the right to a fair trial. However, it wasn't until the November 17, 1991, Stinchcombe case that the Supreme Court of Canada ruled that the Crown has a duty to fully disclose to the defence all of its evidence in a case. When Sophonow was tried, there was little duty to disclose. The extent to which disclosure of evidence occurred depended in part on the province and the Crown prosecutor.

On July 16, 2002, Manitoba Premier Gary Doer announced that Sophonow would be paid $2.6 million in compensation for his wrongful conviction. Sophonow's fight to clear his name was finally over.

Chapter Eleven

Eyewitness Misidentification:
The Michel Dumont Case

Danielle Lechasseur was coming home from mass in Boisbriand, a bedroom community north of Montreal on November 17, 1990. A man grabbed her by the throat and held her at knifepoint. He said that he would kill her if she screamed. He forced her inside her apartment and raped her in an attack that lasted about ninety minutes. After he left, she cleaned up the scene.

Nearly three days later she went to the police to report the assault. She told them that she had cleaned up afterward. The police didn't go to Lechasseur's apartment to see if any physical evidence remained, such as fingerprints or DNA. Lechasseur described her assailant as being five-feet-nine-inches tall, about 175 pounds, and chubby. He also had tattoos on his forearms and didn't wear glasses. The police created a composite sketch of her attacker, but Lechasseur wasn't completely satisfied that it adequately represented the man who assaulted her. Although she felt the sketch was only 70–80 percent accurate, police used it to try to find the perpetrator. It was published in regional newspapers.

This led to an anonymous call pointing to a clerk at a local convenience store in Boisbriand. The father of two young children was in his thirties, stood five-feet-eight-inches tall and weighed 130 pounds. He had no criminal record. Believing that he had nothing to hide, he agreed to participate in a police lineup. When Lechasseur looked at the photos the police presented to her, she said that she believed Dumont was her attacker but she needed to see the suspect's hands in order to be sure she had identified the right man. Police never gave her that opportunity.

Dumont couldn't see without his glasses and didn't have any tattoos. He told police that he had spent the evening of the assault playing cards at home with friends. Nearly half a dozen friends supported his alibi. There was also no physical evidence linking Dumont to the crime — only the victim's eyewitness statement. Nevertheless, he was arrested on December 20, 1990, just days before Christmas. The lawyer that Dumont hired to defend him was Paul Gélinas, a civil lawyer with little experience in criminal cases.

Dumont's trial was held at the courthouse in Saint-Jérôme in the Court of Quebec on April 30 and May 24, 1991. Justice Céline Pelletier presided. During the trial, at least five people, including his wife, testified they had been playing cards with him at his house the evening that Lechasseur was attacked. The judge dismissed the testimony of these witnesses as not being credible. Instead, she opted to rely solely on the victim's eyewitness identification. It was the only evidence against Dumont, since the police had not attempted to take fingerprints nor DNA at the scene of the crime. On June 25, 1991, he was found guilty of sexual assault, kidnapping, and uttering death threats. On January 6, 1992, Dumont was sentenced to fifty-two months in prison. He was released on bail on January 27 pending his appeal of the verdict.

The victim of the sexual assault had never been completely satisfied with the composite sketch of her assailant. In March of 1992, she entered a video store in her neighbourhood to rent some films. She came face-to-face with a man, holding a child's hand, who could have been Dumont's double. The initial reservations she had had about her identification of Dumont as her assailant crystallized into doubts that she'd fingered the right man. "I really froze," she later said. "It completely called into question the identification I made of Michel Dumont. I couldn't keep that to myself."[1] "I was very scared because it became clear ... that Michel Dumont wasn't the one."[2] Lechasseur informed Crown prosecutor Nathalie Du Perron Roy and the police.

Roger Lemay, an officer with the Boisbriand Police Force, waited about two months before going to see Lechasseur to question her about her change of heart. Lechasseur wasn't aware that Dumont was out on bail at the time, but she categorically denied that the man she saw was Dumont. For his part, Dumont confirmed that he never went to the video store in question. Lemay didn't check to confirm whether Dumont was a member of that store.

Lechasseur signed a sworn statement on June 23, 1992, recanting her identification of Dumont as her assailant. The Crown claims the information was forwarded to Dumont's lawyer, Paul Gélinas, but the defence lawyer claimed he was never informed of its existence. Neither the Crown nor the defence raised the matter in court when Dumont's appeal was heard on February 14, 1994. Regardless of whether or not the defence lawyer received a copy of the victim's statement, it does raise questions about whether the role of the Crown is to convict the guilty or win their case. Is the Crown required to divulge to the court information that could cast doubt on the guilt of the accused and free the very person they are prosecuting? If they don't inform the court, does this constitute negligence on their part?

Dumont's appeal was rejected. Police picked him up in July 1994 and sent him to Cowansville Penitentiary in Quebec's Eastern Townships to serve his sentence. Sex offenders are not treated kindly by other inmates; Dumont was threatened his first night behind bars. Over the course of his incarceration, he was assaulted and repeatedly taunted and threatened. His arms were covered with bruises from beatings by other inmates. Prisoners left urine and feces on his mattress and cell walls. Fearing for his safety, he started eating his meals in his cell. Despite the physical assaults and taunts, Dumont refused to ask to be segregated for his own protection. "I told myself that if you go into hiding, you have something to hide," he said.[3] He continued to maintain his innocence and refused to participate in programs for sex offenders. After his appeal, youth protection services took his two young children into custody and placed them in foster care.

Solange Tremblay, the woman whom Dumont had met while he was out of jail pending his appeal, refused to give up on him. The two first met while attending a meeting for people who are separated or divorced. He told his story to the slim, blond mother of three. Then he steeled himself for rejection. Tremblay's intuition told her the gentle-mannered man hadn't committed the crime for which he was convicted. The couple had known each other for barely a year when police came to take Dumont back to prison. He thought that she would leave him, but Tremblay visited Dumont every week, long after his own father had cut him out of his life. She proposed to him through the visitors' partition while visiting him in prison one day. They got married in the prison chapel.

Tremblay was convinced of his innocence and determined to get him out of jail. She contacted lawyers, but couldn't find one who would take the case, because she didn't have the money to pay. She decided to take matters into her own hands. With no legal training, she began carefully reading through the file of the case against Dumont. As she pored over some 1,300 pages of court transcripts of his trial and police reports, she jotted down any inconsistencies and holes she found. She was so committed that she sometimes woke up in the middle of the night to make a note of an idea that had just occurred to her. "I just had to get him out of jail," she said. "And I knew that if I didn't do it, no one would."[4]

In 1995, Tremblay began writing the first of many letters to federal justice minister Allan Rock and his successor, Anne McLellan, asking that Dumont's case be reviewed under Section 690 of the Criminal Code. That provision of the Criminal Code allows someone who has been convicted of an offence to make an application for mercy to have the minister of justice review their case.

It took Tremblay three years of painstaking work to assemble the file for the federal department of justice. Along with her letters, she included copies of her notes and the victim's statement recanting her identification of Dumont as her attacker. When money was needed to cover legal bills, she cashed in the $10,000 RRSP she had painstakingly squirreled away when she worked in a factory. Then the couple waited for a response from the justice minister.

They weren't the only ones trying to exonerate Dumont. Danielle Lechasseur continued to proclaim that she had erred in identifying Dumont as her attacker. On September 28, 1994, and November 4, 1994, she told two different investigators that she had misidentified Dumont as her attacker. She recanted again during two television interviews in 1997, one on Télé-Québec's show *Mongrain* on February 27, and the other on the CBC French television network on the September 10 episode of *Enjeux* on Société Radio-Canada. "I cannot believe that someone with so much goodness in his face could have spent so many years in prison when he wasn't the one, and I kept saying so," she said on

Radio-Canada.[5] She had waited for him outside the prison gates when he was finally released on May 23, 1997, to apologize for her mistake that led to his incarceration.

Dumont felt no bitterness toward Lechasseur. "It's the Crown and the police who hid evidence that it wasn't me," he told Radio-Canada. "The victim, she alerted police before the appeal. Therefore, she did what she needed to do. It was up to the police to do their job and the Crown."[6]

Reunited at last, Dumont and Tremblay began putting the pieces of their lives back together. During his incarceration, he had gone two-and-a-half years without seeing his two children. The first order of business was to get them out of foster care and back home. The couple hired a lawyer and went to court to fight to regain custody. His daughter returned home in late 1997 and his son was brought back in 1999. They also began planning to buy a house.

Tremblay continued to hold out hope for her husband's exoneration. She approached criminal lawyer Jean-François Longtin for assistance. He had helped Laval pipefitter Réjean Hinse win an acquittal after serving eight years for a 1961 armed robbery that he didn't commit. Longtin agreed to take Dumont's case. Federal Justice Minister Anne McLellan ordered an independent investigation of Dumont's case. In February 1998, lawyer Isabel Schurman took Lechasseur's statement recanting her identification of Dumont. McLellan referred the case to the Quebec Court of Appeal on October 4, 2000. The question was whether Lechasseur's statements of doubt could be considered admissible as new evidence. If so, could this evidence have potentially influenced the case's verdict had the information been available at trial or during the appeal? The Quebec Court of Appeal heard the case on February 13, 2001.

On February 22, 2001, the three appeal court justices acquitted Dumont. He was the victim of a miscarriage of justice. It was the first time that section 690 of the Criminal Code had been successfully used in Quebec. "The label 'rapist' has been a heavy burden to bear," Dumont said in a barely audible voice after the decision. "Today, it is lifted." His wife stood by his side, clutching his hand. The acquittal came more than ten years after Danielle Lechasseur picked Dumont out of a photo lineup in a case of eyewitness misidentification.[7]

In August 2001, Dumont launched a civil suit in Quebec Superior Court against the provincial and federal governments and the municipality of Boisbriand. He asked for $8.7 million in compensation for himself and his family. He wanted $1.2 million for each of his children, who were abused in foster care, and another $500,000 for the work his wife did and the money she spent on his case. She had used up her savings in her efforts to free him. "Instead of being compensated, we have debts," she told a television reporter. "Those debts, I think, don't belong to us. It's a judicial error. The government should compensate us so that we can pay those debts and live in peace."[8]

Finally, he claimed $5.8 million for the time he spent in prison, loss of income, loss of reputation, and psychological damages. "From a human perspective, no amount of money is enough," Dumont said at a news conference. "It will never replace 14 years since this nightmare began. But it will help us to live normally."[9]

Dumont's lawyer, Jean-François Longtin, pointed to two troubling aspects of the case. The first was weaknesses in the victim's identification of Dumont during the initial investigation. She wasn't happy with the composite sketch that led to Dumont's arrest, and she also wasn't completely certain that Dumont was her attacker. When she identified Dumont, "the victim said 'I believe he is my attacker' — so there was already an element of ambiguity."[10]

A second question the case raised centred around the Crown prosecutor's authorization of criminal charges against Dumont. "When you have an identification, you also need circumstantial evidence, physical evidence," Longtin said. "In the Dumont case, there was nothing, no DNA evidence, nothing."[11] According to the New York-based Innocence Project, eyewitness misidentifications contributed to wrongful convictions in more than 75 percent of the 220 cases in the United States that were later overturned by post-conviction DNA evidence.

Nonetheless, traditional eyewitness identifications are one of the most commonly used and compelling pieces of evidence in court. Misidentifications can occur for a number of reasons. When using a police lineup, for instance, the person who is administering it usually knows which person is the suspect. Research has found that they often provide unintentional cues to the eyewitness about which person to pick. Also, when an eyewitness is shown a group of people, or individual photographs simultaneously, they tend to choose the one who looks the most like the perpetrator rather than one who looks like their mental image of the perpetrator. Furthermore, since the witness often assumes that the perpetrator is included in the police lineup, this may lead them to pick someone as the perpetrator despite doubts they might have that they selected the right person.

As the Innocence Project notes, there are a few ways to address the issue of eyewitness misidentification. They include having a lineup administrator who doesn't know which person is the suspect, instructions to the eyewitness that *the suspect may or may not be present in the lineup*, having a lineup of people who look like the witness's description of the perpetrator rather than the suspect, ensuring the suspect doesn't stand out from the others in the lineup in any way, and presenting the police lineup one at a time. A sequential approach has been shown to significantly increase the overall accuracy of eyewitness identifications.

Dumont's lawsuit dragged on for years. Federal-provincial guidelines were established in 1988 to compensate victims of wrongful convictions. It was argued that an acquittal isn't sufficient to be eligible for compensation; an appeals court must find "that the person did not commit the offence."[12] In February 2006, the Quebec government decided that Dumont wasn't entitled to compensation because, in their view, he wasn't wrongfully convicted. The Court of Appeal didn't say he was innocent, a spokesman explained, it merely said that he shouldn't have been convicted. His "factual innocence" had not been established. Dumont couldn't be compensated unless he was declared factually innocent. That would only happen if Dumont either found the real perpetrator or produced DNA evidence that would exonerate him. The problem was that the police never went to the victim's apartment to check for fingerprints or any possible DNA evidence.

The lawsuit against the City of Boisbriand, whose police department investigation led to Dumont's arrest, was settled for an undisclosed amount. The civil trial for Dumont's $2.5-million lawsuit against the Canadian and Quebec governments got underway in February 2009.

At the heart of it was the question of why Lechasseur's change of heart about her testimony wasn't mentioned during the first appeal. Was Dumont's lawyer aware of the recanted statement? Paul Gélinas, the man who could answer that question, had since died. The two opposing lawyers could only speculate about what he knew. Crown prosecutor Michel Deom said that the defence lawyer was informed but failed to bring the information to the court's attention during the first appeal; Longtin argued that he was not informed. But nobody knew for sure. In July 2009, Dumont lost his civil suit. Superior Court Justice Benoit Emery ruled that prosecutors made no mistake in the case. Nor did they act with malice or in bad faith. He believed they had sent a letter to Dumont's then-lawyer informing him about the victim's doubts. The fault, the judge believed, lay with Dumont's lawyer — not the Crown. Dumont was denied compensation.

However, the question remains: Is it the Crown prosecutor's job to bring to the court's attention information that could free a defendant? Is it to seek justice or is it to win their case? Where does justice lie? The Crown in the Dumont case had information that could have cleared him — but they chose not to bring it up in court. Is that justice? One would like to think that delivering justice trumps winning cases. In 2005, Dumont told *The Globe and Mail,* "I want them to say sorry. It won't relieve the burden, it won't erase what happened, but it would provide some comfort."[13]

Chapter Twelve

Questionable Tactics: The Case of Gordon Folland

Gordon Folland and his best friend Shawn Harris spent the evening of November 22, 1993, drinking with a twenty-six-year-old female friend as they helped her paint her house in Hamilton, Ontario. Harris and the woman had dated at one time, and he'd recently rented the second floor of her house. That night, he made some offensive overtures toward her. The woman locked her door and went to bed. The two men fell asleep in her living room.

Later that night, in the wee hours of November 23, 1993, the woman woke up in her darkened bedroom. Someone was raping her. As she screamed for help, she reached out and felt the man's forehead. He had no hair. *It must be Folland,* she thought: Folland was balding. Her assailant fled, but he left a pair of men's underwear with the label "K. Beeching" on her bed.

The victim went to the telephone to call police. Harris tried to stop her, threatening to kill her if she reported the assault. He also made comments to the effect that he was the one who had assaulted her. In fact, Harris initially told one of the investigating officers that he had assaulted the woman and that Folland was asleep on the couch at the time and never left the room. But a few days later he refused to give police a signed statement. He also claimed that he had had consensual sex with the woman several times prior to the assault. The last time was the night before she was attacked. The victim got dressed and went to the hospital, where she was examined.

The fact that the victim believed her assailant was balding pointed to Folland, not Harris. The police charged him with sexual assault. Folland voluntarily gave them a DNA sample, but test results revealed that semen on the discarded underwear wasn't his. Harris, the only other person with Folland and the victim the night of the assault, wasn't asked for a DNA sample, so the police couldn't test it. Folland's defence lawyer repeatedly asked the Crown, in writing, to have the police pursue a more complete investigation of Harris's role in the crime. He also suggested that the Crown call Harris as a witness. The Crown opted not to call Harris to the stand to testify; neither did Folland's lawyer. Efforts by the defence to serve Harris with a subpoena were unsuccessful. Defence lawyer Dennis Reardon decided not to request that Harris appear as a material witness because he had grown concerned that Harris would support the Crown's case by denying any involvement in the assault.

At Folland's trial by jury, the victim testified that Harris had admitted to assaulting her, but that she then overheard Folland confess to Harris. The victim's testimony that she had felt her assailant's bald head formed the bulk of the evidence against Folland. A jury took just ninety minutes to decide that he was guilty. Folland was convicted on March 16, 1995, and sentenced to five years in prison. As he was led away, his daughter shouted, "Daddy, I love you."

Folland continued to maintain his innocence. While he was behind bars, he told prison officials that he needed treatment for alcoholism. He believed his trouble with alcohol started after his wife died of leukemia. Prison officials had other ideas; they wanted him to participate in a treatment program for sex offenders. He refused, which made it difficult for him to obtain parole. The National Parole Board decided that he was "in strong denial," and refused his application for parole.

While Folland was in prison, two of his friends met Harris in a bar. They convinced him to provide hair samples and spit into a tissue to obtain his DNA. The Centre of Forensic Sciences in Toronto tested it. They discovered that a pair of clean underwear the victim had put on after the assault contained semen that matched Harris's DNA. Harris's DNA was also found in the semen in the underwear the attacker left behind the night of the attack.

Folland was released on bail in November 1997, nearly halfway through his five-year sentence, pending an appeal of his conviction. Lawyer James Lockyer of the AIDYWC agreed to take his case. In early December 1998, Lockyer presented the new DNA evidence during a hearing before the Ontario Court of Appeal. The defence also said they had statements from five witnesses who claimed they had heard Harris confess that he had sexually assaulted the victim. Lockyer told the court that circumstantial evidence pointed to Harris rather than Folland.

Crown prosecutor Hugh Ashford tried to dismiss the significance of the evidence against Harris. Ashford argued that it had not been determined that the victim's attacker had, in fact, ejaculated. Therefore, it was irrelevant that traces of Harris's semen had been found on both pairs of underwear. Besides, Harris and the woman had been intimate in the weeks leading up to the attack. Harris could have inadvertently deposited the stains, during a consensual encounter, which were later matched to him. The judges of the Ontario Court of Appeal didn't agree with the Crown's assessment.

The Ontario Court of Appeal overturned Folland's conviction on January 20, 1999, and ordered a new trial. However, Justice Marc Rosenberg wrote that the Crown might want to consider whether it would be in the public interest to have a new trial. After spending two-and-a-half years behind bars for a crime that he didn't commit, Folland was relieved. "The disgrace of a charge like this is so great," he told *The Globe and Mail*. "It was wrong for me to have to live with it."[1] He looked forward to seeing his daughter graduate from Brock University in St. Catharines, Ontario, in the spring.

The following May, Folland found himself before the same Ontario Superior Court judge who had sentenced him four years earlier. Crown prosecutor Tim Power withdrew the charges against Folland in light of the DNA tests that pointed to Harris. He announced that there would be no retrial, but stopped short of recommending an acquittal. Folland wept as the judge offered him an emotional apology. "On behalf of the administration of justice, I sincerely apologize to you and to your family," Justice Walter Stayshyn said. "You have been imprisoned improperly for a considerable period of time."[2] Folland was touched by the apology, particularly since it came from the same judge who had presided over the trial leading to his conviction.

Folland launched a malicious prosecution suit against the Hamilton Police and the Crown prosecutor's office. He said that the police should have obtained a DNA sample from Harris prior to the trial. His lawyer could have used the results of the DNA test to apply for a material witness warrant to compel Harris to testify. He also decided to sue Dennis Reardon, the lawyer who had defended him during his trial. He alleged that Reardon was negligent in his defence and that he failed to obtain a DNA sample from Harris, which led to Folland's wrongful conviction and incarceration.

Justice Peter Jarvis of Ontario's Superior Court dismissed the case in January 2004. He said that he found no evidence of egregious error. Folland appealed. Six years after the Ontario Court of Appeal quashed Folland's conviction for a sexual assault he didn't commit, the Court of Appeal granted Folland the right to continue his lawsuit against Reardon.

In a unanimous ruling in Folland v. Reardon, the three judges said that lawyers shouldn't be judged by different standards than other professions. "Without diminishing the difficulty of many judgments that counsel must make in the course of litigation, the judgment calls made by lawyers are no more difficult than those made by other professionals," Ontario Court of Appeal judges David Doherty, Marvin Catzman, and Robert Armstrong said. Justice Doherty wrote that, "An individual being defended in a criminal case is entitled to expect that his lawyer will perform as a reasonably competent defence counsel."[3] The judges said that lawyers mistakenly believe they can't be sued unless they made "egregious" errors of judgment. However, they could be negligent if they failed to measure up to a standard of reasonable competence.

In Reardon's case, failing to obtain DNA samples from Harris to test against the semen-stained underwear constituted negligence. "The DNA evidence offered potentially significant support for the claim that Harris, and not Folland, was wearing that underwear," the court said. "Given that there were only two potential assailants, Harris or Folland, this evidence could have turned the tide in favour of Folland."[4] Folland was also willing to admit that he had stolen a forty-ounce bottle of vodka the day of the assault. However, Reardon presented the evidence in such a way during the trial that he made it look like Folland was trying to hide the theft.

The appeal court judges made a distinction between errors in judgment that a lawyer could justifiably make over the course of a case and outright negligence. "Lawyers make many decisions in the course of a lawsuit. Those decisions require the exercise of judgment. Inevitably some of those decisions, when viewed with the benefit of hindsight will be seen as unwise," the judges noted. "The standard demands that the lawyer bring to the exercise of his or her judgment the effort, knowledge, and insight of the reasonably competent lawyer. If the lawyer has met that standard, his or her duty to the client is discharged, even if the decision proves to be disastrous."[5] Reardon denied that he had been negligent. Both of Folland's lawsuits were settled in November 2005, but the terms of the settlements remain confidential.

Appendix A

Other Cases of Wrongful Conviction in Canada

In Chronological Order

Steven Truscott was fourteen years old when the body of a schoolmate was found near a Clinton, Ontario, air force base in June 1959. Twelve-year-old Lynne Harper had been raped and strangled to death. Police focused their attention on Truscott, who had given Harper a bicycle ride before her death. They did not inquire about other possible suspects. Truscott was tried three months later, found guilty, and sentenced to hang. His death sentence was commuted to life in prison. He was released in 1969, moved to Guelph, Ontario, and adopted a new identity. The federal justice minister referred his case to the Ontario Court of Appeal, which overturned his conviction in August 2007. In July 2008, the Ontario government announced that it would pay Truscott $6.5 million in compensation.

Réjean Hinse was convicted in 1964 of an armed robbery in Mont-Laurier, Quebec, in 1961. He was sentenced to fifteen years in prison, partly on the basis of eyewitness testimony. He spent five years in prison but continued to seek exoneration. The Supreme Court of Canada acquitted him in 1997. Following a lawsuit against the Quebec and federal governments, Hinse was awarded $13.1 million in April 2011.

Romeo Phillion was convicted in 1972 of the stabbing death of Ottawa firefighter Leopold Roy in August 1967. He had confessed while in custody on a robbery charge, then immediately recanted and continued to maintain his innocence. He spent thirty-one years in prison. In 2009, the Ontario Court of Appeal struck down Phillion's conviction and ordered a new trial, in part because a police report that Phillion had been 200 kilometres away from the murder when it occurred was never given to his defence lawyer. In April 2010, the Crown withdrew the charges.

Erin Walsh was convicted of second-degree murder in the 1975 killing of Melvin (Chi Chi) Peters in Saint John, New Brunswick. He was sentenced to life in prison with no parole for ten years. His appeals to the New Brunswick Court of Appeal were dismissed in 1982. New evidence surfaced in 2006, from jailhouse conversations, which suggested that someone else had shot Peters. In 2008, the New Brunswick Court of Appeal acquitted Walsh and overturned his conviction, clearing his name. He died of colon cancer on October 14, 2010.

Norman Fox was sentenced to ten years in prison in 1976 in Vancouver for rape and related offences. He served eight years in prison. He was granted a pardon in 1984 after new evidence indicated that he had been mistakenly identified. He received $275,000 in compensation.

Richard Norris was convicted of sexual assault in 1980 after the Fergus, Ontario, victim mistakenly identified him as her assailant. He served eight months in jail and was acquitted in 1991 after an acquaintance admitted that he had assaulted the woman. Norris was awarded $507,000 two years later.

Benoit Proulx was convicted in 1991 of murdering his former girlfriend, nineteen-year-old France Alain. The Quebec Court of Appeal said there wasn't enough evidence to support a conviction and he was acquitted in 1992. He sued Quebec's attorney general for malicious prosecution and was awarded $1.1 million.

Ivan Henry was convicted in British Columbia in 1983 on ten counts of rape and indecent assault involving eight women. He was acquitted in 2010 after serving twenty-seven years in prison. The appeal court found the witness identifications weak and that the trial judge erred in his instructions to the jury.

Wilfred Truscott was convicted of assault and mischief causing damage to personal property. He was sentenced to eighteen months in jail in 1984. It was later learned that the complaint had been fabricated. The Alberta government awarded him $36,000 in compensation in 1986.

Anthony Hanemaayer was charged with assault after a fifteen-year-old girl was attacked at knifepoint in Toronto. On the advice of his lawyer, he pleaded guilty to avoid a lengthy sentence and was sentenced to two years less a day in jail. In a prison interview in 2006, convicted murderer and rapist Paul Bernardo confessed to the crime. The Ontario Court of Appeal acquitted Hanemaayer on June 25, 2008.

Michael McTaggert was convicted of armed bank robbery, but his conviction was overturned in 1990 after it was learned that a string of robberies, similar to the one of which he was accused, had continued while he was in jail. Evidence surfaced in 2000 that the prosecution had failed to tell his defence lawyer that two bank tellers had identified another man. In 2001, he was awarded $380,000 in compensation for his twenty months of imprisonment.

Peter Frumusa was convicted of first-degree murder in the 1988 killing of a Niagara couple, largely on the testimony of a jailhouse informant. He was sentenced to twenty-five years in prison. The Ontario Court of Appeal ordered a new trial in 1996, and the charges were withdrawn in 1998. He had served eight years in prison.

Jack White was charged with sexual assault in 1993 after a co-worker alleged that he had seen White assault a patient at the mental health care facility where they both worked. The patient was unable to speak. White was convicted in 1995 after a trial that lasted less than two hours. The Superior Court of Ontario withdrew the charges on November 26, 2010, after it was demonstrated that White's accuser had ample reason to lie.

James Driskell was convicted of shooting his friend Perry Harder in the chest several times in September 1990. He was sentenced to life in prison. The RCMP said they had found three of Harder's hairs in Driskell's van. Subsequent tests performed in Britain found that none of the hairs were Harder's. The federal justice minister quashed the conviction in 2005 and ordered a new trial. The Manitoba government decided instead to end the case. Driskell was awarded $4-million in compensation.

Kyle Unger was convicted of first-degree murder in 1992 after sixteen-year-old Brigitte Grenier was found beaten, strangled, and sexually mutilated near Roseisle, Manitoba, in 1990. He was acquitted in 2009 after new DNA testing suggested a strand of hair that was used to convict Unger did not come from him and other evidence also unravelled. He had spent fourteen years in prison.

Robert Baltovich was convicted of first-degree murder following the 1990 disappearance of his girlfriend, Elizabeth Bain. Neither her body nor a murder weapon has ever been found. In 2000, evidence was presented that suggested that Bain was a victim of convicted killer Paul Bernardo. The Ontario Court of Appeal quashed Baltovich's conviction in April 2008, twelve years after he was convicted.

Gregory Parsons was convicted of murder after his mother Catherine Carroll was killed in her St. John's, Newfoundland, home in 1991. The conviction rested largely on the hearsay evidence of witnesses who said Carroll was afraid of her son. DNA evidence cleared him in 1998. A former family friend was later charged with Carroll's murder. Parsons received $1.3 million in compensation.

Steven Kaminski spent seven years in prison after being convicted in 1992 for the sexual assault of a co-worker. He said the sex was consensual. A new trial was ordered in 2002 but did not proceed. It was learned that Kaminski's accuser had had sex with the Mountie assigned to investigate the case and a man who had testified against Kaminski. Kaminski received a $2.2-million settlement from the federal government.

Herman Kaglik was convicted in 1992 of raping his thirty-seven-year-old niece in Inuvik, Northwest Territories, based on her testimony. He was sentenced to four years in prison. A year later, he was charged with additional rapes and sentenced to another six years in prison. He served fifty-two months, before DNA tests exonerated him in 1998. In 2000, he was awarded $1.1 million in compensation by the federal government.

Randy Druken was convicted of murder after his girlfriend Brenda Marie Young was found stabbed to death in her St. John's, Newfoundland, home in 1993. The conviction was set aside in 2000 after a jailhouse informant recanted his testimony that Druken had confessed to the murder. The government of Newfoundland and Labrador awarded him $2.1 million in compensation.

Sherry Sherrett-Robinson was charged with first-degree murder after her son Joshua died. At the preliminary hearing, now-disgraced pathologist Dr. Charles Smith speculated that Joshua's death wasn't an accident. An intimidated Sherrett-Robinson agreed to plead guilty to a lesser charge of infanticide in 1999 and served eight months in jail. Her other son, Austin, was adopted by another family. Sherrett-Robinson later appealed the decision in light of inconsistencies surrounding Dr. Smith's evidence. The Ontario Court of Appeal acquitted her on December 7, 2009.

Appendix B

Compensation for Wrongful Convictions

Name	Jurisdiction	Conviction	Exoneration	Incarceration	Compensation	Year Awarded
Ronald Dalton	NL	1989	2000	8 years	$750,000	2007
James Driskell	MB	1991	2005	12 years	$4 million	2008
Randy Druken	NL	1995	2000	6 years	$2.1 million	2006
Norman Fox	BC	1976	1984	8 years	$275,000	1985
Clayton Johnson	NS	1994	2002	5 years	$2.5 million	2004
Herman Kaglik	Federal	1992	1998	4 years	$1.1 million	2001
Steven Kaminski	AB	1992	2002	7 years	$2.2 million	2006
Donald Marshall	NS	1971	1982	11 years	$1.5 million	1990
Simon Marshall	QC	1997	2004	6 years	$2.3 million	2006
Michael McTaggert	ON	1987	1990	20 months	$380,000	2001

David Milgaard	SK	1970	1997	23 years	$10 million	1999
Guy Paul Morin	ON	1992	1995	18 months	$1.25 million	1997
Richard Norris	ON	1980	1991	8 months	$507,000	1993
Greg Parsons	NL	1994	1998	6 weeks	$1.3 million	2002, 2005
Benoit Proulx	QC	1991	1992	1 year	$1.1 million	2001
Thomas Sophonow	MB	1983, 1985	2000	45 months	$2.6 million	2002
Gary Staples	ON	1971	2002	2 years	Undisclosed	2002
Steven Truscott	ON	1959	2007	10 years	$6.5 million	2008
Wilfred Truscott	AB	1984	1986	18 months	$36,000	1986
Réjean Hinse	QC	1964	1997	5 years	$13.1 million	2011
William Mullins-Johnson	ON	1994	2007	12 years	$4.25 million	2010

Appendix C

Commissions of Inquiry into Wrongful Convictions in Canada

Name:	**Royal Commission on the Donald Marshall, Jr., Prosecution**
Jurisdiction:	Nova Scotia
Established:	October 1986
Commissioner:	Justice Alexander Hickman, Chief Justice of the Newfoundland Supreme Court's trial division
Hearings began:	September 9, 1987
Report issued:	January 1990
Recommendations:	82
Report available:	*http://www.gov.ns.ca/just/marshall_inquiry/ default.asp*

Name:	**Commission on Proceedings Involving Guy Paul Morin**
Jurisdiction:	Ontario
Established:	June 1996
Commissioner:	Justice Fred Kaufman, retired judge of the Quebec Court of Appeal
Hearings began:	February 10, 1997
Report issued:	April 1998

Recommendations:	119
Report available:	*http://www.attorneygeneral.jus.gov.on.ca/english/ about/pubs/morin/*

Name:	**Inquiry Regarding Thomas Sophonow**
Jurisdiction:	Manitoba
Established:	June 2000
Commissioner:	Retired Supreme Court of Canada Justice Peter Cory
Hearings began:	October 2000
Report issued:	September 2001
Recommendations:	43
Report available:	*http://www.gov.mb.ca/justice/publications/ sophonow/toc.html*

Name:	**Lamer Inquiry**
Jurisdiction:	Newfoundland and Labrador
Established:	March 2003
Commissioner:	Retired Supreme Court of Canada Chief Justice Antonio Lamer
Hearings began:	September 23, 2003
Report issued:	June 2006
Recommendations:	45
Report available:	*http://www.justice.gov.nl.ca/just/publications/ index.html#g6*

Name:	**Commission of Inquiry Into Certain Aspects of the Trial and Conviction of James Driskell**
Jurisdiction:	Manitoba
Established:	December 2005

Commissioner:	Justice Patrick LeSage, former Chief Justice of the Ontario Superior Court
Hearings began:	July 24, 2006
Report issued:	February 2007
Recommendations:	21
Report available:	*http://www.driskellinquiry.ca/*

Name:	**Inquiry into Pediatric Forensic Pathology in Ontario**
Jurisdiction:	Ontario
Established:	April 2007
Commissioner:	Justice Stephen Goudge, Ontario Court of Appeal
Hearings began:	November 12, 2007
Report issued:	October 2008
Recommendations:	169
Report available:	*www.goudgeinquiry.ca*

Name:	**Commission of Inquiry into the Wrongful Conviction of David Milgaard**
Jurisdiction:	Saskatchewan
Established:	February 2004
Commissioner:	Justice Edward MacCallum of the Alberta Court of Queen's Bench
Hearings began:	January 17, 2005
Report issued:	September 2008
Recommendations:	13
Report available:	*http://www.justice.gov.sk.ca/milgaard/DMfinal. shtml*

Appendix D

Resources

CANADA

Association in Defence of the Wrongly Convicted (AIDWYC)
111 Peter Street, Suite 626
Toronto, ON
M5V 2H1
Phone: (416) 504-7500
Toll Free: (800) 249-1329 (Canada Only)
Fax: (416) 203-9088
Email: contact@aidwyc.org
Website: *www.aidwyc.org*

Osgoode Hall Innocence Project
Osgoode Hall Law School, York University
4700 Keele Street
Toronto, ON
M3J 1P3
Phone: (416) 736-5174
Fax: (416) 736-5736
Email: InnocenceProject@osgoode.yorku.ca
Website: *http://www.osgoode.yorku.ca/innocence_project/*

The McGill Innocence Project
Innocence McGill
McGill Faculty of Law
3644 Peel Street
Montreal, QC
H3A 1W9
Website: *http://www.mcgill.ca/innocence/*

UBC Law Innocence Project
Faculty of Law, 1822 East Mall
University of British Columbia
Vancouver, BC
V6T 1Z1
Phone: (604) 827-3616
Fax: (604) 827-3585
Email: innocenceproject@law.ubc.ca
Website: *http://www.innocenceproject.law.ubc.ca/*

Criminal Conviction Review Group
Department of Justice Canada
Website: *http://www.justice.gc.ca/eng/pi/ccr-rc/index.html*

UNITED STATES

Innocence Project
40 Worth Street, Suite 701
New York, NY
10013
USA
Phone: (212) 364-5340
Email: info@innocenceproject.org
Website: *http://www.innocenceproject.org/*

Centurion Ministries, Inc.
221 Witherspoon Street,

Princeton, New Jersey
08542-3215
USA
Website: *http://www.centurionministries.org/index.html*

BRITAIN

Criminal Cases Review Commission
Alpha Tower
Suffolk Street Queensway
Birmingham
B1 1TT
United Kingdom
Phone: 0121 633 1800
Fax: 0121 633 1823
Email: info@ccrc.gov.uk
Website: *http://www.ccrc.gov.uk/*

Innocence Project
University of Leeds
Leeds
LS2 9JT
United Kingdom
Email: innocenceproject@leeds.ac.uk
Website: *http://www.law.leeds.ac.uk/prospective-students/
undergraduates/extra/innocence-project.php*

Innocence Network UK (INUK)
School of Law
University of Bristol
Wills Memorial Building
Queens Road, Bristol
BS8 1RJ
United Kingdom
Website: *http://www.innocencenetwork.org.uk*

Appendix E

Further Reading

Anderson, Dawn and Barrie Anderson. *Manufacturing Guilt: Wrongful Convictions in Canada.* Second Edition. Winnipeg: Fernwood Publishing, 2009.

Carter, Rubin "Hurricane" and Ken Klonsky. *Eye of the Hurricane: My Path from Darkness to Freedom.* Chicago: Lawrence Hill Books, 2011.

Finkle, Derek. *No Claim To Mercy.* Toronto: Penguin Canada, 2004.

Gould, Jon B. *The Innocence Commission: Preventing Wrongful Convictions and Restoring the Criminal Justice System.* New York: New York University Press, 2009.

Harris, Michael. *Justice Denied: The Law Versus Donald Marshall.* Toronto: Macmillan of Canada, 1986.

Karp, Carl and Cecil Rosner. *When Justice Fails: The David Milgaard Story.* Toronto: McClelland & Stewart, 1998.

Makin, Kirk. *Redrum The Innocent.* Revised Edition. Toronto: Penguin Canada, 1998.

Milgaard, Joyce and Peter Edwards. *A Mother's Story: My Battle To Free David Milgaard*. Toronto: Doubleday Canada, 1999.

Scheck, Barry, Peter Neufeld, and Jim Dwyer. *Actual Innocence: Five Days to Execution, and Other Dispatches From the Wrongly Convicted*. New York: Doubleday, 2000.

Sher, Julian. *"Until You Are Dead": Steven Truscott's Long Ride into History*. Toronto: Vintage Canada, 2002.

Notes

Introduction

1. Kirk Makin. "The Lawyer Who Has 'A Cause For A Client'" *The Globe and Mail,* May 12, 1999.
2. Kirk Makin. "The Innocence Industry." *The Globe and Mail,* July 7, 2001.
3. "Freed Man Worried About Fate Outside Jail." *The Ottawa Citizen,* December 14, 1985, final edition.
4. Jane Orydzuk. "CBC Betrays Family of Slaying Victim." *Edmonton Journal,* October 20, 1999, final edition.
5. Deborah Wilson. "N.S. Justice System Undermined by Old-Boys' Network, Judge Says." *The Globe and Mail,* May 18, 1988.
6. Kirk Makin. " Judicial Accountability Urged in Wrongful-Conviction Cases." *The Globe and Mail,* June 13, 2005.
7. Ann Carroll. "Quebec Justice Proves Elusive for Wrongfully Convicted Man." *The Gazette.* May 11, 2005, final edition.

Chapter 1 — Unreliable Witnesses: The David Milgaard Case

1. Joyce Milgaard and Peter Edwards. "The Fight to Free My Son." *Reader's Digest,* May 2000, 172-212.
2. *Ibid.*

Chapter 2 — Racism: The Donald Marshall Jr. Case

1. Alan Story. "How Donald Marshall Case Unfolded." *Toronto Star*, June 8, 1986.
2. Drew Fagan. "Marshall Trial Witness Claims Fear, Pressure Caused Him to Tell Lies." *The Globe and Mail*, September 16, 1987.
3. Alan Story. "How Donald Marshall Case Unfolded."
4. Alan Story. "The Tangled Trial of Donald Marshall: Racial Prejudice and Perjury Helped Put Him Behind Bars." *Toronto Star*, June 9, 1986.
5. Alan Story. "Racist Remark About Marshall by N.S. Judge Triggers Outcry." *Toronto Star*, February 4, 1988, final edition.
6. Sandra Martin. "From Victim to Native Rights Hero." *The Globe and Mail*, August 7, 2009.
7. "Bragging Police Chief Cited." *The Vancouver Sun*, January 18, 1988, fourth edition.
8. Michael Harris. "Facing the Replay of a Nightmare." *The Globe and Mail*, June 18, 1982.
9. Michael Harris. "Marshall Acquittal Urged by Crown." *The Globe and Mail*, February 17, 1983.
10. Michael Harris. "Marshall's Ordeal Far From Over Yet." *The Globe and Mail*, May 13, 1983.
11. Michael Harris. "Acquitted in Killing, Marshall Is Jubilant." *The Globe and Mail*, May 11, 1983.
12. Michael Harris. "Frustration Mounts for Jobless Marshall Out of Prison But Not in the Clear." *The Globe and Mail*, May 6, 1983.
13. Michael Harris. "N.S. Jurors Deliberate in Slaying for Which Wrong Man Went to Jail." *The Globe and Mail*, September 14, 1983.
14. "Cheap Marshall Compensation Was Aim." *The Vancouver Sun*, June 6, 1988, fourth edition.
15. Michael Harris. "Canadian Justice Failed Marshall, Lawyer Contends." *The Globe and Mail*, September 27, 1984.

Chapter 3 — Cooking up Evidence: The Jason Dix Case

1. Kerry Powell. "No Struggle as Pair Murdered, Says Constable;

Evidence Based on Blood-Spatters; SATELLITE TESTIMONY." *Edmonton Journal*, April 29, 1998, final edition.

2. Kerry Powell. "Wife Made Terrifying Find — Then Became a Murder Suspect." *Edmonton Journal*, April 30, 1998, final edition.

3. *Ibid.*

4. *Ibid.*

5. Gordon Kent. "'We Really Screwed Up,' Officer Says: Defence Outlines Case in $14.2M Jason Dix Lawsuit." *Edmonton Journal*, November 6, 2001, final edition.

6. Gordon Kent. "Dix Wary of Joining Criminal Gang, But Says 'Money Was a Bigger Draw.'" *Edmonton Journal*, October 16, 2001, final edition.

7. Gordon Kent. "'Whack at Yahk' Ploy Fails." *The Windsor Star*, October 12, 2001, final edition.

8. Kerry Powell. "Motives for Murder a Mystery to Mistress; Dix had No Call To Be Jealous Of Co-Worker. A CASE IN POINTS." *Edmonton Journal*, May 9, 1998, final edition.

9. Gordon Kent. "'You Really Screwed Up,' Cops Told Dix." *Edmonton Journal*, October 3, 2001, final edition.

10. Gordon Kent. "'I'm Not a Murderer,' Dix Says During 11-Hour Grilling: Remains Silent for Most Of RCMP Interviews." *Edmonton Journal*, October 5, 2001, final edition.

11. Florence Loyie "'They Were Trying to Scare Me': Jason Dix Handed a Gun in Marathon Interrogation Aimed at a Confession." *Edmonton Journal*, October 6, 2001, final edition.

12. Gordon Kent. "I'm Not a Murderer.'"

13. Kerry Powell and Charles Rusnell. "Project Kabaya: Mounties' Elaborate Ruse That Fizzled." *Edmonton Journal*, January 17, 1999, final edition.

14. Florence Loyie. "'They Were Trying to Scare Me."

15. Gordon Kent. "Dix Suicidal After RCMP Questioned His Son, 4, on Killings." *Edmonton Journal*, October 10, 2001, final edition.

16. Gordon Kent. "The Case of Jason Dix: What Started as a Murder Investigation Became the Basis For a $14.2-Million Lawsuit." *Edmonton Journal*, February 23, 2002, final edition.

17. Gordon Kent. "Dix Suicidal After RCMP Questioned His Son, 4, on Killings."

18. Kerry Powell and Charles Rusnell. "The Snitch Trap." *Edmonton Journal*, January 17, 1999, final edition

19. Gordon Kent. "The Case of Jason Dix: What Started as a Murder Investigation Became The Basis for a $14.2-Million Lawsuit."

20. Kerry Powell and Charles Rusnell. "The Snitch Trap"

21. Kerry Powell and Charles Rusnell. "Unreliable Sources; Informants Provided Little to Bolster a Flawed Case." *Edmonton Journal*, Jan 17, 1999, final edition.

22. Gordon Kent. "The Case of Jason Dix: What Started as a Murder Investigation Became The Basis for a $14.2-Million Lawsuit."

23. Kerry Powell and Charles Rusnell. "The Snitch Trap."

24. Gordon Kent. "Jailhouse Informant's Letter Aimed at 'Exposing Police Plots.'" *Edmonton Journal*, October 13, 2001, final edition.

26. Kerry Powell. "Motives for Murder a Mystery to Mistress; Dix Had No Call to Be Jealous of Co-Worker. A CASE IN POINTS." *Edmonton Journal*, May 9, 1998, final edition.

27. Kerry Powell. "Prosecutor Booted off Dix Case; Allegation Tests Crown's Reliability, Judge Says. A MURDER WRAP?" *Edmonton Journal*, May 20, 1998, final edition.

28. Gordon Kent. "Crown Prosecutor in Dix Case Feared for his Reputation, Trial Hears: Lawsuit Against Police and Gov't Seeks $14.2 Million." *Edmonton Journal*, Jan 25, 2002, final edition.

29. Lisa Gregoire. "Dix Launches $15M Lawsuit; Spent 22 Months in Jail Before Case Fell Apart." *Edmonton Journal*, February 2, 1999, final edition.

30. Gordon Kent. "Crown Prosecutor in Dix Case Feared for his Reputation."

31. Bob Weber. "'Vindication' for Innocent Man: Victim Awarded $765,000 for Malicious Prosecution." *Kingston Whig-Standard*, June 18, 2002, final edition.

32. Tom Olsen. "Albertans Will Be on the Hook for $500,000." *Edmonton Journal*, June 18, 2002, final edition.

33. Jill Mahoney. "Police, Prosecutor 'Cloaked in Malice.'" *The Globe and Mail*, June 18, 2002.

Chapter 4 — False Confession: The Simon Marshall Case

1. Graeme Hamilton. "Innocent Man Freed After Five Years in Prison." *National Post,* August 11, 2005, national edition.
2. Tu Thanh Ha. "Quebec Man Spent Five Years in Jail." *The Globe and Mail,* September 24, 2005.
3. *Ibid.*
4. Kevin Dougherty. "$2.3 Million for Wrongful Jailing." *The Gazette,* December 22, 2006, final edition.
5. Marianne White. "Quebec Officer a Scapegoat, Group for Wrongly Convicted Says; Man Jailed for Sex Crimes He Did Not Commit." *National Post,* April 30, 2008.
6. Katherine Wilton. "Bar Seeks Changes To Justice System; Clarity Needed; Recommendations Aim to Help Mentally Ill." *The Gazette,* March 25, 2010.
7. *Ibid.*

Chapter 5 — Withholding Evidence: The Gary Staples Case

1. Carol Phillips. "The Morin Ripple Effect: Man Seeks Compensation for Wrongful Conviction." *The Hamilton Spectator,* July 28, 1997, final edition.
2. Cheryl Stepan. "Victim's Sons Back Accused; Wrong Man Jailed in Dad's Murder." *The Hamilton Spectator,* June 6, 2001.
3. *Ibid.*
4. Carol Phillips. "The Morin Ripple Effect."
5. Cheryl Stepan. "Victim's Sons Back Accused."
6. Alan Gilday. "Key Evidence Withheld, Claims Staples Suit." *Dunnville Chronical,* June 6, 2001.
7. Cheryl Stepan. "Victim's Sons Back Accused."
8. John Burman. "Police Will Examine Decades-Old File; Determine Need for New Investigation." *The Hamilton Spectator,* June 6, 2001.
9. Krista Smith. "Staples Seeks Apology for Wrongful Murder Conviction." *The Flamborough Review,* June 15, 2001.

Chapter 6 — Jailhouse Informants and Faulty Forensics: The Guy Paul Morin Case

1. Peter Cheney. "Secret Tapes Made Police Suspect Morin, Trial Told." *Toronto Star*, January 14, 1986, final edition.
2. *Ibid.*
3. Drew Fagan. "'Little Girls Grow Up to Be Corrupt,' Jessop Murder Suspect Told Police." *The Globe and Mail*, January 14, 1986.
4. Harold Levy. "Why Venue Was Changed for Morin Trial." *Toronto Star*, February 15, 1986.
5. "Morin Admitted Killing Girl, Cellmate Says." *Montreal Gazette*, January 16, 1986.
6. Peter Cheney. "Trial Told Morin Said: 'I Killed That Little Girl.'" *Toronto Star*, January 15, 1986, final edition.
7. *Ibid.*
8. *Ibid.*
9. Peter Cheney. "Too Busy to Search for Girl, Morin Says." *Toronto Star*, January 29, 1986, final edition.
10. Peter Cheney. "Morin Admitted Killing Girl, Trial Told Murder Jury Hears Chilling Account of Christine Jessop's Death." *Toronto Star*, January 10, 1986, final edition.
11. *Ibid.*
12. Drew Fagan. "'Little Girls Grow Up to be Corrupt,' Jessop Murder Suspect Told Police."
13. Drew Fagan "Fibres Taken From House, Car. Hair Color Questioned In Jessop Case." *The Globe and Mail*, January 23, 1986.
14. Peter Cheney. "Hair from Morin's Car Matched Slain Girl's, Murder Trial Told." *Toronto Star*, January 22, 1986, final edition.
15. Peter Cheney. "Morin Is Insane Defence Expert Tells Stunned Jury." *Toronto Star*, January 31, 1986, final edition.
16. *Ibid.*
17. Drew Fagan. "Don't Fall into Trap, Defence Urges Morin Murder Trial Jury." *The Globe and Mail*, February 6, 1986.
18. Peter Cheney. "Ontario Seeks a New Trial for Morin." *Toronto Star*, March 6, 1986, final edition.
19. Peter Cheney. "Lawyer Won Morin's Freedom with Daring

Courtroom Tactics." *Toronto Star*, February 9, 1986.

20. Peter Cheney. "Fear, Distrust Linger in Queensville Two Years After Christine's Murder." *Toronto Star*, October 3, 1986, final edition.

21. *Ibid.*

22. *Ibid.*

23. Jack King. "The Ordeal of Guy Paul Morin: Canada Copes with Systematic Injustice." *Champion Magazine*, August 1998.

24. Justice Fred Kaufman. "Report of the Kaufman Commission on Proceedings Involving Guy Paul Morin." April 1998.

25. *Ibid.*

Chapter 7 — Deadly Cereal: The Ronald Dalton Case

1. Bonnie Belec. "Wife Killer Seeks Retrial." *The Telegram*, December 6, 1997.

2. Bonnie Belec. "Dalton Freed, Awaiting Retrial: Time Delay Concerns Court." *The Evening Telegram*, June 11, 1998.

3. Bonnie Belec. "Change of Venue Granted: Judge Says Man Will Receive Fairer Trial in St. John's." *The Evening Telegram*, June 29, 1999.

4. Bonnie Belec. "Woman Not Strangled: Doctor." *The Evening Telegram*, May 31 2000.

5. Richard Foot. "Pathologist Sued Over Wrongful Conviction: Newfoundland Case: Doctor Seeks Dismissal Under 'Witness Immunity.'" *National Post*, March 6, 2002.

6. *Ibid.*

7. Dene Moore. "Nfld. announces Sweeping Public Inquiry into Three Wrongful Convictions." *The Canadian Press*, March 21, 2003.

8. Dene Moore. "First Phase of Nfld. Wrongful Convictions Inquiry Hears From Last Witness." *The Canadian Press*, September 26, 2003.

9. Kirk Makin. "Prosecutors Must Share Blame for Botched Cases, Report Says." *The Globe and Mail*, June 22, 2006.

10. "Nfld. to Compensate Man Jailed for Years Awaiting Appeal." *The Globe and Mail*, October 27, 2007.

Chapter 8 — Down the Stairs: The Clayton Johnson Case

1. Kirk Makin. "Did Clayton Johnson Kill His Wife?" *The Globe and Mail*, March 31, 1998.
2. *Ibid.*
3. Tracey Tyler "Not Guilty; 'Clearly, The Crown Has a Conscience.'" *Toronto Star*, February 19, 2002.
4. Kirk Makin. "Did Clayton Johnson Kill His Wife?"
5. Alison Auld. "Murder Conviction Could Be Overturned." *Kingston Whig-Standard*, February 18, 2002.
6. Jack Batten and Derek Finkle. "James Lockyer's Quest for Innocence: Founder of the Association in Defence of the Wrongly Convicted Is a Champion of 'Lost Causes.'" *National Post*, November 23, 2002.
7. "An 'Extraordinary Remedy.' Petitioners Hope Federal Justice Minister Will Examine Case of Clayton Johnson." *The Windsor Star*, April 1, 1998.
8. Rachel Boomer. "Johnson Free on Bail Pending Hearing." *StarPhoenix*, September 26, 1998.
9. Kirk Makin. "'Murdered' Wife's Body to Be Dug Up for Truth. Some Doctors Suspect Death Was Accidental." *The Globe and Mail*, November 19, 1998.
10. *Ibid.*
11. Graeme Hamilton. "Doctors to Report on Wife's Exhumed Body: Forensic Evidence Will Figure into Murder Case Appeal." *National Post*, December10, 1998.
12. Kirk Makin. "Forensic Science Backs Freak-Fall Theory." *The Globe and Mail*, February 19, 2002.
13. Tracey Tyler. "Not Guilty; 'Clearly, The Crown Has a Conscience.'"
14. Kirk Makin. "Wrongly Convicted Man Cleared in Wife's Death." *The Globe and Mail*, February 19, 2002.
15. Alison Auld. "N.S. Police Suffered Tunnel Vision In Wrongful Conviction: Experts." *New Brunswick Telegraph Journal*, February 23, 2002.
16. Francine Dube. "Judge Criticizes 'Hired Gun' Experts: Relationship with Lawyers 'Insidious,' Biases Testimony." *National Post*, November 18, 2002, Toronto edition.
17. Tracey Tyler. "'I'll Always Have Hate,' Wrongly Convicted Man Says." *Toronto Star*, November 17, 2002.

18. Kirk Makin. "Did Clayton Johnson Kill His Wife?"
19. "An 'Extraordinary Remedy.' Petitioners Hope Federal Justice Minister Will Examine Case of Clayton Johnson."
20. Michael Tutton and Rick MacLean. "'The Truth Is Out There.'" *New Brunswick Telegraph Journal*, April 1, 1998.

Chapter 9 — Natural Causes: The William Mullins-Johnson Case

1. "A Death in the Family." *The Fifth Estate*. CBC Television, January 7, 2009.
2. Harold Levy. "'Murderer' Didn't Do It, Forensic Experts Say." *Toronto Star*, September 13, 2005.
3. Joe Friesen. "Report Casts Doubt on Murder Conviction." *The Globe and Mail*, September 13, 2005.
4. Harold Levy. "'Murderer' Didn't Do It, Forensic Experts Say".
5. "A Convicted Killer's Quest for Justice." *Toronto Star*, September 13, 2005.
6. Harold Levy. "Pathologist Lost Vital Evidence." *Toronto Star*, March 30, 2005.
7. Harold Levy. "After 12 Years, A Taste Of Freedom." *Toronto Star*, September 22, 2005.
8. Harold Levy. "Pathologist Argues Crown Immunity in Lawsuit." *Toronto Star*, Jan 26, 2006.
9. *Ibid.*
10. April Lindgren and Shannon Kari. "Judge, Experts to Run Inquiry Into Pathologist." *The Ottawa Citizen*, April 26, 2007.
11. Shannon Kari. "Court Removes 'Scarlet Letter.'" *National Post*, October 16, 2007.
12. Kirk Makin. "Formal Acquittal not Enough for Tearful Mullins-Johnson." *The Globe and Mail*, October 16, 2007.
13. Shannon Kari. "Court Removes 'Scarlet Letter'; Uncle Acquitted of Girl's Death After 12 Years in Prison."
14. Tracy Tyler. "Acquittal And Apology; After 12 Years in Jail for Molesting and Killing his Niece, He Describes the Toll; 'It Destroyed Me.'" *Toronto Star*, October 16, 2007.

15. Kirk Makin. "Wrongfully Convicted, But Not 'Innocent.'" *The Globe and Mail*, October 20, 2007.

16. Kirk Makin. "Smith Apologizes for Critical Autopsy Errors." *The Globe and Mail*, November 13, 2007.

17. Kirk Makin. "Smith Describes Himself as 'Profoundly Ignorant.'" *The Globe and Mail*, January 29, 2008.

18. Theresa Boyle. "Smith Delivers Tearful Apology." *Toronto Star*, February 1, 2008.

19. Jordana Huber. "Inquiry Blasts Ontario Pathologist; Judge Calls for Review of 142 Cases; Report Calls for Sweeping Changes to Flawed Pediatric Forensic Pathology System." *The Ottawa Citizen*, October 2, 2008.

20. *Ibid.*

21. Trevor Wilhelm. "$4.25M to Help Rebuild His Life; Wrongfully Convicted." *The Windsor Star*, October 22, 2010.

Chapter 10 — Prosecutorial Misconduct: The Thomas Sophonow Case

1. "Murder Conviction Comes Quickly After 'Psychic' Juror Is Dismissed." *The Globe and Mail*, March 18, 1985.

2. *Ibid.*

3. David Roberts and Ravi Uhba. "Wrongfully convicted Sophonow ready to forgive." *The Globe and Mail*, June 9, 2000.

4. "Police apology ends legal ordeal." *Sudbury Star*, June 9, 2000.

5. Janice Tibbetts. "Man weeps as he's cleared of '81 murder." *The Ottawa Citizen*, June 9, 2000.

6. Tracey Tyler and Harold Levy. "Memories of a 'Prisoner Of War.'" *Toronto Star*, June 11, 2000.

7. David Staples. "Jailhouse Testimony a Tougher Sell." *Edmonton Journal*, June 29, 2003.

8. Justice Peter Corey. "Commission of Inquiry Regarding Thomas Sophonow." Province of Manitoba, 2001.

Chapter 11 — Eyewitness Misidentification: The Michel Dumont Case

1. Jane Davenport. "Acquittal delivers man to freedom." *The Gazette*,

February 23, 2001.

2. Ingrid Peritz. "How a Woman's Love Corrected an Injustice." *The Globe and Mail*, March 3, 2001.

3. Jane Davenport. "Acquittal Delivers Man to Freedom." *The Gazette*, February 23, 2001.

4. *Le Telejournal/Le Point*, May 3, 2004, Société Radio-Canada.

5. "Quebec: Man Who Spent Three Years in Prison Acquitted." *National Post*, February 24, 2001.

6. *Le Telejournal/Le Point*, May 3, 2004, Société Radio-Canada.

7. "Man Wants Cash for False Rape Conviction." *Sudbury Star*, May 4, 2004.

8. Jane Davenport. "Acquittal: 'No Cause for Probe.'" *The Gazette*, February 24, 2001.

9. Isabelle Mathieu. "Condamnes par de faux souvenirs." *Le Soleil*, March 10, 2001.

10. "Dumont's due." *National Post*, October 6, 2005.

11. Les Perreaux. "Quebec Lagging in Wrongful-Conviction Payments, Victim Says." *The Globe and Mail*, Apr 27, 2005.

12. Graeme Hamilton. "Man Wants Charest's Good Name: Trying to Clear his Own." *National Post*, June 30, 2006.

13. Les Perreaux. "Quebec Lagging in Wrongful-Conviction Payments."

Chapter 12 — Questionable Tactics: The Gordon Folland Case

1. Kirk Makin. "Appeal Court Overturns Sexual-Assault Conviction; DNA Evidence Points to Victim's Ex-Boyfriend." *The Globe and Mail*, January 21, 1999.

2. Tracey Tyler. "Wrongly Convicted Man Given Apology." *Toronto Star*, May 22, 1999.

3. Kirk Makin. "Wrongly Convicted Has Right to Sue Lawyer, Court Rules." *The Globe and Mail*, January 27, 2005.

4. *Ibid.*

5. Julius Melnitzer. "Competency Standard: Barristers, Solicitors Face Same Music." *Law Times*, February 7, 2005. Vol. 16, No. 5.

Acknowledgements

The idea for *Justice Miscarried* began germinating in my head about six years ago after I wrote a magazine article about two Toronto lawyers who were working *pro bono* to exonerate the wrongfully convicted. The passion that David Bayliss and Lon Rose displayed for their work stayed with me. I decided to write a book profiling the stories of twelve men who were wrongly convicted, and the errors that put them behind bars.

If it takes a village to raise a child, it takes a supportive community of family and friends to publish a book. Tracey Arial made helpful suggestions about structuring the book's sections. Julie Barlow, author of *Sixty Million Frenchmen Can't Be Wrong* and *The Story of French* read my book proposal and offered valuable advice. Agent Robert Mackwood found a receptive publisher with Michael Carroll at Dundurn. Marian Scott dug around for some of the articles I needed while researching the book. Many thanks to photographers Milan Chvostek, Linda Martin, and Michael Di Massa for kindly traipsing out to take some photos for the book. My thanks also to Sandra Phinney, Tourism Hamilton, Justices Alexander Hickman, Fred Kaufman, Stephen Goudge, and Dr. Michael Pollanen for graciously contributing photos.

Halifax lawyer Dale Dunlop, who had more than enough work on his own plate, was kind enough to read the manuscript for legal accuracy. If any errors remain, they are entirely my own. He also took me on fascinating trips down memory lane with his connections to virtually every story. My sister Catherine Katz, who has been watching over me since I was born, eyeballed the manuscript and provided valuable suggestions for improving the text. Editor Nicole Chaplin asked for clarifications in the right spots. My partner in life, Mike Couvrette, spent months looking at my back as I lived at the computer. He kept me fed and watered throughout and handled some of my chores at our alpaca farm as the manuscript deadline loomed.

Index